# Criminal

MW01681657

# Profiling

## Serial Killers

### Understanding & Prevention

**FLORENCE MCLEAN**

Copyright © 2026

All Rights Reserved

No part of this book may be reproduced or transmitted in any form or by any means, electronic or mechanical, including photocopying, recording, or by any information storage and retrieval system without the written permission of the author, except where permitted by law.

*This book is dedicated to all the victims of violent crime.*

# Acknowledgements

I would like to express my gratitude to the universities and the professors who had an invaluable patience and valuable feedback throughout my Master of Science in Psychology (2004) and Criminal Profiling (2023).

The Universities:

Department of Psychology and Behavioural Sciences

Aarhus BSS, Aarhus University, Bartholins Allé 11, D

K - 8000 Aarhus C – Denmark

Evidentia University of Behavioral & Forensic Sciences

111 E. Monument Ave. Unit 401-09

Kissimmee, Florida, 43741 - USA

Gratitude and thanks to Professor Ask Elklit at *Aarhus University* to Professor Klaus Nielsen, PhD at *Aarhus University.*

Gratitude and thanks to the following professors: Rafael López, PhD. (President of Evidentia University and professor for my capstone project) Mark Safarik, M.S., V.S.M., Eric Hickey, PhD., María José Garrido, PhD., Ángel Cuñado, PhD., Adrián Rodriguez, PhD., Javier Sanz (Director of University Communications), Jorge Jiménez (Crime Science Director), Nestor García-Barcelóp, PhD., Sergio Martinez, Silvestre Cabezas (Student Recruitment Director), Marta Grau and Mercedes Diéguez from *Evidentia University* of Behavioral & Forensic Sciences.

A special thanks to John E. Douglas, who helped me in 2000-2004 regarding my thesis and understanding the method of criminal profiling for my master's degree and to my friend and mentor Bent Isager-Nielsen.

His merits: Knight of the Dannebrog; education: Military and police; studies with the FBI in the USA, Scotland Yard in England, and RCMP in Canada; and Police Superior Leader Training.

# Contents

# 1. INTRODUCTION

The present book *"Criminal Psychology and Profiling - Serial Killers - Understanding and Prevention"* is a merger of all my work from 1997 to 2025, about serial killers: my thesis *"Serial Killers – Understanding and Prevention"* (2004) Aarhus University; my research report *"Prevention: A Case Study of Arthur Shawcross"* (2012) Aarhus University in collaboration with the Danish psychological union to become a specialist, the capstone project for my MSc in Criminal Profiling *"Serial killers - Prevention Through Deconstructing Criminal Profiling"* (2023); and lastly my 3 books: *"Serial Killers - The Man Behind the Monster"* (2021), *"The Psychology of Evil - Profiles of Serial Killers"* (2023), and *"A disturb Mind – Behind the Serial killers Mask"* (2025) all published in Denmark by Lindhardt & Ringhof publisher.

My interest in criminal profiling and serial killers started in 1997 when I watched a series of TV programs (FBI-Files/Crime Night) where the criminal profiling method was reviewed, which is a method for clarifying the type of murderer you are facing by examining the crime scene and the victims. I started studying psychology in 1997 at Aarhus University in Denmark, wondering why someone chose to be a serial killer. I thought that if we can spot a serial killer from the method of criminal profiling, maybe we can find them before they kill. If we take the theory from criminal profiling and turn it around, is it then possible to find serial killers before they kill? That was what I wanted to examine in my thesis.

I contacted the FBI's training department because I needed to talk to a person who knew about the criminal profiling method, someone who could help me with contacting serial killers and gathering information. I was given the contact information of John E. Douglas, a former FBI agent and profiler. Together with his team, he had developed the FBI's criminal profiling method.

In 1998 I joint the "Forensic Network," which was a forensic/criminological e-mail list, that was established to provide an information network for academics, students, clinicians, and other professionals. When I encountered John Douglas, I was added to his bulletin board "John Douglas Mindhunter Bulletin Board."

I was provided the contact information for the 34 serial killers for my investigation. From all the information, I wrote my thesis, "*Serial Killers - Understanding and Prevention*," in 2004, in which I surveyed 34 serial killers in the USA, UK, and Australia. Most of the serial killers were on death row, some had multiple life sentences, and some were in closed psychiatric wards.

The overall goal of the book is to investigate whether using the theories behind criminal profiling, we can find a method that can find potential serial killers. I have used the personality and socio-cultural theories I discovered by analyzing criminal profiling, together with the causal factors that are relevant to the development of serial killers, to formulate a proposal for a method that can predict whether a child or young person is at risk of becoming extremely violent, self-destructive, a serial rapist or a serial killer. This model is "McLean's Multifactor Model," and it consists of 29 factors, which are divided into three areas: 10 problems in childhood, 13 behavioral strategies, and 6 psychological problems. I will go through the model in Chapter 8.

In this book, I will go through and discuss the existing research about serial killers, their demographics, paraphilias, psychological characteristics, and motives. Then, I will give my hypothesis and my understanding of why someone develops into a serial killer.

I will examine the method behind criminal profiling and see if we can use it for prevention. That way, some of the psychological and sociological theories behind criminal profiling will be examined and revealed.

Can we use the theory behind criminal profiling to find potential serial killers before they commit their first murder with a psychological underlying view?

One of the serial killers I communicated with after completing my thesis was Dennis Rader. I contacted him in 2022 because I wanted him to answer my questionnaire from 2004. It was not an easy task because he wanted something (money or other valuable) in return, and I would not give him that. But Dennis Rader volunteered to answer in 2023, but I have never received it back, and the communication stopped because the law enforcement agencies suspected him of committing some cold cases.

Dennis Lynn Rader was born on March 9, 1945, who is convicted of 10 murders. Rader is known as BTK, an epithet he gave himself, he is an American serial killer who murdered at least 10 people in Wichita and Park City, Kansas, between 1974 and 1991. Although he occasionally killed or attempted to kill men and children, Rader targeted was females. His victims were often bound, sometimes with objects from their homes, and either suffocated with a plastic bag or manually strangled with a ligature. In addition, he stole souvenirs from his female victims, including underwear, driver's licenses, and personal items.

Rader often sent taunting letters to police and media outlets, describing his crimes in detail. In 2004, after a thirteen-year hiatus, he resumed sending letters, leading to his 2005 arrest and subsequent guilty plea.

Rader is currently serving ten counts of first-degree murder and sentences of ten consecutive life sentences and is incarcerated at the El Dorado Correctional Facility.

# 2. SERIAL KILLERS

The term "serial killer" is commonly attributed to former Federal Bureau of Investigation special agent Robert Ressler, who first used the term "serial homicide" in 1974 at a lecture at the Police Staff College in Bramshill, Hampshire, England.

But in 1930, the term can be traced back to Germany where the concept was first used by criminologist Ernst Gennat (1930), who described Peter Kürten as a Serienmörder (serial murderer) in his article *Die Düsseldorfer Sexualverbrechen* in 1930.

In 2005, the FBI hosted a multidisciplinary symposium in San Antonio, Texas, convening 135 experts on serial murder from various fields and specialties with the goal of identifying the commonalities of knowledge regarding serial murder. The group also established a consensus on a definition of serial murder that is currently accepted by FBI investigators as their standard: "The unlawful killing of two or more victims by the same perpetrator(s) in separate incidents." Serial homicide researcher Enzo Yaksic has found that the FBI's decision to lower the victim threshold from three to two victims is justified, given that serial murderers from these groups tend to share similar psychopathologies.

Before the terminology serial killer was used officially, we had the original co-ed killer, John Norman Collins, who is one of the serial killers I am still in contact with.

# CASE: JOHN NORMAN COLLINS

***Epithets: The Co-Ed Killer, the Michigan Murderer, the Ypsilanti Killer, the Ypsilanti Ripper.***

John Norman Collins was born June 17, 1947, in Center Line, Michigan, to Loretta Collins. Shortly after Collins' birth, his father abandoned him and his mother. Loretta Collins remarried; however, the marriage only lasted one year, and then she remarried for a third time. Loretta's last husband was an alcoholic and abusive towards her and her children. In the period spanning from 1949 to 1950, Collins' stepfather used physical violence against his mother, throwing her across the car in his presence. On another occasion, he used Collins as a shield when he was confronted by another man with a gun.

In 1951, at the age of four, the family relocated from Canada to Detroit. Loretta married William Collins, who adopted all three children. William was also an alcoholic, and the family dynamic was marked by violence. This union ultimately dissolved in 1956. By this time, Collins had encountered three different father figures and had been subjected to considerable domestic violence.

During Collins' high school years at St. Clement's in Center Line, which he completed in 1965, he demonstrated academic excellence as an honors student. He participated in three sports and served as the president of the C-Club for lettermen, excelled as a pitcher on the baseball team, and held the position of tri-captain for the football team. Those who were acquainted with him characterized him as polite, quiet, respectful, and very nice. However, his former romantic partner noted that his mood was predominantly angry.

In 1966, at the age of 19, he enrolled at Eastern Michigan University, where he pursued a degree in education and was an active member of the Theta Chi fraternity. However, he was expelled from the fraternity on suspicion of theft.

During his sophomore year at Eastern Michigan University (EMU), his academic performance exhibited a decline. One professor accused him of cheating. This led to a pattern of petty theft, often driven by a sense of impulsive excitement. During this period, he met Andrew Manuel, who would become an accomplice in some of these crimes.

In the period spanning from 1966 to 1967, Collins' sister became pregnant, a development that caused considerable problems in the family. Collins' reaction was to confront his sister's partner; and there was a physical altercation ensued, and he inflicted a serious injury upon his sister.

There is some encounter of Collins' behavior. It is noteworthy to say that the description is made by other people afterward and, of course, cannot be verified, but it does show a pattern. It is stated that when Collins went out, he often behaved aggressively and sexually towards females and made some misogynistic comments that could be interpreted as a reason for some of his actions. One of his former girlfriends remembered one time when he walked her across the school grounds and then started touching her in a sexual way. Suddenly, he held her away from him and angrily asked if she was on her period. She said she was, and he yelled, "That is really disgusting!" Then, he walked away.

Another college student recalled a time when he took her to a wooded area and asked if she would be scared if he were the co-ed killer. Collins said that she could be the next victim because she was alone with him. She thought he was joking, but he looked serious, which made her uneasy.

Furthermore, a girl who said she had met a man who looked like Collins when he accosted her from his car remembered him saying that he couldn't stand girls with pierced ears "because they leave holes that defile their bodies." He also told some people that he had strangled a cat with a length of clothesline, and to make his point, he put his hands on the girl's throat so hard it left a mark.

Collins had also expressed some beliefs that bordered on psychopathy.

He had told a girl that if a man had to kill, he would kill. If he decided it was right for him to do it, then he had to do it. The perfect crime, he told her, was when there was no guilt. Without guilt, a person could not get caught. He had said something similar in a college English paper: "If someone wants something, he alone is the deciding factor of whether to take it, regardless of what society thinks may be right or wrong. If someone points a gun at someone, it's up to them to decide whether to take that person's life or not. The point is: it's not society's judgment that's important, but the individual's own choice of will and intellect."

Collins apparently thought he could get away with murder because he had decided it was the right thing for him to do.

**The first** official considered victim**:** On August 7, 1967, Mary Fleszar's body was found in an old farmhouse two miles north of Ypsilanti, Michigan, after she had been missing since July 9. She had been stabbed approximately 30 times to her chest and abdomen with a knife or other sharp object; her feet had been severed just above the ankle; the thumb and sections of the fingers of one hand were missing; and one forearm had been severed from her body (these severed body parts were never found). Despite the advanced state of decomposition, the pathologist was also able to locate multiple linear abrasions upon the victim's chest and torso, indicating that Fleszar had been extensively beaten before her death. Although police theorized that she had been raped, the advanced state of decomposition of the corpse had erased any conclusive evidence of sexual assault.

**The second** official considered victim**:** On June 5, 1968, Joan Elspeth Schell's (20 years old) body was found. Her body was discovered at a construction site in Ypsilanti. She had been sexually assaulted and murdered with a knife. It was hypothesized that, although she had been deceased for several days, her body had only been in its discovered location for less than 24 hours.

The third incident was on March 21, 1969, the remains of 23-year-old Jane Louise Mixer were discovered in the vicinity of the Ypsilanti cemetery. She had been reported missing earlier that day. The preliminary investigation indicated that the victim had been subjected to sexual assault, physical assault, and was killed by stabbing.

**The fourth** official considered victim**:** On March 25, 1969, a construction worker unearthed the body of Maralynn Skelton in the same construction site where the body of Joan Schell had been discovered 8 months earlier. She had been reported missing four days earlier, on the same day as Jane Louise Mixer. She had sustained severe physical trauma, including lacerations to the abdomen and head, and a branch had been forcefully inserted into her vaginal cavity.

**The fifth** official considered victim**:** On April 16, 1969, the body of 13-year-old Dawn Louise Basom was discovered alongside a country road in Ypsilanti. The victim had been missing for a mere 24 hours. She had been subjected to sexual assault, asphyxiated by an electrical cord, and had suffered a stab wound around her body to her breast, buttocks and stomach.

**The sixth** official considered victim**:** On June 9, 1969, the body of Alice Elizabeth Kalom (21 years old) was found by three teenage boys in an abandoned farmhouse. She had sustained a gunshot wound to the head, been sexually assaulted (either before or after death), and repeatedly stabbed. Kalom had received multiple slash and stab wounds to the body (including two stab wounds that had pierced her heart) and a gunshot wound to the forehead before her neck had been cut through to the spine.

**The seventh** official and the only victim Collins is convicted of killing**:** On July 27, 1969, 18-year-old Karen Sue Beineman was discovered by a physician and his spouse in a wooded gully. She had sustained severe trauma, including rape, blunt force trauma to the head, and asphyxiation, with her undergarments being forcibly inserted into her oral cavity.

Not officially considered victim: On July 13, 1969, the remains of 17-year-old Roxie Phillips were discovered by two individuals searching for fossil sites in Pescadero Canyon. Her body exhibited advanced stages of decomposition. She was unclothed and had a belt tightly wrapped around her neck. She had been missing for two weeks before she was found.

Not officially considered victim: In January of 1968, the body of 13-year-old Eileen Adams was discovered in a location just south of Ypsilanti. She had sustained severe trauma, including rape, strangulation with an electrical cord, and blunt-force trauma to the head. Her bra was tied around her neck, and a three-inch nail had been hammered into her skull. The body was discovered in a highly visible location.

John Norman Collins was apprehended on suspicion of the murder of Karen Sue Beineman (the 7th victim). At the trial, the sole basis for the defendant's prosecution was the murder of Karen Beineman, as there was physical evidence against him. There were several main prosecution witnesses who testified during the trial. Among them was Diane Goshe, who owned a wig shop where Beineman was last seen. She witnessed Collins accompanying Beineman on a motorcycle shortly before her disappearance. Another key witness was Arnold Davis, a friend of Collins. He stated that he had observed Collins remove a blanket and a box of women's clothing from his vehicle's trunk. Following his initial police interview, Davis claimed to have seen Collins dispose of these items. Collins also entrusted a knife to Davis for safekeeping, which Davis then relinquished to the detectives investigating the case.

Collins attempted to use Davis as an alibi for the period of the Beineman abduction and murder, stating, "Don't forget we went motorcycle riding in the afternoon on July 23," which was the day Beineman disappeared.

Corporal Leik and his spouse, Sandra, offered testimony detailing Collins' use of their residence during their vacation, as well as the evidence that culminated in his eventual arrest. Collins received a life imprisonment sentence in August 1970, and when the sentence was announced, he made a statement, "I never knew a girl named Karen Sue Beineman. I never took the life of Karen Sue Beineman." This was the extent of his public statements regarding the murder at the time.

On August 19, 1970, Collins was convicted of the murder of Karen Beineman and sentenced to life imprisonment without the possibility of parole.

In the early 1980s, he legally changed his last name back to Chapman, which was his mother's maiden name, and formally requested a transfer to a penitentiary in Canada. This request was denied.

Notably, an unreleased movie about the murders was partially filmed in Ann Arbor during the summer of 1977. The film starred Victoria Bayley as one of the murder victims, and Bob Purley played the role of Collins, although the names were all changed in the movie to avoid legal complications. This film, which cost over a million dollars to produce, was shot at locations in Southern California as well, given the suspicion of Collins' involvement in a series of killings there. The film was named *Now I Lay Me Down to Sleep,* and its screenplay was based on the book *The Michigan Murders.*

Collins, while imprisoned, granted an interview to William Treml, during which he expressed dismay at the film project's potential to hinder his efforts in the appeal process to regain his freedom. The producer William Martin stipulated, that the production would halt if Collins were to take and pass a lie detector test, a stipulation that Collins never did.

In 1979, an escape attempt by Collins and six other inmates from the maximum-security prison in Marquette led to the creation of a two-foot-wide tunnel dug 19 feet beneath the prison's foundations. The prisoners had dug another 25 feet toward their goal of freedom but were impeded by a guard who discovered the tunnel's entrance.

As of marts 2026, at the age of 78, John Norman Collins (Chapman) remained incarcerated at the Marquette Branch Prison in Michigan.

Source: Fournier, 2016, Ramsland, 2015, Holmes & Holmes, 2002, McLean, 2004 and Ressler, 1992.

***

Serial killers have a lot of internal pressure that they release at some point in their lives. They often plan extensively. They want power and control and have some psychological issues they live out through the murders. They are somewhat disturbed, so they have often been diagnosed with different personality disorders, but they are seldom insane. The serial killers I examined in 2000-2004 displayed the same pattern of behavior.

This book will explore whether criminal profiling theories can be used to identify potential violent offenders. The goal is to prevent extremely violent serial crimes. I believe it is very important to try to prevent crimes, and to do that, you need to understand the psychology and behavior of the perpetrator. Law enforcement around the world can and does often use criminal profiling to better understand serial crimes. Especially cases and cold cases where we have serial murder, robbery, arson, or serial rape, criminal profiling can help the investigation.

Criminal profiling creates a profile of the offender. The profile can include gender, age, behavior, personality, work, hobbies, and more. The profile is created from, examining the crime scene information, walk-through, autopsy results, crime scene photos, blood spatter analysis, crime scene analysis, link analysis, geographic profiling, forensic examination, victimology, which is the study of the victim where we examine the victim's personality, and behavior found at the crime scene regarding the case or cases.

The focus is mainly on serial killers in this book. I could also have chosen serial rapists because serial killers and serial rapists often display the same psychological profile.

When I examined serial killers, I found that they usually have a childhood characterized by violence and abuse. This could be physical, psychological, sexual abuse, rape, or other traumas. Or they have experienced abuse between the parents or siblings in their own family. Children who experience violent events are more likely to be traumatized in some form. They may turn their destructiveness inwards and become alcoholics, sex workers, suffer from anxiety and depression, or practice self-mutilation, or they can turn it outwards and commit violent crimes, murder or ultimately, become serial killers.

A different way to examine serial killers could be to look at what they have in common with non-serial killers and not solely focus on what's abnormal or different about them. In their day-to-day lives, most serial killers act normal, marrying, having children, and working. This is one of the reasons why they can murder for years or decades without being detected. They benefit from the fact that we think we can tell if someone is a serial killer.

As part of my study from 2000-2004, I decided to ask the serial killers I examined different questions than they were used to. Ideally, if I conducted more research on them, I would investigate them as whole individuals. I would examine both their normal functioning and destructive characteristics. In my thesis, I argued that studying serial killers poses several difficulties. In addition, I criticize criminal profiling and the methods to identifying potential serial killers.

My psychological perspective is eclectic, with an emphasis on psychodynamic. I will argue that the psychodynamic approach is relevant to human understanding. Therefore, I focus on the importance of childhood and human relationships in shaping our behavior and personality. Furthermore, my studies also examine serial killers' own perception of the reasons why they are killing people repeatedly.

The book also examines whether criminal profiling theories can be used to design a method to identify potential serial killers. What is criminal profiling? How is the method applied, and is it an art or a science? What theories is criminal profiling built on? What are serial killers like? Are they mentally ill? What personality disorder does serial killers have? Why do some become serial killers? Can we use these theories to design a method to find potential serial killers? What are the advantages and disadvantages of the method?

## UNDERSTANDING SERIAL KILLERS

Understanding serial killers is useful for many reasons. Law enforcement, criminologists, psychologists, and psychiatrists is still trying to understand why. It can be difficult because of many parameters, and there is no firm consensus about the definition. It is crucial to define serial killers before continuing this book.

According to Liebert (2000), there is no common psychological model for serial killers. However, in the literature I reviewed, there have been several aspects of general agreement.

Throughout the next chapter, I will outline a definition of serial killers. I will examine what serial killers are, whether it is a psychotic outburst or they have personality disorders, and why some become serial killers.

In this chapter, I will define different types of multiple murders: mass murderers, spree killers, and serial killers. Next, I will examine demographic and gender differences in relation to serial killers. Then, I will look at some hypotheses about whether serial killers are mentally ill, have personality disorders, or are sane. I will review and discuss various psychiatric disorders related to serial killers. Lastly, I will discuss paraphilias and fantasies related to sexuality, which play a significant role in becoming serial killers.

## DEFINITION

The literature generally distinguishes between three types of multiple murderers: mass murderers, spree killers, and serial killers, which I will go through even there is other classification for example familicide and contract killers.

Mass murderers kill multiple people in the same location. This could be someone in a restaurant or school. They kill as many people as they can at once. The mass murderer often knows one of the people they murdered or has a relationship with some of the victims or the location. Mass murderers are often shot by law enforcement (commit suicide by cop), commit suicide, or surrender when law enforcement comes to the scene.

A mass murder may be further classified as a mass shooter or a mass stabber.

FBI defines mass murders as: "Generally, mass murder was described as a number of murders (four or more) occurring during the same incident, with no distinctive "cooling off" period between the murders. These events involved a single location, where the killer murdered a number of victims in an ongoing incident" (e.g., the 1984 San Ysidro McDonald's incident in San Diego, California; the 1991 Luby's Restaurant massacre in Killeen, Texas; and the 2007 Virginia Tech murders in Blacksburg, Virginia) (FBI, 2005).

I will argue that the intent of killing multiple persons is a more practical definition. In my opinion, the intent is the important issue, not how many people they murder, because we have cases like the mass murder which took place on April 17, 2025, in Tallahassee, Florida where 20-year-old student opened fire at Florida State University, killed two people and injured six others, before being shot and injured by the police. I will argue that he is a mass murderer, even though he "only" killed two people, because his intent was to kill them all (Payne & Fischer, 2025).

# CASE: CHARLES JOSEPH WHITMAN

***Epithets: The Texas Tower Sniper***

Charles Joseph Whitman was born on June 24, 1941. He was an American mass murderer and Marine veteran who gained notoriety for his actions as the "Texas Tower Sniper." On August 1, 1966, Whitman perpetrated a series of homicides by using knives to kill his mother and his wife in their homes. He then proceeded to the University of Texas at Austin (UT Austin) with multiple firearms and proceeded to shoot randomly at people. Whitman fatally shot three individuals inside UT Austin's main building and gained access to the 28th-floor observation deck on the building's clock tower, where he proceeded to fire at random for 96 minutes.

This attack resulted in a total of 17 deaths and 31 people were injured, before Whitman was fatally shot by members of the Austin Police Department. The total number rose to 18 victims succumbing to injuries sustained in the attack, 35 years later. Whiteman was killed by law enforcement when he was shooting at people and died on August 1, 1966.

Charles Whitman's background was characterized by an early period of exemplary behavior. He was a devout Roman Catholic altar boy, a newspaper delivery boy, a pitcher on his parochial school's baseball team, and a manager of its football team.

At the age of twelve years and three months, he was an Eagle Scout, a distinction he shared with few others in his cohort. The family in which he was raised in Lake Worth, Florida, included two younger brothers, a mother, and a father who was a moderately successful plumbing contractor, so they appeared to be a typical American family.

From an early age, Whitman and his brothers received training in the use of firearms, a practice that was passed down from their father, Mr. Whitman, the 47-year-old gun enthusiast. By the age of 16, Charles Whitman had mastered the proficiency of shooting a squirrel in the eye. In the Marine

Corps, he achieved a rating as a sharpshooter, second only to the expert level, by scoring 215 points out of a possible 250.

Charles Whitman graduated from St. Ann's High School in West Palm Beach in 1959. In July 1959, at the age of 18, he enlisted in the Marines. He enrolled at the University of Texas in August 1962. However, beneath the surface, there were some unusual undercurrents. His time in the Marines was not without incident. He was demoted from the rank of corporal and was sentenced to 30 days of hard labor for illegally possessing a pistol. In addition, he was reprimanded for threatening to inflict harm upon a fellow Marine.

Charles Whitman preferred sporting activities, including hunting, scuba diving, and karate. Behind the family facade, tensions prevailed. Mr. Whitman, Charles' father, has been described as an authoritarian figure in the family, a perfectionist, and an unyielding disciplinarian who has been known to demand a great deal from his sons. He also admitted to having a history of physically abusing Charles Whitman's mother.

In February 1962, at the age of 20 years, Charles Whitman met Kathleen Frances Leissner, who was an education major. Leissner was Whitman's first serious girlfriend. They dated for five months before announcing their engagement on July 19. On August 17, 1962, Whitman and Leissner were married in Leissner's hometown of Needville, Texas. They had chosen the 22nd wedding anniversary of Charles' parents as the date for their wedding.

Whitman's family drove from Florida to attend the event. Leissner's family and friends approved of her choice of husband, describing Whitman as a "handsome young man" who was both intelligent and aspirational.

Because of low grades, Whitman was ordered back to duty as an enlisted man in the Marine Corps on February 12, 1963. Although his grades improved somewhat during his second and third semesters, the Marines considered him insufficient for the continuation of his scholarship. He was ordered to active duty in February 1963 and went to Camp Lejeune in North

Carolina for the remainder of his five-year enlistment. While still in the service, he attended East Carolina State College in the summer of 1964. He was discharged on December 4, 1964, and returned to Austin, where he reentered the University of Texas in the spring of 1965 to study architectural engineering. In the summer of 1965, he attended Alvin Junior College and then continued at the University of Texas in the 1965–66 school year. He also worked part-time and was a scoutmaster in the spring of 1966.

In March 1966, Mrs. Whitman left Charlie's father. She called him from Austin to assist her in making the decision to leave, presumably because of the concern that his father might resort to violence. While his mother was arranging her belongings, a police car from Lake Worth was stationed outside the residence. After the separation, to be in closer proximity to Charles, Mrs. Whitman relocated to Austin.

The parents' separation caused significant distress for Charles Whitman, and on March 29, 1966, he sought consultation with Dr. Maurice Heatly, a staff psychiatrist at the University of Texas. During a two-hour session, Charles Whitman disclosed that, like his father, he had engaged in physical altercations with his wife on a few occasions. He indicated that he was making "intense efforts" to manage his temper, but he expressed concern that he might lose control. In his notes from the session, Dr. Heatly described Whitman as a "massive, muscular youth" who "seemed to be oozing with hostility." Notably, he documented only a single direct quotation from Whitman, which indicated a desire to ascend the tower with a deer rifle and commence a shooting spree. This did not cause significant concern for Dr. Heatly, as he acknowledged that it was a common sentiment among students who visited the clinic and contemplated drastic actions at the tower. Nevertheless, he encouraged Whitman to return the following week for a new therapy session. However, Whitman did not comply, opting instead to act within the months. On the eve of his planned ascent to the tower, Whitman ensconced himself within a dilapidated portable typewriter in his unassuming brick cottage. His wife, Kathy, who had been his companion for the preceding four years, was at her place of employment.

Whitman commenced his note with the following words: "I am at a loss to comprehend the motivations that compel me to inscribe these words. I have been besieged by trepidation and violent impulses. I have been afflicted by severe headaches. I am prepared to perish." Following his demise, he requested an autopsy to ascertain the presence of any mental disorders.

Additionally, he expressed his intention to kill his wife after she returned from work, citing a desire to avoid subjecting her to the potential embarrassment his actions might cause her.

The motive was thought to be founded on homicidal ideation, mental illness, and possibly caused by a brain tumor. Dr. Coleman de Chenar, who was a neuropathologist at Austin State Hospital, reported that he discovered a pecan-sized brain tumor, above the red nucleus, in the white matter below the gray center thalamus, which he identified as an astrocytoma with slight necrosis, but medical authorities disagreed if it influenced Whitman's actions.

Source: Barr, 1966, Lavergne, 1997, Time, 1966 and Flippin, 2007.

***

Spree killers (see next case) kill multiple people in different locations over a relatively short period of time, hours, days, or weeks. They don't have a cooling-off period like serial killers. They don't worry about being caught; therefore, they don't care if they leave clues at the crime scene.

## CASE: WADE STEVEN WILSON

### Epithets: Deadpool Killer

Wade Steven Wilson was born May 20, 1994, and is an American spree killer who was convicted of the 2019 murders of Kristine Melton and Diane Ruiz in Cape Coral, Florida. Due to a shared name with the Marvel character

Deadpool, Wilson has been referred to in the media as the "Deadpool Killer." He was sentenced to death in 2024 after being found guilty of two first-degree murders, together with six other charges and was sentenced to death in 2025. Prior to the murders, Wilson had a criminal history dating back to 2012, including convictions for burglary, grand theft, and firearms offenses.

Life and Early Crimes: Wade Steven Wilson was born on May 20, 1994, to teenage parents. He was adopted by Steve and Candace Wilson and raised in Tallahassee, Florida, where he attended Chiles High School. During his youth, Wilson was often described as "troubled" and was reportedly involved in minor criminal activities and substance abuse.

In an interview with *Newsweek,* a male high school classmate of Wilson's described him as "troubled." He went on and stated, "People that were on track for college, I'd say, weren't his acquaintances." He further told *Newsweek* about who Wilson allegedly surrounded himself with. "The kids that got into trouble, he would hang out with them, mostly."

The classmate added that Wilson "always pushed the boundaries as far as crazy things he would do," including allegedly "trespassing and breaking into cars and all that stuff" after high school. "Just like, ... why would you do that?" the man said. "Even if he didn't get anything monetarily out of it, it was just something he liked to do."

Wilson also sustained several head injuries during his childhood and adolescence, which he later cited as contributing to his feelings of instability.

Wilson's encounters with the law began in 2012 in Leon County, where he was involved in various incidents, including burglary, assault, and firearm-related offenses. In November 2013, he was sentenced to prison for burglary and grand theft, serving until September 2014. In 2015, he stood trial for sexual battery and kidnapping after a woman accused him of assaulting her in his vehicle following a party. However, he was acquitted of these charges by a jury.

By 2017, Wilson was incarcerated again for stealing firearms, serving until July 2018. In 2018, his name surfaced in connection with the case of Denise Williams, who stood accused of conspiring to murder her husband. Allegedly, Wilson attempted to fabricate evidence and even offered to kill Williams during this period.

In February 2019, Wilson's former girlfriend reported an incident in which he had allegedly assaulted and strangled her. Although she initially accused him of kidnapping and rape, investigators did not pursue these charges due to the lack of evidence and an existing no-contact order. On July 1, 2019, Wilson was arrested again for battery.

On October 7, 2019, he committed two murders within hours. The first victim, Kristine Melton, was strangled in her home after Wilson had met her at a live music bar. Later, the same day, Diane Ruiz, a mother of two who also worked as a bartender, was strangled and run over multiple times with a car, after being lured into Melton's car, which Wilson had stolen from her. Wilson called his biological father, Stephen Testasecca, and confessed to murdering Ruiz and Melton. Testasecca and his wife contacted the authorities, resulting in Wilson's arrest the following day. During his interrogation, Wilson expressed a willingness to commit the same act again with no remorse at all.

During the legal proceedings, evidence pertaining to Wilson's mental health was presented, including testimony regarding his brain injuries. A neurologist provided expert testimony, stating that brain scans revealed trauma and impairment that could potentially explain some of Wilson's impulsive behaviors. However, experts for the prosecution argued that drug abuse was a more significant factor in his actions. The defense claimed that Wilson's drug abuse could have impaired his judgment at the time of the crime, and they argued that he was not guilty for that reason. They argued that his use of flakka (alpha-PVP), a dangerous street *drug* that is commonly known as "bath salt" and can cause paranoia, hallucinations, odd and bizarre behavior, and can be uncontrollable. The forensic psychiatrist Dr. Mark Mills testified on behalf of Wade Wilson, saying Wilson suffered from "some kind of psychotic disorder" based on the results of Eisenstein's interview and testing of Wilson. However, Mills' assessment of Wilson's condition was deemed invalid by the prosecutor due to the subject's exaggeration of symptoms during the testing.

Dr. Mark Mills stated his inability to provide a definitive diagnosis due to Wilson's premature termination of an interview, based on his belief that corrections personnel were monitoring him. Miller further elaborated that Wilson's paranoia thinking could contribute to his diagnosis of paranoid delusions, which could be indicative of schizoaffective disorder. However, Wilson did not exhibit any symptoms of delusions or hallucinations during his interaction with Miller, he stated.

In a line of questioning focused on the potential presence of disturbing and antisocial behaviors, defense lawyer Kevin Shirley asked Miller about Wilson's tattoo art, which should be a sign of mental instability.

Both defense experts asserted that jail records substantiated their opinions, citing documentation indicating that Wilson had been diagnosed with schizoaffective disorder, depression, anxiety, and adjustment disorder and had been prescribed antipsychotic medications by the jail staff. The experts clarified that their conclusions did not extend to offering an assessment of his psychological state during the commission of the criminal acts.

Wilson's biological father, Stephen Testasecca, testified against him in court, recounting details of his confession over the phone. Testasecca stated that his son realized that Ruiz was not yet dead and proceeded to run over her, offering no further explanation for his actions beyond stating, "I just wanted to do it." The jury's recommendations for the death penalty for Wilson were 9 for the murder of Melton and 10 for the murder of Ruiz. Judge Nicholas Thompson, having the authority to accept or reject the jury's recommendation, imposed two death sentences. Wilson is currently appealing the decision to the Supreme Court of Florida.

Wilson's sentencing garnered significant public attention and provoked a range of reactions, including numerous appeals for Wilson to be declared innocent by reason of insanity or just declared innocent by different individuals. The case raised significant questions regarding the intersection of mental health, criminal behavior, and the justice system. It attracted extensive media coverage, partly because of the striking similarity between Wilson's name and that of the well-known fictional character Wade Wilson, the secret identity of the Marvel Comics character Deadpool. Public reactions were mixed, with some expressing sympathy due to his mental health issues while others focused on the brutality of his crimes.

Source: The trial can be seen in its full length on "LIVE: FL v. Wade Wilson - Strangled Women Murder Trial" on Court-TV, et al. 2024, Law & Crime Network, 2024, Keller, 2024.

***

Serial killers operate differently from mass murderers and spree killers. Holmes & DeBurger (1988) define serial killers as: "...consisting of repetitive killings which are one-on-one with rare exception, where the relationship between victims and the offender is that of a stranger or slight acquaintance, and the motivation to kill and apparent motives are lacking."

Egger (1998) agrees with Holmes & DeBurger (1988) but added: "...the motive is not for material gain [but rather] the murderer's desire to have power or dominance over his victims" and that "victims may have symbolic value for the murderer and/or are perceived to be prestige less and in most instances are unable to defend themselves or alert others to their plight."

Using Hickey's definition from 1991, more women fall under the category of serial killers: "...anyone who kills in sequence over time, regardless of motive - period of days, weeks, months, or years."

There is a significant difference between multiple murderers who murder for money and those who kill for control, power, and some psychological issues that they outlive. Therefore, it makes sense to separate serial killers who have different motives.

FBI's definition was three or more murders, but after a serial murder symposium: "Serial Murder: Multi-Disciplinary Perspectives for Investigators (FBI, 2005), held from August 29 to September 2, 2005. The goal of the symposium was to bring together a group of respected experts on serial murder from a variety of fields and specialties, to identify the commonalities of knowledge regarding serial murder." From the FBI symposium: "The topic of serial murder occupies a unique niche within the criminal justice community. In addition to the significant investigative challenges they bring to law enforcement, serial murder cases attract an overabundance of attention from the media, mental health experts, academia, and the public. While there has been significant, independent work conducted by a variety of experts to identify and analyze the many issues related to serial murder, there have been few efforts to reach a consensus between law enforcement and other experts regarding these matters, in an effort to bridge the gap between the many views of issues related to serial murder" (FBI, 2005, p. vii).

The definition of a serial killer is a person who murders at least two people in two different locations, with an emotional cooling-off period between murders. This cooling-off period can last from days to months to years. It is unique and sets the serial killer apart from other multiple murders. Furthermore, many serial killers plan their murders down to the smallest detail. They can spend several months, some even years, planning the murder. Serial killers spend a lot of time fantasizing about murders.

Some serial killers murder the same type of person with a common denominator. This could be gender, hair color, or other special traits. Others choose their victims randomly. The choice of victim can change over days, weeks, or years, so you can never be sure what type of person a serial killer will attack next. Serial killers can also kill people close to them. Some murder their own family members or friends.

According to Turvey (2012) and Ressler (1992), serial killers and serial rapists have the same profile. They have the same behavior and motivation to commit the crime. When comparing serial killers and serial rapists, the motive is not the act itself. Instead, the act is a behavior that expresses a need that the perpetrator fulfills in this way. There are sexual aspects involved in many serial murders, be it rape or other sexual contact with the victim or the corpse. I define the sexual component and rape as an extreme violent act with sex as the weapon.

In nearly hundred years, multiple definitions of serial murder have been used by law enforcement, clinicians, academia, and researchers. While these definitions do share several common themes, they differ on specific requirements, such as the number of murders committed, the types of motivation, and the temporal aspects of the murders. So, for that reason, apart, the symposium in 2005 where the aim was to define a serial killer, the conclusion was that a serial killer is a person who murders two or more people, in different locations, with an emotional cooling-off period between those murders. This cooling-off period can last from days to months and is unique and sets the serial killer apart from other multiple killers, like mass murderers and spree killers" (FBI, 2005). The different discussion groups at the symposium agreed on a number of similar factors to be included in a definition. These included:

- One or more offenders.
- Two or more murdered victims.
- Incidents should occur in separate events, at different times.
- The period between murders separates serial murder from mass murder.

In combining the various ideas put forth at the symposium, the following definition was crafted:

"Serial Murder: The unlawful killing of two or more victims by the same offender(s), in separate events" (FBI, 2005, p. 9).

In this book, I will make a distinction between multiple killers that have a clear motive as for example robbery, contract killers, jealousy or revenge, and serial killers where the motive is the murders itself. I will concentrate exclusively on serial killers based on Holmes & DeBurger's (1988), Egger's (1998) and McLean (2004) definition:

A serial killer/murder is the unlawful killing of two or more victims by the same offender(s), in separate events with a period without murder in-between the murders, which can be from hours, days, months and years, and they can stop killing. The motive is power, control and dominance, and they have some psychological issue they are reliving.

## DEMOGRAPHICS

Serial killers are extremely dangerous. Especially those who are not caught quickly or at all. Some serial killers murder many people in their lifetime. In the worst cases, this can amount to several murders a week. Some serial killers have been identified quickly, after a few weeks or months, and others remain at large for up to 25 years. There remain many unsolved serial murders in the world, and some serial killers are never found. On average, it takes four years to catch a male serial killer. Although serial killers are feared, the likelihood of encountering them is low. But if you encounter an active serial killer, the outcome is nearly always death. Very few have escaped alive from a serial killer.

I use the database from Radford University's Department of Psychology for the information, and Dr. Michael G. Aamodt's (2023) work. For the database, they have collected information about serial killings from 1900 to 2020 and include serial killers from over 115 countries.

To be included in their database, the following must have occurred:

1. A person illegally killed two or more people in separate incidents.

2. The murders were discovered by law enforcement.
3. The murders were tied by law enforcement to the same killer.
4. The identity of the killer was identified by law enforcement.
5. The name of the killer and the number of victims, or the names of the victims, were publicized in the media or other publicly available sources of information.
6. The publication of the murders was at some point documented in English.

Because all 6 of the above conditions must be met, the database is much more likely to contain killers from countries such as the United States that have effective law enforcement agencies, openly publish information about crimes, and communicate those results in English.

Since there is considerable disagreement among experts regarding the definition of a serial killer (Reid, 2016), they decided to use the 2005 FBI definition as a base (the unlawful killing of two or more victims by the same offenders in separate events) and then provide subtypes that will allow individual researchers to remove individuals who do not reflect the researcher's personal definition of a serial killer. "Although each of us has our own ideas as to whom we might count as a serial killer, we felt it important that the database be broad enough to allow individual researchers to make that call for their own research purposes" they stated.

I am using the narrower definition: A Serial killer/ is the unlawful killing of two or more victims by the same offender(s), in separate events with a period without murder between the murders, which can be from hours, days, months or years, and they can stop killing. The motive is power, control and dominance, and they have some psychological issue they are reliving. But in the following the short definition is used.

Table 1. Serial killers by country with at least 10 identified serial killers

| Country | % of Serial Killers | % of Serial Killers | Country's Share of World Population | Ratio |
|---|---|---|---|---|
| US | 3,690 | 64.16 | 4.24% | 15.12 |
| England | 182 | 3.16 | 0.68% | 4.66 |
| Russia | 164 | 2.85 | 1.87% | 1.52 |
| Japan | 138 | 2.40 | 1.62% | 1.48 |
| India | 130 | 2.26 | 17.70% | 0.13 |
| S. Africa | 129 | 2.24 | 0.76% | 2.95 |
| Canada | 125 | 2.17 | 0.48% | 4.49 |
| Germany | 99 | 1.72 | 1.07% | 1.60 |
| Italy | 95 | 1.65 | 0.78% | 2.13 |
| Australia | 92 | 1.60 | 0.33% | 4.89 |
| France | 89 | 1.55 | 0.84% | 1.85 |
| China | 68 | 1.18 | 18.46% | 0.06 |
| Mexico | 64 | 1.11 | 1.65% | 0.67 |
| Brazil | 42 | 0.73 | 2.73% | 0.27 |
| Hungary | 28 | 0.49 | 0.12% | 3.93 |
| Poland | 28 | 0.49 | 0.49% | 1.00 |
| Spain | 28 | 0.49 | 0.60% | 0.81 |
| Austria | 24 | 0.42 | 0.12% | 3.61 |
| Colombia | 24 | 0.42 | 0.65% | 0.64 |
| Netherlands | 20 | 0.35 | 0.22% | 1.58 |
| Belgium | 17 | 0.30 | 0.15% | 1.99 |
| Czech Republic | 16 | 0.28 | 0.14% | 2.03 |
| Turkey | 15 | 0.26 | 1.08% | 0.24 |
| Scotland | 14 | 0.24 | 0.07% | 3.59 |
| Sweden | 14 | 0.24 | 0.13% | 1.88 |
| Argentina | 14 | 0.24 | 0.58% | 0.42 |
| Kenya | 13 | 0.23 | 0.69% | 0.33 |
| Thailand | 13 | 0.23 | 0.90% | 0.25 |
| Iran | 13 | 0.23 | 1.08% | 0.21 |
| Nigeria | 13 | 0.23 | 2.64% | 0.09 |
| Ukraine | 12 | 0.21 | 0.56% | 0.37 |
| Greece | 11 | 0.19 | 0.13% | 1.43 |
| South Korea | 11 | 0.19 | 0.66% | 0.29 |
| Pakistan | 11 | 0.19 | 2.83% | 0.07 |
| New Zealand | 10 | 0.17 | 0.06% | 2.81 |
| Finland | 10 | 0.17 | 0.07% | 2.45 |
| Switzerland | 10 | 0.17 | 0.11% | 1.57 |
| Ireland | 9 | 0.16 | 0.06% | 2.47 |

**Reference:** Radford University's Department of Psychology: Uploaded and revised August 2023. Note: the list changes all the time, as new killers get incarcerated and convicted.

For instance, the US is the country with the most recorded serial killers, at 3,613 since 1900. That is 67%. Canter et al. (1996) calculated that 74.1% of serial killers are from the US. For a country with 4.35% of the world's population, it is significant.

Table 2

| Over 100 serial killers from 1990 – 2020 in the World | |
|---|---|
| US | 3,613 |
| England | 176 |
| Japan | 137 |
| South Africa | 123 |
| India | 121 |
| Canada | 119 |

**Reference:** Michael G. Aamodt: Radford University| Radford Department of Psychology. Radford/FGCU Serial Killer/ Multiple murders Database: Uploaded and revised August 2023. Note: the list changes as new serial killers get incarcerated and convicted.

Another interesting aspect is the number of victims of serial killers. It looks like the highest number of serial killers and the most victims in the US are in the 80s. But when you compare the figure with the rest of the world's, serial killing peaks in the 1990s, 10 years after the US.

Table 3: Number of serial killers by decade: 1900-2020

| **Decade:** | **US** | **Canada** | **Other countries** | **total** | **%US** |
|---|---|---|---|---|---|
| 1900-1910 | 53 | 0 | 32 | 85 | 62.4 |
| 1910-1920 | 62 | 0 | 33 | 95 | 65.3 |
| 1920-1930 | 70 | 3 | 40 | 113 | 61.9 |
| 1930-1940 | 67 | 0 | 34 | 101 | 66.3 |
| 1940-1950 | 61 | 4 | 52 | 117 | 52.1 |
| 1950-1960 | 93 | 1 | 50 | 144 | 64.6 |
| 1960-1970 | 255 | 8 | 79 | 342 | 74.6 |
| 1970-1980 | 673 | 20 | 175 | 868 | 77.5 |
| 1980-1990 | 840 | 24 | 246 | 1,110 | 75.7 |
| 1990-2000 | 729 | 18 | 441 | 1,118 | 61.4 |
| 2000-2010 | 438 | 26 | 364 | 828 | 52.9 |
| 2010-2020 | 215 | 20 | 189 | 424 | 50.7 |
| 2020- .. | 26 | 1 | 20 | 47 | 55.3 |

**Reference:** Michael G. Aamodt: Radford University Radford Department of Psychology. Radford/FGCU Serial Killer Database: Uploaded and revised August 2023.

For further research, I have started my own database with only serial killers that fall under the definition used in this book.

It is interesting to look closer at the reasons for the decline in serial killers in the US and how other countries and the US are getting closer to each other. Even though we only have a small sample, this is one of the topics I want to look closer to in future research. I have delved into it in my other writings, but it is not given much place in this book. It is also important that the numbers that are used refer to identified serial killers. There may be many more serial killers there is not caught.

There are instances when these results match the calculation made by Canter et al. (1996), where 74.1% of serial killers are from the US. If you look closer at the statistics, you might find some answers. One information you can get from the data is the decline in killings by serial killers in the US. The highest number of victims was in 1980-1989: 2,841 in the US.

Table 4: Number of Serial killers Victims by decade: 1900-2020

| Decade: | USA: |
|---|---|
| 1900-1910 | 204 |
| 1910-1920 | 253 |
| 1920-1930 | 264 |
| 1930-1940 | 187 |
| 1940-1950 | 159 |
| 1950-1960 | 233 |
| 1960-1970 | 527 |
| 1970-1980 | 1,884 |
| 1980-1990 | 2,841 * |
| 1990-1920 | 2,224 |
| 2000-2010 | 1,451 |
| 2010-2020 | 544 |

**Source:** Radford University's Department of Psychology

*:highest number. Note: The numbers for 2010-2020 should be interpreted with caution, as there is normally a lag between a murder and the identification of the serial killer (Aamodt, 2016).

The argument for different scientists working in the field is that some of the decline could be attributed to law enforcement has improved detection, which means that serial killers with financial motives are less likely to go undetected and so are either caught before meeting the definition of a serial killer or are put off murdering for financial gain entirely. Scientists argue that there has also been a decline in victims of serial killers and potential serial killers seeking their first victim (Tayler, 2023). But how is it with serial killers with my definition, the killing for the sake of killing, I must examine this in future works.

I think that serial killers are also aware of the risk of being caught and therefore choose low-risk victims for their murders, like sex workers, homeless people, and/or immigrants living outside the community where no one or few will miss them or report them missing (Allison, 2015).

So, can we be sure of this information in the database? What about India and Mexico where they have a lot of unsolved killings of women, and the country's law enforcement does not always acknowledge that a series of murders is committed by the same perpetrator. Therefore, a serial killer could go undetected. Russia states that they don't have serial killers, but if you examine a little further, from what is listed in the literature, there have been several serial killers in Russia. So, it depends on what information you are getting from different countries. There are also many missing persons whose whereabouts are not known whether they have been murdered. There needs to be more research done on this subject to know more about it.

## FEMALE SERIAL KILLERS - GENDER DIFFERENCES

Most serial killers are men (92%). Even though female serial killers are outnumbered, they are as dangerous as men (Davis, 2001). Since women often have a more subdued way of killing, they lack the same popularity as male serial killers in the media. Researching female serial killers is under-prioritized. Ressler (1992) admitted that he was not interested in female serial killers and knew nothing about women who kill.

Female serial killers are often referred to as the silent killers because of their motives (see Table 5). The fact that they kill very differently from male serial killers, I do think it is appropriate to use the term "female serial killers" because they have a unique profile that is important to acknowledge.

In many of the cases with female serial killers, we see that they often are not working alone. For example, Wuornos with Tyrea More, Myra Hindley with Ian Brady, Carol Bundy with Douglas Clark, Karla Homolka with Paul Bernardo, and even Johanna Dennehy with Gary Stretch and Mark Lloyd, who killed 3 men together with her male helpers, acted a bit like male serial killers, and was not acting alone. She did state that she wanted to kill like Bonnie and Clyde.

Bonnie Elizabeth Parker (October 1, 1910 – May 23, 1934) and Clyde Chestnut Barrow (March 24, 1909 – May 23, 1034) are regarded as some of the most infamous outlaws in American history. During the Great Depression (1932–1934), they traversed the Central United States with their gang, committing a series of criminal acts, including bank robberies, kidnappings, and murders.

Their activities garnered significant attention from the American press, which referred to them as "public enemies" and the period referred to as the "public enemy era" (1931-1934). The couple was caught and fatally shot by police in Bienville Parish, Louisiana. It is estimated that they were responsible for the murders of at least nine police officers and four civilians. At the time they were killed by the police (FBI, 1933).

Table 5: Female serial killers account for only 8% of all American serial killers, but they account for 76% of all female serial killers worldwide. Hickey's (2002) subsample of 62 females out of 399 serial killers found the following methods and motives:

| **Methods** | **Motives** |
|---|---|
| 1. Poison (80%)<br>2. Shooting (20%)<br>3. Bludgeoning (16%)<br>4. Suffocation (16%)<br>5. Stabbing (11%)<br>6. Drowning (5%) | 1. Money (74%)<br>2. Drugs, cult, cover up, feelings of inadequacy (24%)<br>3. Control (13%)<br>4. Enjoyment (11%)<br>5. Sex (10%) |

Many killers have several method and motive at the same time, that is why the % is more than 100%.
Source: Hickey, 2002a.

We often see female committed familicide, which is when people murder their own family members, or we see the female serial killer in healthcare or medical murderers. Female serial killers are just as dangerous as male serial killers. There is significant uncertainty about how many murders women commit. But some believe there are far more victims than we want to admit. Women take longer to be discovered when they murder and are better at covering their tracks.

Kelleher (1998) estimates that female serial killers are more successful, cautious, precise, and systematic than male serial killers and therefore they are more difficult to catch. Kelleher (1998) studied 100 female serial killers from 1900 to 1996 and found that it took an average of 8 to 20 years for female serial killers to be caught.

There is a significant difference between how men and women murder. To date, there are only a few examples of women who stalk their victims in the same way as men do: plan the attack and then kill their victims. Most women murder their husbands, children, or other family members, and their motives are mostly money, drugs, cult, cover up, or feelings of inadequacy and jealousy (see table 5).

Aileen Carol Wuornos (see next case) is often called the world's first female serial killer. She is one of the most portrayed female serial killers, but not the first, the only, nor the most heinous murderer, and for sure not the last. Wuornos was a sex worker, but sometimes when she picked up a John, she would then shoot the man and steal whatever valuables they had. She was convicted of murdering seven men.

## CASE: AILEEN CAROL WUORNOS

***Epithets: First female serial killer***

Aileen Carol Wuornos was born in Rochester, Michigan, on February 29, 1956, as Aileen Carol Pittman. Her mother, Diane Wuornos (born August 12, 1939), was 14 years old when she married Aileen's father, 18-year-old Leo Pittman (1936-1969), on June 03, 1954. On March 14, 1955, Diane gave birth to Aileen's older brother, Keith. After less than two years of marriage, and two months before Aileen was born, only 16 years old Diane filed for divorce, before she had Aileen.

Wuornos never had contact with her father. In 1967, Leo Pittman (Aileen's father) was sentenced to life imprisonment for kidnapping and raping a 7-year-old girl. Pittman was diagnosed with schizophrenia; he committed suicide by hanging in prison on January 30, 1969.

In January 1960, when Wuornos was almost 4 years old, Diane abandoned her children and left them in the care of their maternal grandparents, Lauri and Britta Wuornos. Both were alcoholics who legally adopted Keith and Aileen on March 18, 1960, who were Finnish Americans who were born in Finland and later moved to Michigan. Her alcoholic grandfather had sexually abused and beaten her when she was a child. Before beating her, he would force her to undress.

At the age of 11, Wuornos began engaging in sexual activities at school in exchange for cigarettes, drugs, and food. She was allegedly molested and raped by her big brother. In 1970, at the age of 14, she became pregnant. She had been raped by a family friend, and there has been testimony that Wuornos was raped multiple times.

On March 23, 1971, Wuornos delivered a baby boy at a home for unmarried mothers, and the child was put up for adoption. Several months after her son's birth, she quit school around the same time her grandmother died of liver failure. When Wuornos was 15, her grandfather kicked her out, and she began living in the woods near her old home, supporting herself through prostitution.

On May 27, 1974, Wuornos, age 18, was apprehended in Jefferson County, Colorado, for driving under the influence, disorderly conduct, and discharging a .22-calibre pistol from a moving vehicle, which she did not appear to.

In 1976, Wuornos hitchhiked to Florida, where she met Lewis Gratz Fell, the 69-year-old president of the yacht club. The couple got married and was featured in the local newspaper's society section. Wuornos repeatedly engaged in altercations at their local bar and was imprisoned for a brief period for assault. She also physically assaulted Fell, which resulted in him obtaining a restraining order against her within weeks of their marriage that was annulled on July 21, 1976, after a period of only nine weeks.

Wuornos returned to Michigan, where, on July 14, 1976, she was apprehended at Bernie's Club in Mancelona, Antrim County, and charged with assault and disturbing the peace for throwing a cue ball at a bartender's head.

On July 17, her brother Keith passed away from esophageal cancer, and Wuornos received $10,000 from his life insurance.

In August 1976, Wuornos was fined $105 for driving under the influence of alcohol. She utilized the financial resources she had inherited from her brother to settle the fine. She used the remaining money within two months on luxury items, including a new automobile, which she damaged in an accident.

In 1978, at the age of 22, Wuornos made a suicide attempt by discharging a firearm at her abdomen. Between the ages of 14 and 22, she made six suicide attempts.

May 20, 1981, Wuornos was arrested in Edgewater, Florida, for the armed robbery of a convenience store, where she stole $35 and two packs of cigarettes. She was sentenced to imprisonment on May 4, 1982, and released on June 30, 1983.

May 1, 1984, she was arrested for attempting to pass forged cheques at a bank in Key West. On November 30, 1985, she was named as a suspect in the theft of a revolver and ammunition in Pasco County.

January 4, 1986, she was arrested in Miami and charged with car theft, resisting arrest, and obstruction of justice for providing identification bearing her aunt's name. Miami police officers found a .38 caliber revolver and a box of ammunition in the stolen car.

June 2, 1986, Volusia County deputy sheriffs detained Wuornos for questioning after a male companion accused her of pulling a gun in his car and demanding $200. It was discovered that she was in possession of spare ammunition, and a search of the vehicle revealed a .22 pistol concealed under the passenger seat.

In 1986, 30-year-old Wuornos met 24-year-old Tyria Moore, a motel maid, at a Daytona Beach gay bar called Zodiac. The pair moved in together. They cohabited, and Wuornos supported them financially with her earnings as a sex worker. On July 4, 1987, the Daytona Beach police detained Wuornos and Moore at a bar for questioning regarding an incident in which Wuornos was accused of assault and battery with a beer bottle.

March 12, 1988, Wuornos accused a Daytona Beach bus driver of assault, claiming that he had pushed her off the bus following a confrontation. Moore was listed as a witness to the incident.

Regarding the murder of Peter Siens, Wuornos and Tyria Moore abandoned his car after being involved in an incident where Rhonda Bailey, had been present, provided police with a description of two women, which later led to a media campaign to locate them. Furthermore, police found some of the victims' belongings in pawnshops. Wuornos' fingerprint was found on a receipt at one of the pawnshops that matched the print that was left in Siems' car. She had a criminal record in Florida, and samples of her prints were in a database.

Wuornos was arrested on January 9, 1991, at the Last Resort bar in Volusia County. The following day, Moore was arrested in Pittston, Pennsylvania. Moore agreed to elicit a confession from Wuornos in exchange for immunity from prosecution and returned to Florida with the police, being accommodated in a motel. Thereafter, she made repeated phone calls to Wuornos requesting assistance in establishing her innocence, in accordance with police guidance. Three days later, on January 16, 1991, Wuornos confessed to the murders. She claimed that the men had attempted to commit rape, and that she killed them in self-defense. In November 1991, Wuornos was formally adopted by 44-year-old Arlene Pralle, with whom she had no previous contact or relation, after Pralle saw Wuornos' photograph in a newspaper.

On January 14, 1992, Wuornos stood trial for the murder of Richard Charles Mallory. It is generally inadmissible for the prosecution to use evidence of previous convictions in criminal trials, under Florida's Williams Rule.

On January 27, 1992, Wuornos was convicted of Mallory's murder, with assistance from Moore's testimony and the prosecution was permitted to introduce evidence relating to previous convictions to demonstrate a pattern of criminal activity. On January 31, 1992, psychiatrists for the defense provided testimony that Wuornos was mentally unstable and diagnosed her with borderline personality disorder and antisocial personality disorder.

On February 04, 1992, she was sentenced to death. During the trial, Wuornos' defense made efforts to introduce evidence that her victim Mallory had been previously convicted for attempted rape in Maryland and was detained in a maximum-security correctional facility for the treatment and observation of sexual offenders. Records obtained from the correctional institution showed that from 1958 to 1962, Mallory was committed for treatment and observation, resulting from a criminal charge of assault with intent to rape. These records also reflect eight years of overall treatment from the facility. In 1961, it was observed that Mr. Mallory exhibited "strong sociopathic trends." However, the presiding judge declined to permit the admission of these records as evidence and denied Wuornos' request for a retrial.

On March 31, 1992, Wuornos entered a plea of no contest to the murders of Charles Richard Humphreys, Troy Eugene Burress, and David Andrew Spears, stating that she wished to "atone with God." In her statement to the court, she stated, in part, "I wished to confess to you that Richard Mallory did violently rape me as I have told you, but these others did not. They only began to start to."

On May 15, 1992, Wuornos was sentenced to death on three more occasions. In June 1992, Wuornos pleaded guilty to the murder of Charles Edmund Carskaddon. In November of the same year, she received her fifth death sentence. In February 1993, Wuornos pleaded guilty to the murder of Walter Jeno Antonio and was sentenced to death once again. However, no charges were brought against her for the murder of Peter Abraham Siems, as his body was never found. In total, Wuornos received six death sentences.

It is noteworthy that Wuornos provided several inconsistent accounts of the killings. Initially, she claimed that all seven men had either raped or attempted to rape her while she was working as a sex worker, but later recanted the claim of self-defense, citing robbery and a desire to leave no witnesses as the reasons for murder, which makes her a predatory killer. During an interview with documentarian Nick Broomfield, believing the cameras were not recording, she disclosed that, in fact, it was self-defense, but that she could not bear to remain on death row, where she had been for a decade at that point, and she really wished to die. Aileen Carol Wuornos was executed by lethal injection on October 9, 2002.

Source: Berry-Dee & Aileen, 2006, CCPA, 2008; Chesler, 2021, Case No. SC00-1199, 2001, Chesler, 2021 and Clary, 1991.

***

Looking at Wuornos' life story, it is very similar to that of male serial killers. She was sexually abused and abandoned by her mother. When she was only 6 years old, Aileen started causing problems at home when she started taking an unhealthy interest in fire. While trying to start a fire with lighter fluid, she suffered scarring facial burns. She also began working as a sex worker as a teenager. It's not clear when examining Wuornos' case whether the motive was money or revenge against men in general. However, it is claimed that she had a strong hatred for men, compared to men's hatred of women, because she had been abused. There is evidence on the contrary, for example, in the bar's eyewitnesses said that she often frequented, and that she had many male friends and could get close to some of them, which was also reported by the undercover cop. But this is also seen in male serial killer, they are often married and have female friends and girlfriends.

The FBI has characterized most serial killers as predominantly White males who have experienced childhood abuse, often involving arson or animal torture and killing, and social isolation. Their motives are frequently characterized by sexual interests, such as fetishes, partialism, or necrophilia. Additionally, some have been motivated by anger, seeking thrills or attention, or financial gain. Additionally, many of these individuals have a history of mental illness, engage in petty criminal activities, face challenges in maintaining stable employment, and often resort to low-level criminal activities.

A notable aspect of the FBI's classification is the association with low IQ scores, particularly among those who exhibit a disorganized or impulsive behavior pattern and tend to be loners with few social connections. The question of whether women can also be classified as serial killers is an intriguing one. The characteristics of serial killers, as outlined by the FBI, bear a striking resemblance to those of Wuornos. A review of her background reveals a history marked by childhood trauma, social isolation, and a propensity for arson, and a suggesting of a possible low IQ (81-82). Additionally, her history of post-traumatic stress disorder (PTSD) and mental illness, along with challenges in maintaining employment, further underscore the complexity of her situation. Notably, her tendency towards petty crimes and independent killing sprees, which resulted in the death of many victims, is particularly noteworthy. However, a closer examination reveals additional layers to her case.

At the age of 13 or 14, she was raped and forced to give up her child for adoption, an event that this typically can give some psychological and psychiatrically problems for most women, this is not something that men experience in the same way a female. Furthermore, during her childhood, she was subjected to severe physical abuse, yet no one reported the abuse, and no one intervened. Furthermore, when she was compelled to sleep outside in the snow and an abandoned car and resorted to selling her body in exchange for cigarettes, beer, food, and drugs, no adult intervened to offer her assistance.

Not a single social worker or school counselor provided her with help and a place to live, a crucial step that her loving but alcoholic grandmother or mother failed to take (Chesler, 2021). When Wuornos did not attend school, no one came to her aid. Individuals in her intimate circle exploited her for monetary gain, exploiting her need for companionship and emotional support.

Wuornos' arrest records included charges as varied as driving under the influence, discharging a firearm while intoxicated, assaulting a bartender, speeding, resisting arrest, and attempting to pass a counterfeit check. Notably, Wuornos had a history of violent confrontations with romantic partners. Wuornos' sense of alienation from societal norms and values was palpable. It is estimated that she made at least one serious suicide attempt and perhaps two more. While in prison, Wuornos was reprimanded for fighting and uncooperative behavior.

In contrast to other known female serial killers of men, Wuornos did kill males who was strangers on the highway, outdoors, not inside at home, and with a gun, not with poison. A notable distinction between Wuornos and other female serial killers is the method of killing. While other female serial killers primarily targeted male intimate partners for financial gain, such as through insurance policies or real property, Wuornos opted for a more public and violent approach.

The most prominent case is that of Belle Gunness, a first-generation Norwegian American who is regarded as the "female Bluebeard with a profit motive." In 1900, Belle Gunness's first husband died under dubious circumstances, resulting in her receipt of a life insurance payout. She remarried. Her second husband was also found dead under confusing circumstances, leading to another insurance payout. Immigrant men, saw Belle's advertisements seeking "partners" and "hired hands," wanted to work for her, only to never be seen again. These men, who were attracted to the notion of marriage, arrived with cash and trunks full of valuables (Schechter, 2018).

Law enforcement officials alleged that Gunness was responsible for at least 25 murders and was suspected of twice that number. She was accused of committing these murders primarily for financial gain, but also for the sheer pleasure it brought her. Gunness methodically slaughtered these men and then buried their bodies on her Indiana "murder farm." This fact became evident when the police excavated their remains. Gunness presumably perished in a fire before she could be apprehended, although some claimed that she had escaped.

Some female serial killers have enticed girls into brothels with false job offers, gang-raping, beating, and addicting them to heroin and cocaine. They have coerced these individuals into becoming sex workers and have then murdered them. The consequences for disobedience were exceedingly severe. A particularly alarming instance of this occurred in Mexico during the 1950s and 1960s, involving Delfina Gonzalez and Maria de Jesus Gonzalez, who enticed and killed hundreds of girls, all of whom "disappeared." In 1963, authorities uncovered the remains of 80 girls buried on the brothel grounds. Those who were alive and were liberated were described as "nervous wrecks." The Gonzalez sisters were sentenced to 40 years, and their collaborators were also apprehended and sentenced (Chesler, 2021).

Another category of female serial killers is characterized by the killing of elderly patients for financial gain, often through the exploitation of their social security checks or insurance policies, which are often signed over to their nurses. This phenomenon is well-documented, with cases being reported globally.

Some female serial killers have a history of being compensated for the placement of out-of-wedlock newborns, killing them and retaining the financial compensation. The pursuit of financial gain, often characterized by the desire to accumulate as much wealth as possible, has been identified as a recurring theme in the motivations of female serial killers.

Wuornos, who, throughout her life, exhibited a narrow approach to financial management, often perceiving that she had "enough" money if she could purchase two days' worth of beer, food, loud music, and a motel room. She showed an inability to plan, and her lack of foresight into her future actions is also a notable characteristic.

But then she got thrown in prison and saw how other people made money from the things she had done on her own. It made her uneasy and she could not stop thinking about it, especially because everyone was talking about her.

She was just as preoccupied with her place in history and all the notoriety that goes with it as loads of other male serial killers who had been imprisoned. Wuornos was much more into negotiating deals than talking about legal defense strategies or appealing her death sentences. Also, a supposed corruption of law enforcement officials who were said to be profiting from movie deals before her arrest.

Was Wuornos a female serial killer, a spree killer, or one of a killer couple? In my opinion, she was a crossover killer, namely a killer couple and spree killer together.

Let us look at another female serial killer Juana Dayanara Barraza Samperi.

# CASE: JUANA DAYANARA BARRAZA SAMPERIO

***Epithets: first El Mataviejitas, then La Mataviejitas/Little Old Lady Killer, La Dama del Silencio/The Lady of Silence***

Juana Dayanara Barraza Samperio was born on December 27, 1957, when her mother was still a teenager. Her mother already had a severe alcohol addiction at the time and supported herself as a domestic worker and sex worker. Her children were often left alone, and, as the eldest, it was Samperio's task to take care of her younger siblings. They often slept on the bare ground, had to find food in rubbish bin, and were not allowed to go to school, which is why she remained illiterate all her life. Samperio was regularly subjected to physical and psychological violence, and several times it was so severe that she was bathed in her own blood.

When Samperio was a teenager, her mother sold her to a 62-year-old man for alcohol, with whom she was held captive, beaten, tied up, and raped. Over time, he rented her out to other men in the area. Samperio became pregnant at the age of 13, and from that time, she went through a series of abortions before becoming a mother for the first time five years later. While staying with the older man, Samperio kept hoping that her mother would come and save her, but what she didn't know was that her mother had told the rest of the family that her daughter had run away with the older man. It was years before her uncles found her and her son. When her mother died a few months later, Samperio said that she felt nothing at all.

More abusive relationships and children followed, and it didn't get any better when her stepfather, whom she loved, died of cancer.

When Samperio was 24 years old, her son was murdered by street robbers. She later described his death as the saddest moment of her life. To support her children, Samperio did various kinds of domestic work in the area where she lived, and when money was tight, she scavenged food in shops and markets. At the same time, she had a remarkable career in lucha libre, the Mexican version of show wrestling, where participants perform in costumes as superheroes and supervillains. Here she called herself La Dama del Silencio, the Lady of Silence, because she was a quiet, introverted person, although it was hard to tell when she appeared in her pink spandex suit with a large pink and silver butterfly mask on her face. She was popular, but even though she toured Mexico, each match brought her no more than 23 dollars, which wasn't enough with four hungry children at home. So, the petty theft turned to theft and burglary, which kept the family afloat, until 2001, when she suffered an injury that left her at risk of paralysis if she continued as a wrestler, forcing her to stop her wrestling career.

How many elderly women Juana Barraza Samperio killed, we may never know. She confessed to the last murder where she was caught in the act. She was convicted of the 16, where forensics found her fingerprints at the scene, but she could have as many as 49 victims on her conscience. Speculation about her motives was many. Some believed she had been seeking excitement after she had to retire from wrestling. Others believed that she was menstruating when she killed and that the full moon had made her even more aggressive. There were also those who pointed out that she often wore red, which they thought was a sign of female anger. She herself had no doubts. She was unrepentant and admitted to the police that she hated older women, who, incidentally, belonged to the same generation as her mother. Samperio told the police that she knows that it is not an excuse and that she doesn't deserve forgiveness from either God or any other person. She said that when she saw the old ladies, she felt a violent rage, which became stronger when they thought they were worth more than her or thought they could humiliate her because they had money.

Samperio is currently in prison serving a sentence of 759 years and will not be eligible for parole until she is 100 years old.

There is no doubt that Juana Barraza Samperio was a deeply traumatized person, which was reflected in her crimes. This is not meant as an excuse, as she was aware of what she was doing and the grief she caused both her own and others' families. But it increases our understanding of the impact that growing up can have on the most vulnerable children in society. Trauma can show itself in the form of difficulty coping with what you have been exposed to. The reactions that should be directed towards the person(s) who hurt them are withheld and then directed to someone else who represents the original abuser. This is seen in many serial killers who are unable to manage their emotions and are therefore unable to respond appropriately. For many children who have grown up with trauma, aggression might be the only thing they feel that keeps them safe in a world they feel has turned against them. For Juana Barraza Samperio, the older woman became the symbol of her mother she couldn't take revenge on because she was already dead, but also because it was emotionally difficult for her. In most cases, revenge against a mother or father, for example, is not possible because the parents still have so much power over the adult child that they need, subconsciously find a surrogate to kill.

Source: McLean, 2023b and Tuckman, 2006.

***

Samperio's case is particularly interesting because she has traits of both female and male serial killers. One last thing worth noting is the feeling of invulnerability that you see in some of the men, like when Dennis Rader sent letters to the press to make sure, he got credit for the murders he had committed. This sense of invulnerability was also seen in Juana Barraza, and there are not many examples of female serial killers who kill like her, where the gender of the killer could be in doubt.

As mentioned, women often have a more subdued approach and do not have the same "popularity" as male serial killers in the media. Investigating female serial killers is an under-prioritized area, and there is therefore great uncertainty about how many murders women commit. I agree with researchers and police officers who believe that there are far more than we want to admit. Women take longer to be discovered when they murder, and they are generally better at covering their tracks. This is perhaps exacerbated by the fact that they are already not on our mental radar when it comes to this type of crime. That's why it's important that we learn more about them, not least about their childhood and upbringing. We know a lot about men, but evidence-based knowledge about women is a scarce commodity. When we do case studies, we see that female serial killers also have long histories of childhood abuse, and they have a problematic family structure. We don't yet know why women often kill differently than men, because methods aside, there are many similarities between the sexes: women are also manipulative, immoral, impulsive, charming and conscienceless. Furthermore, we have started to see a raising in female serial killers murdering unknown victims, so it's about time we look at them with the same seriousness as the males.

As already mentioned, it is relatively rare for women to become serial killers in the same way as we see with men, stalking their victims, and capturing, torturing, raping, and killing them. Depending on the definition and method of counting, about 90-97% of serial killings are committed by men, but when women are guilty of this type of crime, they often go under the radar. This is because most people find it hard to believe that women can commit murder in this way. That's why police in Mexico City insisted that the serial killer was a man. While male serial killers are often caught relatively quickly, within months or a few years, women are on the loose for an average of eight years from the time they commit their first murder, and they also have more victims than men, 8 to 14 on average, compared to 8 to 11 for male serial killers. One explanation could be that female serial killers are typically more cautious and leave fewer clues, while choosing victims and methods of killing that do not necessarily reveal that a crime has been committed.

This was also seen in the case of Gwendolyn Graham and Cathy Wood (The Lethal Lovers). Gwendolyn Gail Graham (born August 6, 1963) and Catherine May Wood (born March 7, 1962) were two American serial killers couples who were convicted of the 1987 murders of five elderly women in Walker, Michigan, a suburb of Grand Rapids. They committed their crimes at Alpine Manor Nursing Home, where they both worked as nursing assistants. No one realized that the old ladies in the nursing home had been murdered until one of the two women confessed to what had happened (Ramsland, 2006).

There was no such doubt in Mexico City, but because the police insisted that they were looking for a man, it took longer to solve the case than it might have if they had listened more to the eyewitnesses. This was also evident in the many articles and reports about El Mataviejitas, which was now called La Mataviejitas instead, when they realized that the suspect was a female.

Both male and female serial killers have the same motive: power and control. And both parties have something psychological that they fulfill by killing. Sex is more important for men, but rape is also power, and remember that when it's not about sex, like exercising power and degradation (rape), you see something similar in women who enrich themselves by murdering their partners, for example, money is also power. That's why you often see a monetary motive in women who kill multiple victims. Revenge against or hatred of a particular person or group is something the two genders also have in common, as I mentioned in the case of Aileen Wuornos. However, it is often the case that serial killers have multiple motives, as was the case with Juana Barraza. Finally, we also see different choices of murder weapons. Both genders can use firearms, but because men are generally stronger, it is easier for them to strangle their victims. Knife is also used by both genders, but it is often the case that men stab far more times than women. If you look at poison killing, it is the domain method for female murderers. An American study of homicides between 1980 and 2008 Cooper & Smith (2011) shows that of all poisoners during this period, 60.5% were men and 39.5% were women. But this is because most murders are committed by men. Looking at individual cases, male killers use poison in around 0.3% of their killings, while women use poison in around 2.5% of their killings. Poison killings are difficult to detect as they require chemical tests, such as blood and hair tests, to detect. And the tests are only carried out if there is a suspicion that a death is not due to natural causes.

Hickey (2002b) studied 399 serial killers and found the following motives for male and female serial killers: for women, the motive was money in 74% of cases, whereas for men, the motive was money in 19% of murders. For men, 55% of murders were motivated by money.

Most men are motivated by sex, but only 10% of women are motivated by sex, and it is when they have a partner in the murders. For men, control was a motive in 29% of the murders, whereas for women, control was only a motive in 13% of the murders (see Table 4).

Of the 399 serial killers, Hickey (2002b) found 62 female serial killers. Of these, he found that the method for women was mostly poisoning (80%). Men mostly used firearms (41%), strangulation (37%), and knives/sharp objects (34%) (see Table 5).

Table 6: Hickey studied 399 serial killers (male and female) and found the following ranking of the most frequently used methods and motives.

| **Methods** | **Motives** |
|---|---|
| 1. Firearms mainly (41%) | 1. sex (55%) |
| 2. Strangulation/suffocation (37%) | 2. Control (29%) |
| 3. Stabbing (34%) | 3. Money (19%) |
| 4. Bludgeoning (26%) | 4. Enjoyment (16%) |
| 5. Firearms only (19%) (16%) | 5. Racism and hatred (11%) |
| 6. Poison (11%) | 6. Mental problems (6%) |
| 7. Drowning (3%) | 7. Cult inspired (5%) |
| 8. Other (2%) | 8. Attention (2%) |
| | 9. Drugs, cult, cover up, feelings of inadequacy (24%) |
| | Source: Hickey, 2002a |

Furthermore, women are more likely than men to be with another person when committing serial murders. Alarid et al. (1996) interviewed female offenders and found that 86% had an accomplice. Wuornos also had a girlfriend with her when she committed the murders.

Hickey (2016) identified and studied 34 female serial killers from 1821 to 1988. The women could roughly be divided into two categories:

- Black Widows: females who murder their husbands, but also often their children, or other family members.
- Angels of Death: Angels of Death nurses or doctors who murder their patients.

The 34 female serial killers Hickey found were responsible for between 261-271 murders. Because not all murders committed by women are convicted, the range is between 261 and 471. They had more victims (8 to 14) than male serial killers (8 to 11). One reason for this difference may be that law enforcement takes twice as long to catch female serial killers.

Feminists have criticized the literature on crime and women for many misconceptions. They argue that women are always perceived as victims, even when they commit murder, especially in popular mythologies. In most stories, both old and modern, the woman is portrayed as the victim. However, American movies have featured female psychopathic serial killers in recent years, but this is the exception. This detracts from the reality that women are mostly victims of violent crime instead of being the perpetrators.

According to Holmes et al. (1991), there is evidence that there are female serial killers who have the same modus operandi as the male serial killers I am dealing with in this book. Often, this type of female serial killer is seen with a male partner. An example of this is Carol Bundy, who murdered women and abused their bodies with her boyfriend, Douglas Clark. But there are a few examples of female serial killers who murder like male serial killers alone. Furthermore, female serial killers seldom murder unknown victims when they are alone.

I will argue that the reason for fewer female sociopaths/psychopaths might be because of the way we diagnose females and males differently. I often see females get diagnosed with borderline personality disorder and not antisocial personality disorder or psychopath. Men get diagnosed as antisocial more than borderline personality diagnoses.

Another important reason for the gender difference in the method used is that it can be somewhat difficult for a female to kill like men, who use their strength, size, and force. Females have another way of killing, but as with everything, some females are powerful, some have more strength than men, and some do use that strength to kill. Females typically have a different upbringing from males. Research shows that small girls are encouraged to resolve conflict by talking and working together; they are taught to be in the relationship and rather back out than stand for their rights (King et al., 2021).

## PARAPHILIA, FANTASY, AND SEX

Paraphilia is a condition where sexual arousal and gratification depend on fantasizing about and engaging in atypical and extreme sexual behavior. There's nothing wrong with this as long as it's with other consenting adults and no one is harmed. However, when the sexual behavior harms others or yourself, it is called a disorder. For example, a couple can engage in role-playing where one assaults the other, but this is a crime if one party hasn't consented to the act.

Although many paraphilias seem strange or extreme, they are easier to understand if you think of them as behaviors that, in less extreme versions, are quite common. For example, for some people, having a partner talk dirty can be arousing, but when talking dirty is the only way sexual arousal or gratification can occur, and the person with that desire forces people to talk dirty to them against their will, it would be considered paraphilia (APA,

2022).

Paraphilia can be classified into primary and secondary paraphilia. For example, pedophilia may be viewed as the dominant or secondary paraphilic behavior of an offender. However, the pedophile may be engaged in a variety of sexually related deviant behaviors such as voyeurism, scatologia—also called coprolalia, a deviant sexual practice in which sexual pleasure is obtained through obscene language or exhibitionism in the development of intimate relationships (APA, 2022). Exploring deviant sexual relationships is paraphilia. While primary paraphilia always has control, it is not manifested in violence.

When I talk about paraphilia, it plays a role in fantasy and sex. Fantasy plays a major role for serial killers. Before the first murder is committed, many serial killer reports that they fantasize about sex, violence, murder, and sometimes sadism. Serial killers report that these fantasies often started as children. Imagining yourself as someone else or in another situation that you really are in, which is something most children (and adults) do, and it is perfectly normal. However, in extreme situations, fantasy can take over a large part of a child's or adult's life, as seen with serial killers (Jackson & Bekerian, 2001).

Prior to any serial crime, many offenders fantasize about the crime. This has been observed in serial offenders for murder, rape, robbery, and arson.

Fantasy is often linked to sexuality. This link is seen in pornography, which often links violence and sexuality together (Dietz et al., 1986). Women in certain pornographic parts are raped and used as fantasy objects. Pornography can reinforce serial killers' hatred of women and provides an outlet for their rage, and they find it triggering (Bahn et al., 1995). An example of this can be seen in serial killer Theodore Robert Bundy's case, who used pornography to gain sexual experience. His peers engaged in this experience with real people, and not only pornography. Bundy had difficulties socializing. When he was young, he didn't know how to interact with others and had difficulty connecting with the type of females he wanted. Over time, he was drawn to the darker side of pornography: sadism and violence. A significant point to remember is that Theodore Robert Bundy was drawn to pornography for release, not as a murderer. There are many people who watch pornography every day without starting to murder and become serial killers.

Even though many serial killers engaged in extremely violent pornography and death pornography, or even films of real torture and murder, which have been found in some serial killers' homes. However, not everyone who fantasizes about sadistic violence wants to live out the fantasy. Conscience may cause people who are drawn to violent or death pornography to not act out the fantasy by thinking about the consequences of the act. However, if it is people suffering from a lack of or disturbed empathy who have these fantasies, there is a danger that their conscience and empathy with the victims and the victim's family will not stop them. Therefore, there is a real risk that they will eventually act out their fantasy and therefore become a murderer.

When the serial killer finally gives in to their fantasy and commits the first murder, it often does not live up to reality. Japanese cannibal Issei Sagawa answers the question of whether his fantasy lived up to reality or if reality did not match up to his fantasy at all. He said that murder is dirty, there was blood everywhere, the body was not as he had imagined, but cold and difficult to handle (HBO, 2002). This disappointment that reality doesn't match the fantasy means that the serial killer may suffer symptoms that look like depression. Therefore, he starts to fantasize and plan the next murder with the aim of getting closer to his fantasy next time. But the urge to kill does not disappear, and sooner or later the fantasies are replaced with actual planning of murder and take over the serial killer's life, again, and then it can be a matter of time before the serial killer feels the urge to kill again and act on the urge (Scott, 2003).

Serial killers can have a sadistic sexual component to their murders. Yet, it is not an unusually strong sex drive that drives them to murder. Instead, the motivation is more about aggression, control, and power. Even when sexual behavior is apparent in serial killers' murders, Schmidt (1983) argues that the sexual act is not the motivation for the crime. Schmidt (1983) wrote: "Sexuality contains not only its autochthonous character, but also qualities of intensity and dynamism from other sexual sources; it gets its intensity and the usage of non-sexual motives and affections."

This is especially true in relation to sadism. According to Stoller's (1975) research, three significant processes occur in sadism where only a small aspect of sexual arousal is involved. The three processes are:

1. The oscillation between anticipation of danger, victory over danger, and taking a risk. Together, this increases sexual desire.
2. The tension between fear and triumph turns sexuality into a battle. Reducing their partner to a non-person and using them as an object that is only used in the sexual act is critical in terms of erotic hostility.
3. Risk-taking and fighting are about resolving a conflict. It may be a victory over unresolved traumas dating back to childhood, or it may have been conflicts or traumas that arose while the child developed their sexual identity.

Stoller's explanation is criticized by, among others, Schorsch (1978), who believes that it is not only hostility that triggers intensive sexuality, but also previous desires from childhood, as well as a desire to relive early pleasurable stages of pure happiness. Goldberg (1975) and Schmidt (1983) call this the secularization of love: "...affections - painful ones such as fear, terror and humiliation, aggressive ones as fury and hate, but also positive ones, such as joy and approval - are transformed into the sexual and are sexually experienced as desire, attraction and excitement. The intensity of sexual desire and experiencing as well as the extent of satisfaction usually depends on non-conscious and non-identifiable meanings of a sexual act that can only be understood with biographical knowledge and not on the strength of the "pressure of instincts.""

Sexuality and paraphilia represent a form of derived hostility. Therefore, it can become more about aggression than sexuality.

But it is important that, before the extreme aggressive motivation ends in murder, which is the real motivated activity, the murderer often has violent fantasies prior to the murder.

Füllgrabe (1992) argues that it is imperative to find out why some people develop sadistic fantasies. In my study of 34 serial killers, I found that 97% of all serial killers had fantasies of rape before 18 years old. The FBI's study of 36 serial killers only found that 56% of all serial killers had fantasies of rape before 18 years old. When examining the fantasies of different serial killers, the fantasies from their childhood (of murdering and torturing) are acted out later in life. Serial killers often kill according to their early fantasies.

Not all children react to violence in their environment with violent fantasies, and not all children act them out. In the FBI's interview study of serial killers, all fantasies and dreams were negative. It was unclear whether the serial killers had positive fantasies or whether the violent fantasies were overshadowed, so that the positive ones were pushed into the background. As I will discuss later, this link between sexuality and violence can either be due to childhood sexual abuse or if they have witnessed abuse by others. Children who have these violent fantasies can be seen expressing them in interactions with other children (Paulus, 1998).

A serial killer reported that at 15, he dragged younger boys into the restroom of his school and then forced them to perform oral and anal sex. In this way, he relived what he had experienced when he was younger. Violent fantasies can predict future death and murder, but only a small portion of people who have violent fantasy will act on them. Death is the ultimate control over another human being.

Psychiatrists Dr. B.R. Johnson and Dr. J.V. Becker (1997) have done a research project at the University of Arizona examining the role of fantasy in serial killer development. They examined nine cases of 14 to 18-year-olds who had clinically significant fantasies about murder and sadism and about becoming serial killers. Johnson and Becker aimed to research whether fantasy can be linked to killing. I have attempted to locate the research project, but their research has not yet been published. This work is significant, as fantasy is critical for serial killers. However, as mentioned, it is equally imperative to research why children have these fantasies.

Apart from sexual masochism, paraphilia predominantly occurs in males. However, we don't know why, but there are some hypotheses about why some people develop paraphilias. Some psychologists believe that paraphilia repeats or return to an earlier habit in their early childhood. Behavioral scientists suggest that paraphilia arises through a process in which objects can become sexually arousing if they are repeatedly associated with pleasurable sexual activity. Sexual acts such as window-gazing or exhibitionism that provide particularly intense erotic pleasure can make people prefer these behaviors. In some cases, there seems to be a predisposing factor where difficulties forming personal relationships lead to atypical sexuality. These difficulties may be rooted in childhood problems, as seen in many serial killers. For example, behavioral research suggests that a child who is a victim or observer of inappropriate sexual behavior may learn to mimic this behavior as they grow older.

The causes could also be physical, and the relationship between hormones, behavior, and the central nervous system. This is especially true when it comes to aggression. Some studies suggest that certain abnormalities in the frontal and temporal lobes of the brain correlate with pedophilic urges. One hypothesis for foot fetishism stems from the fact that the area of the brain that processes sensory information from the feet is presumably adjacent to the area that processes sensory information from the genitals. There is still no definitive answer to how paraphilia occurs. Combining the various suggestions is the key to finding the answer. The important thing is that paraphilia, sexual fantasy, founded on dominance, control, and power, is often present in serial killers.

## CASE: JEFFREY LIONEL DAHMER

***Epithets: The Milwaukee Cannibal, The Milwaukee Monster***

Jeffrey Dahmer was born on May 21, 1960, in Milwaukee, Wisconsin. He was the first of two sons born to Lionel Herbert Dahmer, a Marquette University chemistry student and later a research chemist, and Joyce Annette Dahmer, a teletype machine instructor. Lionel was of German and Welsh ancestry, and Joyce was of Norwegian and Irish ancestry.

Some sources report that Dahmer was deprived of attention as an infant, while others suggest that he was generally doted upon as an infant and toddler by both parents. However, his mother was known to be tense and greedy for both attention and pity, as well as argumentative with both her husband and their neighbors.

As Dahmer entered first grade, Lionel's studies kept him away from home much of the time. At home, Joyce Dahmer, described as a hypochondriac who suffered from depression, demanded constant attention and spent an increasing amount of time in bed. On one occasion, she attempted suicide using Equanil, a short-term medication to treat symptoms of anxiety and nervousness. It acts on certain centers of the brain to help calm the nervous system (source: webmd.com, 2024). The parents, according to the recollections of the son, provided minimal emotional and physical support, fostering an environment of uncertainty and instability. This sentiment was further compounded by the frequent tensions and disputes between the parents, which contributed to an atmosphere of constant anxiety and distress.

At age six, Dahmer underwent hernia surgery. When he woke up from the anesthesia, he was worried someone had cut his genitals. After a long recovery, Dahmer exhibited a notable shift in demeanor, becoming more reserved and subdued. Dahmer had been an energetic and happy child before the operation.

During his elementary education, he was characterized as a reserved and timid child by his father and some peers. Jeffrey Dahmer disagreed; he was only that way at home because of all the tension, so he was always alert and afraid of what might come.

One teacher noted the early indications of abandonment due to the father's absence and the mother's illnesses, which increased when Joyce Dahmer became pregnant with her second child. In elementary school, Dahmer had a small number of friends. In October 1966, the family moved to Doylestown, Ohio.

In the meantime, Lionel obtained a degree and embarked on a career as an analytical chemist in the nearby city of Akron.

In May 1968, the family relocated to Bath Township, Summit County, Ohio. This address marked their third change in residence within two years and the sixth location for the family. The residence was situated on one-and-a-half acres of woodland, near a modest hut, where Dahmer initiated the collection of substantial insects and the skeletons of diminutive animals, such as chipmunks and squirrels. Some of these remains were preserved in jars with formaldehyde and stored within the hut.

Two years later, during a dinner with chicken, Jeffrey Dahmer inquired with Lionel as to the potential outcome of placing chicken bones in bleach. Lionel, recognizing his son's budding scientific curiosity, proceeded to demonstrate the proper method for safely bleaching and preserving animal bones. Jeffrey Dahmer incorporated these techniques into his own bone collection. He also began collecting dead animals, including roadkill's, which he would dissect and bury beside the hut, with the skulls occasionally placed atop of crosses. According to one friend, Dahmer explained that he was curious as to how animals "fit together." In one instance in 1975, Dahmer decapitated the carcass of a dog before nailing the body to a tree and impaling the skull upon a stick in the woodland behind his house. As a "prank," he later invited a friend to view the display, claiming he had found the remains. The same year, Lionel taught his son how to preserve animal bones.

Joyce Dahmer began increasing her daily consumption of Equanil, laxatives, and sleeping pills, further increasing her emotional distance from her husband and children.

From his freshman year at Revere High School, Dahmer was perceived as an outcast. By age 14, he started drinking beer and hard liquor during the day, often concealing his alcohol inside the jacket he wore to school. When a classmate asked why he was drinking Scotch so early in the morning, Dahmer shrugged and said alcohol was "my medicine." Although largely uncommunicative, in his freshman year, Dahmer was seen by staff as polite and highly intelligent but earned only average grades. He was a competitive tennis player and played briefly in the high school band.

When Dahmer reached puberty, he discovered he was gay but did not tell anyone about it and certainly not to his parents. During his early teenage years, he engaged in a brief relationship with another adolescent male. By Dahmer's own words, he began to fantasize about dominating and controlling a completely submissive male partner during his early to mid-teens.

Dahmer's masturbatory fantasies gradually evolved to focus on chests and torsos. These fantasies gradually evolved to include dissection. From the age of 16, he began fantasizing about capturing an attractive male jogger, making him unconscious and engaging in sexual activity with his body.

On one occasion, Dahmer hid in the bushes with a baseball bat in anticipation of catching a jogger whom he saw many times. However, the jogger did not run by on that day. Dahmer later admitted this was his first attempt to attack and subjugate a person.

Dahmer was known to his high school peers as a class clown who often perpetrated practical jokes, these became known as "Doing a Dahmer" and included simulating epileptic fits, seizures, or cerebral palsy at school and local stores. Occasionally, Dahmer would perform these strange behaviors for money to purchase alcohol. By 1977, his grades had declined. His parents hired a private tutor, with limited success.

The same year, to save their marriage, his parents attended counseling sessions. They continued to quarrel frequently. In September 1977, Lionel discovered Joyce's extramarital affair, which led to the couple's decision to divorce, expressing their desire to do so amicably and informing their sons of this intention. However, the divorce proceedings became increasingly contentious, ultimately leading to Lionel's relocation in early 1978. He temporarily resided in a motel on North Cleveland Massillon Road.

In May 1978, Dahmer completed his high school education. A few weeks before the graduation ceremony, Dahmer's teachers witnessed Dahmer sitting near the school parking lot, consuming numerous cans of beer. When the teacher threatened to report this incident, Dahmer disclosed that he was dealing with significant personal challenges, and the school's guidance counselor was aware of these issues. In the spring of that year, Joyce Dahmer, acting in contravention of a court order and without informing Lionel, relocated from the family residence to live with relatives in Chippewa Falls, Wisconsin. At the time, Dahmer had just turned 18 and was residing in the family home, totally alone. His parents' divorce was finalized on July 24, 1978, with Joyce being awarded custody of their younger son and alimony payments, and Dahmer was placed with his grandmother. Shortly before that, June 18, 1978, Dahmer killed his first victim.

Jeffrey Dahmer had been deeply fascinated by bones, bodies, and dissections since childhood. He displayed a preference for deceased animals. This preference may have been initiated during his early years when he observed his father extracting animal remains from beneath their family residence. According to Lionel, Dahmer experienced a peculiar sense of excitement when he heard the auditory resonance produced by the bones, which he initially referred to as his "fiddlesticks." He would periodically search the surrounding area and the family's residence for additional bones and would even explore the bodies of live animals to make sure of the location of their bones.

Dahmer said that he wanted to see what was inside the animals, which gave him a sense of power, a power he did not have in any other places and situations. He then explained that it came as a compulsion, and his fantasy slowly went from animal to humans, where the dismemberment of the animals and humans was exciting to him, but also gave him a huge feeling of control and power.

Jeffry Dahmer described that as a teenager, he began to have sexual fantasies about unconscious or dead partners; he simply explained that he connected violence with sex. He started to have fantasies about taking hitchhikers and killing them. This was a fantasy that started early in his teens, and it went from fantasy to reality with his first victim, who was a hitchhiker. Dahmer was alone in the house, and that made it easier to take his victim home with him. As Dahmer said, "My parents were gone, and I was looking for some pleasure."

On the morning of July 23, 1991, Detective Patrick Kennedy initiated a series of inquiries on Jeffrey Dahmer concerning the homicides he had committed, and the evidence found at his residence. Over the course of the following two weeks, Kennedy and Detective Dennis Murphy conducted a series of interviews with Dahmer, the total duration of which exceeded 60 hours. During these interrogations, Dahmer voluntarily resign his right to legal counsel, stating his intention to confess to the murder of sixteen young men in Wisconsin since 1987, with one further victim, Steven Hicks, who was killed in Ohio in 1978.

Most of Dahmer's victims had been rendered unconscious prior to their murder, although some had died because of having acid or boiling water injected into their brains. Most of these murders involved a ritualistic practice of positioning the victims' bodies in a manner that was suggestive of certain sexual acts, typically with the chest thrust outwards, prior to the dismemberment of the bodies. Dahmer admitted to engaging in necrophilia with several of his victims' bodies, including performing sexual acts with their viscera as he dismembered their bodies in his bathtub. It is noteworthy that a significant amount of blood accumulated in the victims' chests during the postmortem phase. Dahmer's methodical approach involved the extraction of vital organs, followed by the suspension of the torso to allow for blood drainage into a designated bathtub. This was followed by the dismemberment of non-retention organs and the removal of flesh from the carcasses. The bones intended for disposal were either pulverized or acidified using a Soilax solution. Bleach solutions were used to aid in the preservation of the skeletons and skulls he wished to retain.

Dahmer confessed to having consumed the hearts, liver, biceps, and portions of the thigh of three victims he had killed at the Oxford Apartments (Raymond Smith, Ernest Miller, and Oliver Lacy), and to having retained the flesh and organs of other victims for the purpose of consumption.

Typically, Dahmer would tenderize the body parts he intended to consume prior to preparing meals flavored with various condiments.

Referencing his reasons for consuming his victims, Dahmer stated he had initially consumed portions of his victims due to "curiosity" before adding: "I suppose, in an odd way, it made me feel they were even more a permanent part of me."

Describing the increase in his rate of killing in the two months prior to his arrest, Dahmer stated he had been "completely swept along" with his compulsion to kill, adding: "It was an incessant and never-ending desire to be with someone at whatever cost. Someone good looking, nice looking. It pervaded my thoughts incessantly." When questioned about his motivations for preserving a total of seven skulls and the complete skeletons of two victims, Dahmer stated that he had been in the process of constructing a private altar of victims' skulls, which he had intended to display on the black table located in his living room. He had photographed the bodies of many of his victims on this table.

An illustration provided by Dahmer depicted the private altar he had been planning to create at the time of his July 1991 arrest. This display of skulls was to be adorned on each side with the complete skeletons of Miller and Lacy. The severed heads found in his kitchen were to have all flesh removed and incorporated into the altar, as was the skull of at least one future victim. Incense sticks were to be placed at each end of the black table, above which he intended to place a large blue lamp with an extending blue globe light. The entire construction was to be placed before a window covered with a black opaque shower curtain, in front of which he intended to sit in a black leather chair.

When asked in a November 18, 1991, interview to whom the altar was dedicated, Dahmer replied: "Myself... It was a place where I could feel at home." He further described his intended altar as a "place for meditation," from where he believed he could draw a sense of power, adding: "If this had happened six months later, that's what they would have found."

What was the core of Dahmer's acts? Was it mental illness, paraphilia, or his schizotypal and borderline personality disorder? In my opinion, the schizoid personality disorder, together with the paraphilia, which was the wish to be together with a person with whom he did not have to relate as a real person, drove him to the act of killing. It was not the murder Dahmer wanted, but a body he could have 100% control of at any time. That was also the reason he tried to make living people zombies, which was not a success for him, so he kept killing his victims.

If he had not experienced trauma as a child, the constant danger that lurked and uncertainly in the family, he might never have had the wish to gain power and control, which led to the urge to control dead bodies, which started with animals and then later people. In his childhood the interest in what was inside the animals gave him, for the first time in his life, a sense of power; that sense was the chase. But people always have a choice to either kill or not kill, Dahmer chose to kill.

The most important thing for Dahmer was that he wanted total control over his victims. I have a hypothesis about the double hernia operation he had when he was only 3 years old. This could have impacted him a lot and could have been a trauma for him.

I have seen children who have had the same or similar operation, having a psychological reaction to it afterwards, like anxiety, depression, an eating disorder, or conduct disorder. They have a trauma reaction to that because they don't fully understand what is happening, it hurts, and it can damage them psychologically. So, it is crucial that we are aware of that and take that into consideration and talk to the child about the operation, also as they grow up, letting them know what happens exactly, so they don't make their own internal story, that might not be the truth.

The paraphilia (necrophilia) was the gateway to becoming a serial killer for Dahmer, together with getting close to someone. So, all this factors together, with the psychotic and personality disorder, we have a dangerous cocktail for Dahmer, which made him react to his fantasies and wishes.

The alcohol made him numb so he could kill, but it was not the killing that was the endgame.

The diagnoses that were given to Dahmer included borderline personality disorder, substance use disorder (alcoholism), psychotic disorder, schizotypal personality disorder, and necrophilia. Although various diagnosis was proposed, he was not found "guilty by reason of insanity". This was mainly due to the maintenance of his comprehension of the legal and moral wrongfulness of his acts and the steps he took to hide his crimes, as well as his tendency to plan the murders beforehand, proving the crimes were not impulsive and uncontrollable acts in the context of mental illness.

On July 25, 1991, Dahmer was charged with four counts of first-degree murder. By August 22, he had been charged with eleven additional murders committed in Wisconsin. On September 14, investigators in Ohio uncovered hundreds of bone fragments in a wooded area behind the address where he had confessed to killing his first victim. They formally identified two molars and a vertebra using X-ray records of Steven Hicks three days later, authorities in Ohio formally charged him with Steven Hicks' murder.

Dahmer was not charged with the attempted murder of Tracy Edwards, nor with the murder of Steven Tuomi. The district attorney's office only brought charges where murder could be proven. Thus, Dahmer was not charged with Tuomi's murder beyond a reasonable doubt and lacked recollection of committing this homicide due to an absence of physical evidence. During a scheduled preliminary hearing on January 13, 1992, Dahmer entered a plea of guilty but insane, admitting to 15 homicides. Jeffrey Lionel Dahmer was murdered on November 28, 1994.

Source: Borowski, 2017, Dahmer, 1994, 2021, Masters, 1993, Dahmer, Dahmer & Phillips, 1994 and McEvoy, 2023.

In the next chapter, I will examine mental illness and serial killers. Many people think that serial killers are mentally ill, but few are mentally ill; they are more mentally disturbed and have one or more personality disorders, but I will examine that in chapter 3. For now, I will then go through some mental disorders that serial killers have been diagnosed with.

# 3. ARE SERIAL KILLERS PSYCHOTICS?

## DISSOCIATIVE IDENTITY DISORDER

Dissociative identity disorder (DID), previously known as multiple personality disorder (MPD), is a complex psychological condition caused by severe trauma during early childhood, which is usually extreme and repetitive physical, sexual, or emotional abuse. Until 1994 it was known as multiple personality disorder and split personality.

The DSM-5 provides the following criteria to diagnose dissociative identity disorder: two or more distinct identities or personality states are present, each with its own relatively enduring pattern of perceiving, relating to, and thinking about the environment and self. Dissociation means to split or divide and is a partial or complete loss of the normal integration between memory, identity awareness, immediate sensory experiences, and motor control (WHO, 1998: pp. 111-112). In dissociation, the state of consciousness deviates from normal so that only a limited amount of conscious mental activity is available, while the rest is unconscious. Dissociation is a primitive defense mechanism that keeps unpleasant states apart. For example, if a child is being abused, DID can keep awareness of the abuse out of consciousness. This is a method of dealing with fundamental conflicts, where difficult situations are unconsciously absent from the mind (Hemmingsen et al. 1998: p. 101).

DID uses defense reactions. These defense reactions are formed during life. If the person's development is harmonious, the defense response has developed into an agile and flexible personality structure. In most situations, this allows the person to respond appropriately. If the defense mechanism is poorly developed, the person is vulnerable and reacts inappropriately in stressful situations. Under severe stress, the person may use primitive ways of dealing with the situation, such as splitting. Splitting means dividing themselves into more than one identity. There can be many identities, but the most common is between three and five identities.

In splitting, the person may perceive the parents as evil one moment and exclusively good the next. For individuals, there is no connection between the bad and the good. One person can also be viewed as exclusively virtuous, while another is perceived as purely evil. The person may experience splitting with the consequence of shifting experiences from the environment and the self. The separation is so severe that the person is unaware that the other persons are in the same body, so they do not recognize that there is a connection between the split parts (Vestergaard & Sørensen, 1998).

This can also be seen with borderline personality disorders in a milder form, where different personalities can be explained by internal images of early objects. This could be the mother, who has split into a good and a bad mother with borderline. These beliefs later apply to other current objects. The patient has difficulty integrating both the positive and problematic sides of others, but also themselves (Cullberg, 1996).

So, the splitting occurs when a patient with DID personality is divided into multiple personalities/identities, the other personalities, besides maybe one (not the core personality), do not know of the other personalities. The reason for splitting can also be because of trauma, so they don't have to deal with it. This defense mechanism was initially a way of surviving the trauma, which is helpful for the person, but over time, this results in DID and can be harmful to relationships and create difficulties in creating close bonds with other people.

As mentioned, DID can develop when a child is exposed to extremely traumatic experiences. Various researchers (Bradley et al., 1992) have shown that traumatic experiences in childhood remain in the memory for a longer period, whereas normal experiences are forgotten over time. They contain more emotional and perceptual elements than normal events. The impact on memory is different due to the high emotional stress involved. Norris (1989) explains that serial killers often experience massive violence as children, and it can affect them. He writes: "Parents who abuse their children, physically and psychologically, instill in them an almost instinctive reliance upon violence as the first resort to any challenge."

Ross-Gower et al. (1998) found a link between sexual abuse and dissociative psychopathology. They studied 45 women who received psychological help for various undisclosed reasons. Of those, 28 (62.2%) had been sexually assaulted. They were then divided into two groups. One group consisted of 28 women who had been sexually abused, and the other group consisted of 17 women who had not. They were examined using, among other things, Ross' questionnaire, the Dissociative Experience Scale (DES), which is used to diagnose and differentiate dissociative symptoms in patients (Ross, 1997, pp. 107-108). The DES is a 28-item questionnaire that asks about the dissociation degree of dissociation. The scale is structured so that you score from 0, where you do not dissociate, up to 100, where you dissociate in most aspects of life (Ross, 1997, p. 55). Patients with DID cause by sexual abuse or neglect have DES scores between 30 and 40. It was found that the 17 women studied who had not been sexually abused had an average DES score of 12.1. The 28 women with a history of sexual abuse had an average DES score of 21.3, indicating that women who have been sexually abused dissociate more. This allows them to, in their mind, escape sexual abuse (Ross-Gower, 1998).

Alice Miller (1998) states that the child's trauma becomes subconscious and always remains in the background. Whenever the child remembers what happened, it is catastrophic. Therefore, it becomes repressed and unconscious. As an adult, an abused child's unconscious drives them to constantly replay traumatic scenes. They are trying to escape the anxiety that the abuse has left them with without knowing it. It doesn't have to be persistent abuse, but it can also be a single trauma. If the child, as an adult, experiences violence or transgressive behavior towards them, that can be the trigger.

The serial killers who have claimed to suffer from DID over the years have claimed that it was another personality who committed the murders without the subject's knowledge (Lane, 1996).

An example of this is serial killer Kenneth Alessio Bianchi, who was examined by psychiatrist Dr. John Watkins (1984). Bianchi's lawyer believed he suffered from DID. Dr. Watkins interviewed and filmed Bianchi for 17 hours. In the film, he switches between two different personalities. During the interview, a new persona, Steve, emerged, who was supposedly the person who murdered the woman Bianchi was charged with. Steve had a more aggressive personality than Kenneth, and the footage shows him cheerfully recounting the murders with his cousin and alone. Steve says Kenneth is stupid and doesn't understand anything (Discovery, 2003).

In the footage, we can see that Bianchi changes his personality. However, some factors question whether he suffered from DID. It is difficult to know for sure if someone struggles with DID, as there is no way to measure or test for the disorder. Diagnosis is solely based on clinical examination. In Bianchi's case, he revealed himself by sometimes referring to himself in third person when he should be Steve. People with DID do not talk about themselves in third person when they are the main personality. So, when Steve was the person who was in front, he should speak in first person. DID patients switch between two or more distinct personalities. Sometimes one personality is present, sometimes another, and they often don't know about each other. Only when they are in treatment, and you integrate the personalities, do they realize there are other personalities in them. And as stated, it is never the basic person (the original personality) who knows about the other personalities, but other personalities know each other. Furthermore, Bianchi initially had only two personalities until one of the psychiatrists who examined him told him that DID patients have at least three personalities. Soon after, Bianchi developed a third personality (Summers, 2002). This also indicates that Bianchi didn't have DID but tried to make it look like he had.

Danny Harold Rolling is also an example of a serial killer who tried to claim DID. It is not conclusively established whether he suffered from DID, as he had a long history of psychiatric disorders throughout his childhood and adolescence (Bahn et al., 1995).

There are no valid studies to substantiate whether serial killers have developed or suffer from DID.

In Chapter 9, you will find more information about Arthur John Shawcross, who also claimed that he had DID. He was diagnosed with dissociative disorder but not DID. Dissociative disorder is a milder form of DID, where you only split the trauma away from you and experience a loss of connection between thoughts, memories, feelings, surroundings, behavior, and identity. These conditions include escape from reality in ways that are not wanted and not healthy, but you do not split your identity into different personalities.

During the trial, psychologist Dr. Dorothy Otnow Lewis tried to convince the jury and judge that Shawcross suffered from DID. Lewis hypnotized Shawcross, and during the hypnosis, multiple personalities emerged. Hypnosis is not used anymore to diagnose people with DID (APA, 2022). So, when trying to determine if a person has DID, family and friends can help determine if the disorder only appears when the person is examined by a professional or if the family has noticed that the person has unusual or bizarre behaviors that may explain the multiple personalities. If family members, friends, or colleagues see this behavior, it could be indicative of the diagnosis. If the patient is extremely forgetful, does not always know where he or she is, and, at times, clearly changes personality to such an extent that it appears to be a different person than the original, this together could be a sign that the person suffers from DID.

Ross believes that even though serial killers suffer from DID, they are not diagnosed because, in the USA, they do not want serial killers to be declared insane. If they are declared insane, they are innocent and can avoid the death penalty if they are "not guilty by reason of insanity" (Ross, 1997, p. 75).

Ross (1997) proposes a solution to this problem. He suggests holding the trial in two stages: first, determining if the person is guilty. The trial ends here if the person is innocent, but if the person is guilty, the judge and jury decide the punishment. Once this has been determined, it must be decided whether the offender is mentally ill. Treatment in prison is established. This will rule out the possibility that some people want to declare themselves insane without being insane. So, this is not a way to avoid punishment. At the same time, people who need treatment can receive it in prison. There are some states in the USA that use this approach to date.

As mentioned, there is disagreement about whether serial killers suffer from DID. Turvey (1995) writes that some violent sex offenders develop other personalities completely dissociated from their vicious criminal personality. In this way, they do not stand out from society and appear normal. Fantasy further enables serial killers to dissociate. If the fantasy is complicated, the victim can be seen as an object. It can create more distance between violent behavior and personality. Disfiguring the victim and staging the crime scene further dehumanizes the victim and allows serial killers to further distance themselves.

Pincus (2002), a psychiatrist at Georgetown University in Washington, studied 100 serial killers who denied being abused in childhood, even though there was evidence that they had been mistreated (medical reports, family accounts, or scars and burns). Pincus found that those who denied abuse had a memory disorder, suggesting dissociation. Holmes & Holmes (2002) say that many serial killers suffer from split identity. Split identity cannot be categorized as DID, but serial killers report that they establish a dividing line between the killer and the person who acts normally in society, which they call Fractured Identity Syndrome.

There has been some debate about Fractured Identity Syndrome (FIS), which is a theory that combines Charles Cooley's "Looking-Glass Self" and Erving Goffman's "Virtual and Actual Social Identity theories." FIS suggests that a social event, or series of events, during one's childhood or adolescence results in fracturing the person's personality. The term fracture is defined as a small break in the personality that is not visible to the outside world. Fragmentation occurs during adolescence.

Social scientists have long theorized that social deviants are a product of traumatization in life. Traumatic events affect different people in different ways. It is possible for some people to experience a traumatic event, and it will not be of any significance in their lives; they will simply move on. For other people, these traumatic events are a precursor to crime, delinquency, and mental health issues (Holmes et al., 1999).

There has been interest in clarifying whether other forms of dissociation are significant for serial killers. First, I will go through a case where DID was present, and after that, I will discuss dissociative amnesia and dissociative fugue.

## CASE: KENNETH ALESSIO BIANCHI

### *Epithets: The Hillside Strangler*

Kenneth Alessio Bianchi is an American serial killer, kidnapper, and rapist. He is known for the ten murders committed from 1977 to 79 with his cousin Angelo Buono Jr. and for murdering two other women in Washington.

Bianchi tried to fake multiple personality disorder (MPD), but it was concluded that he was faking, and the diagnosis of antisocial personality disorder with sexual sadism was concluded instead.

Kenneth Bianchi was born on May 22, 1951, in Rochester, New York, to a 17-year-old alcoholic sex worker who gave him up for adoption two weeks after his birth. He was adopted in August 1951 by Nicholas Bianchi and his wife, Frances Scioliono-Bianchi; he was their only child.

The family had a hostile environment, with his mother and father fighting, and there have been reports of violence towards Kenneth Bianchi. Bianchi had many behavioral problems and was prone to temper tantrums as well as insomnia. He urinated in his own bed, for which he was frequently examined by doctors for the involuntary urination problem, which caused him great humiliation. Bianchi's older cousin and Frances' nephew, Angelo Buono, also experienced Bianchi's involuntary urination when he came to stay with him and his family in 1957. Bianchi was barely 6 years old, and Buono only remembered Bianchi as a restless, irritated child who kept wetting his pants.

Bianchi was deeply troubled from an early age, with Frances Scioliono-Bianchi describing him as a "compulsive liar" from the time he could speak. When Bianchi was 5 and a half years old, he would often fall into inattentive, trance-like daydreams in which his eyes would roll back in his head. Based on these symptoms, a doctor diagnosed him with petit mal seizures (now called absence seizures, which is a form of epilepsy that causes him to blankly stare into space for a few seconds). They usually don't cause any long-term problems.

Bianchi was sent to a private Catholic elementary school to try to correct his behavior, which did not affect him.

Frances Scioliono-Bianchi also took him to a psychiatrist several times. Bianchi was diagnosed with *passive-aggressive personality disorder at the age of ten, and both Bianchi and his mother were advised to go to therapy, but neither of them went to therapy. At age 11, Kenneth Bianchi was seen by Dr. Dowling at the DePaul Clinic, where the *psychological evaluation* report stated in summary that "Kenneth was a severely repressed individual, characterized by profound anxiety and loneliness."

**Passive-aggressive personality disorder: The fifth edition of the Diagnostic and Statistical Manual of Mental Disorders (DSM-5) does not include PAPD.*

*This is partly due to the broad nature of the terminology. PAPD is characterized by a tendency to procrastinate, dawdle, be stubborn, or be intentionally inefficient. Individuals with PAPD may also "forget" appointments or misplace important materials. These behaviors are interpreted as passive expressions of underlying negativism. This pattern persists, even when individuals can engage in more adaptive behaviors, and often impedes success in various domains, such as occupations, domestic life, and academic pursuits. The disorder was classified in an appendix of DSM-IV-TR for proposed diagnostic categories needing further study and given an alternative name, negativistic personality disorder, in accordance with the theoretical proposals of Theodore Millon. However, it has been incorporated into DSM-5 and DSM-5-TR under "Other Specified Personality Disorder" (APA, 2022).*

Bianchi's intelligence was measured at 116 at the age of eleven. Despite his above-average intelligence, he was an underachiever and was twice expelled from school for failing to get along with teachers. Frances Scioliono-Bianchi described him as "lazy," and his teachers stated he was working below his potential. He had various behavioral problems.

After his adoptive father died suddenly of pneumonia when he was 13 years old, Bianchi refused to cry or show any other signs of grief. After her husband's death, Scioliono-Bianchi had to work while her son attended public high school, and she was known to keep him home from school for long periods of time.

Bianchi dated frequently and joined a motorcycle club. Shortly after graduating from Gates-Chili High School in 1970, he married his high school girlfriend, Brenda Beck, at 18. The marriage ended after a few months, and he claimed it was annulled. He said he had very high standards for her, but it was standards that he by no means could keep up with himself.

Bianchi decided he wanted to be a police officer and enrolled at Monroe Community College to study police science and psychology. He dropped out after one semester and drifted through a series of menial jobs, ending up as a security guard at a jewelry store. His work as a security guard gave him the advantages that he could exploit so he could steal, which, in his opinion, he was entitled to, without notice. So, he took the opportunity to steal valuables, which he often gave to girlfriends or sex workers to buy their loyalty. He applied for a job with the sheriff's department several times but was rejected.

Due to his many petty thefts, Bianchi was constantly on the move. In 1976, he moved to Los Angeles, California, and began spending time with Angelo Buono, who impressed Bianchi with his flashy clothes, jewelry, and talent for getting any woman he wanted and, as he said, "putting her in her place." Soon they were working together as pimps, and by the end of 1977, they had escalated to committing what would become known as the Hillside Strangler murders.

Bianchi (27 years old) moved to Bellingham, Washington, with his girlfriend, Kelli Boyd, whom he had met in 1977 through his work while he was employed at the title company. The couple soon began live together. In June of 1977, he proposed marriage to Boyd, who was skeptical and declined his offer. However, she continued to live with him. His demeanor became morose, and he began spending nights away from home with Angelo Buono. He also began lying to Boyd about the activities he engaged in during these nights where he was not at home.

In May 1978, Bianchi worked as an armed security officer, from where he was captured in 1979.

For preparing for the trial, on March 29, 1979, the defendant entered an insanity defense because of multiple personality disorder (MPD) before the Bellingham court. If successful, the defense would result in the dismissal of the death penalty, and potentially, Bianchi could get free because of "the not guilty by reason of insanity" claim. attributing the alleged crimes to an alternate personality he identified as "Steve Walker."

To find a way to use an insanity defense, the defense attorney assembled a team of psychologists and psychiatrists to examine him. He was examined by six court-appointed psychiatrists, two other psychiatrists, and three psychologists. Only the two appointed by the prosecuting attorney said he was faking.

Dr. Martin Lunde was a psychologist and a clinical associate professor of psychiatry. He said: "The thing that puzzled me was that there were some things he seemed not to remember or had different versions of, which had no relation to the crime. And the two that stand out the most in my mind are his descriptions of his mother as a wonderful, saintly kind of woman when I knew from records from childhood, that that was not the case; and secondly the fact that he had no memory, he had a loss of memory, amnesia as we would call it, for various events in his childhood including periods when he was in psychiatric treatment and so I was puzzled by this. But other than that, I say, he seemed like a nice enough fellow."

Dr. John Watkins, a professor of psychology at the University of Montana, was asked by Bianchi's lawyers to use hypnosis to try to unblock his memory. Dr. Watkins visited him in the Bellingham jail. It was there that over 60 hours of interviews were videotaped.

Dr. Watkins' arrival produced a sensational turning point in the case. He stated that in a true multiple personality, there are from two to several completely separate personalities within the same body. Each one has its own identity, behaviors, mannerisms, and speech, and when one is present, the person with MPD may be completely unaware of the existence of the others.

The presiding judge faced a challenging dilemma. Initially, the defendant had refused to enter an insanity defense, but he changed his mind, and a panel of experts was appointed to determine whether the defendant truly had MPD. Dr. Ralph Allison, a California psychiatrist specializing in multiple personality, was then consulted by the judge, who was independent of both the defense and the prosecution. In his report, he wrote that Bianchi exhibited amiable qualities, presenting as pleasant, courteous, and ordinary, as would be expected from a middle-class working individual with a family. He expressed a complete lack of understanding regarding his involvement in the situation, finding it utterly perplexing. During the session, Bianchi entered a "trance state," during which a malevolent personality emerged, identified itself as "Steve," and confessed to the homicides, displaying a blatant disregard for human life.

Dr. Watkins' report for the judge stated: "that he is a dual personality, and he had been since the age of nine. At that time, he created an alter personality which took the name of 'Steve Walker.' This was while he was hiding under the bed in his bedroom, trying to escape his mother's vicious tongue and punishing hand. As time elapsed, 'Steve Walker' became increasingly independent in action and was able to take over the body of Kenneth Bianchi, causing a great deal of trouble in the family and later in the world outside the family."

Dr. Watkin went on, stating: "Then I concluded that Ken Bianchi can understand what he is charged with, but he has amnesia for the actual incidents during which his body was under the control of Steve Walker. Therefore, he has not been able to discuss his whereabouts, actions and all this with his attorney since all that time is completely unknown to him. 'Steve Walker,' on the other hand, does not consider Mr. Brett (Bianchi's attorney) to be his attorney. Therefore, at the present time, I would not consider Ken Bianchi or Steve Walker competent to stand trial for the crimes charged."

But the problem for the defense was that no one could confirm that Bianchi had MPD, no one in his own life, not his girlfriend, co-workers, persons he grew up with, or any other.

The investigators did not believe that Bianchi had MPD, so the prosecutor brought in their own psychiatrists, notably Dr. Martin Orne, a professor of psychology and psychiatry at the University of Pennsylvania and an expert in hypnosis, to challenge Bianchi's claims. When Dr. Orne mentioned to Bianchi that in genuine cases of the disorder, there tend to be three or more personalities, Bianchi promptly created another alias, "Billy" to prove that Bianchi had lied about having multiple personalities to avoid being prosecuted. Dr. Orne tested him by introducing him to his "invisible" lawyer, who was not present. Bianchi interacted with the imaginary lawyer. He tried to greet the non-existent attorney with a gesture of his imaginary hand. This phenomenon, termed "tactile hallucinations," is an occurrence that, according to experts, is seldom, if ever, observed during hypnosis or other forms of neurological-event-triggered hallucinations. Dr. Orne then brought in his real lawyer, flustering Bianchi, who claimed that the imaginary lawyer had vanished. Dr. Orne had never encountered a genuine instance of "tactile hallucination" during his career, thereby suggesting that this was a complete fabrication.

Bianchi's defense lawyer, Dean Brett, stated that they obtained the psychiatric records of Kenneth Bianchi to illustrate that he was referred to various medical professionals, presenting with a series of physical ailments. These included ocular motility, tics, falling, and what were interpreted as petit mal seizures. The medical professionals recommended consultation with a psychiatrist. As stated before, his mother brought him to the De Paul Clinic, and their report included the following observations: "When Bianchi was eleven years old, Dr. Dowling reported that: 'Kenneth is a profoundly hostile boy who exhibits an acute need for dependence that his mother fulfills. He expressed a profound reliance on his mother for survival, expending considerable energy to regulate his hostility... "There appeared to be a fundamental confusion regarding his own identity, as he made a concerted effort to appease his mother, who consistently expressed dissatisfaction."

Investigators found through their investigation that the name "Steven Walker" came from a student whose identity Bianchi had previously attempted to steal for the purpose of fraudulently practicing psychology. Police also discovered a small library of books on modern psychology in

Bianchi's home, which further suggested his ability to fake the disorder.

The impact was that it broke the multiple personality defense; they were able to prove and document the fact that Stephen Walker really did exist, and it was not an alter ego of Kenneth Bianchi. Because of that, Kenneth Bianchi withdrew his plea of not guilty by reason of insanity. In a plea bargain, the state of Washington dropped its demand for the death penalty in exchange for an agreement from Bianchi to plead guilty to the Bellingham murders and to testify against Angelo Buono in Los Angeles because Bianchi was faced with the compelling police evidence on Stephen Walker and with Dr. Oven's investigation that cast huge doubts on the psychiatric evidence of MPD.

Dr. Oven consulted Margaret Thaler Singer, a psychologist and professor of psychology at the University of California at Berkeley. Her conclusion was that from childhood, Bianchi's history was that of a typical psychopath and that he was a true psychopath. Singer stated that even his own mother said that he was a compulsive liar, and he has a history of lifelong, almost pointless lying, which is the mark of a psychopathic kind of habitual lying and that the lying is done usually just to try to persuade a person or to make the psychopath feel better at the moment.

Margaret Singer saw some of the love letters Bianchi wrote to different women as evidence of the lies and manipulative charm of a psychopath and stated that psychopaths never quit. Some of the letters were addressed to hairdresser Angie Kinderberg, who was just one of the people Bianchi tried to provide with an alibi for the murders he had committed.

Singer stated that psychopaths just don't stop; they don't give up and continue the same style. He is sane, he knows the difference between right and wrong, he was able to form the intent for their murders, and they were highly planned and organized murders both before and afterwards, so he is sane and can stand trial.

Dr. Ralph Allison changed his opinion after he had left private practice to become a prison psychiatrist. He said that he had changed his mind about

Bianchi because of his experience in prison, which opened his eyes, and he saw that there was no reason to believe anything they said. Allison had been used to believing what his patients told him and working from that. But in prison, he found out that you can never believe a prisoner, but four experts kept believing Bianchi had MPD.

On November 3, 1981, the judgment was that Bianchi faked both the hypnosis and MPD. The conclusion was based on the circumstantial evidence acquired by the investigators, the contradictory testimony of Bianchi regarding his mental status, the opinions voiced by the psychiatrist, Dr. Orne, and the circumstantial evidence involving Steve Walker's personality. Also, in Bianchi's home, the investigators found over 21 books about hypnosis, psychiatry, and psychology. Some of the books were found in his bookshelf, and some of them were found in a basement in boxes. Among these books were *Dictionary of Behavioral Science, Psychoanalysis of Behavior Therapy, Psychology and Behavioral Therapy, Modern Clinical Psychology, Diagnostic Psychological Testing, Hypnotic Techniques, Elements of Psychology, Supervision of Police Personnel, Infant Psychiatry, Criminal Procedure Law and Juvenile Delinquency.*

All this led Bianchi to confess his fabrication of MPD, ultimately resulting in a diagnosis of antisocial personality disorder with a sexual sadism disorder. He consented to testify against Buono for a reduced sentence. However, during his testimony, he exhibited a pattern of uncooperativeness and self-contradictions, seemingly aiming to circumvent a conviction. However, these efforts were ultimately unsuccessful, as Buono was convicted and sentenced to life imprisonment without the possibility of parole. Bianchi plead guilty to 5 of the Hillside murders and was ultimately sentenced to six terms of life imprisonment.

In 1980, Bianchi initiated a relationship with Veronica Lynn Compton, a woman he had met in prison. Compton was an aspiring actress and playwright who suffered from drug-induced psychosis and was fascinated by serial killers. She authored a screenplay titled *The Mutilated Cutter*, which was about a female serial killer, and sent Kenneth Bianchi a copy of the script, hoping to gain his opinion about it. During Bianchi's trial, she testified for the defense, providing the jury with a false and vague account of the crimes to clear him. She also admitted to wanting to purchase a mortuary with another convicted murderer for necrophilia. She was later convicted and imprisoned for attempting to strangle a woman she had lured to a motel to convince authorities that the Hillside Strangler was still on the loose. Bianchi had allegedly provided her with semen during a prison visit to plant on the victim to make it look like a rape/murder committed by the Strangler.

There were, in total, 13 other alibis. For example, Bianchi had asked his mother to type an alibi letter for him with rubber gloves on so there'd be no fingerprints on it and wanted her to fly to Seattle, Washington, still with rubber gloves on and mail it so that that would establish an alibi. He also tried to blame the murders in Washington on a dead motorcyclist whom he knew was dead.

Bianchi is currently serving a life sentence in the Washington State Penitentiary for these crimes (aged 74).

Source: O'Brien, 2017, Barnes et al., 1984, Iginla, 2019, Lindsey, 1979, Orne et al., 1984 and McClary, 2008.

***

Could a person have MPD/DID and commit murder as the "other" person? Yes, that is possible, but that does not mean that the person is not guilty. In my opinion, it is still the same person. The personalities are in the same body, so that does not mean that one personality cannot be guilty. Many murderers will tell you that they did not feel like themselves when they committed murder, but that does not mean that they are not guilty. The person must be seen as one person and not as more than one person, so I am a huge advocate for seeing the person, even with multiple personalities, as one person.

In the case of Kenneth Bianchi, there are many red flags that reveal that he was faking it. A way around is to first find out if the person is insane or not; afterward, find out if the person is guilty of the crime. If the person is found insane, the person should then have treatment in a psychiatric facility, not to let the person go free of the crime.

## DISSOCIATIVE AMNESIA AND DISSOCIATIVE FUGUE

Dissociative amnesia causes memory loss. The cause must be psychological, as organic causes are rarely seen. The disorder is activated by stressful events such as war, natural disasters, or other traumatic events.

According to DSM-5, there are four types of dissociative amnesia, with each type forming differently depending on the type of trauma the person is exposed to (Hickey, 2016, p. 84; Morrison, 1995). The four types are:

1. Selective amnesia is when a person remembers parts of events over a certain period. For example, a person who has been abused can only remember parts of the abuse.
2. Generalized amnesia is when a person's entire life cannot be remembered.
3. Coherent amnesia is when the person cannot remember parts of events that happened at a specific point in time. This can be up to the present or over a continuous period.
4. Systematized amnesia is when the person cannot remember specific facts, which can be anything. For example, a person suffering from this type of amnesia cannot remember anything about a particular family member (APA, 2022, pp. 229-232).

Dissociative fugue is described in DSM-5 as a temporary psychological escape or psychological disturbance resulting from traumatic events. Individuals suffering from dissociative fugue will experience identity change due to their lack of self-identity.

For some people, it is too painful to recall certain events or people. As a defense mechanism, certain parts or the entire event is excluded from memory. It can be a normal mechanism, and many people need to forget some events from time to time. It could be a severe divorce or mistakes we have made that we don't want to remember. But for some people, dissociation has become a survival mechanism. Memory can be highly selective when dealing with threatening or anxiety-provoking information. This is seen, for example, if the person has been sexually assaulted. Then, they can use dissociation in the sense that while the assault is occurring, they can imagine it is happening to someone else. In the case of chronic abuse, the person may have amnesia about what occurred, and the event is completely removed from their consciousness, but the event remains in their subconscious. In this way, they can live as if nothing had happened.

## OTHER PSYCHIATRIC DISORDERS

In history, we have seen a few serial killers who suffer from schizophrenia. For example, Herbert Mullin was psychotic. He heard his father's voice telling him to murder some people. He also believed that murder prevented earthquakes and floods. Mullin was declared sane by the courts, even though everyone knew he was mentally ill and paranoid.

Richard Thenton Chase (The Vampire of Sacramento) had paranoid schizophrenia. He thought he would die if he did not drink human blood (see the next case).

Psychotic serial killers are often easier to catch as they often leave many clues at the crime scene. In addition, they are often not as calculated as non-psychotic serial killers. What makes serial killers so dangerous is that they appear to function normally and do not stand out from their surroundings.

Although many argue that serial killers are not insane, I believe more serial killers are mentally ill than some of the literature suggests (Bahn et al., 1995). Serial killers may be psychotic if they have diminished sensory experiences, such as an impaired sense of smell. The inability to smell may be due to brain damage or psychosis. The impaired sense of smell may explain how serial killers can live with bodies in their homes for long periods of time. Some serial killers have the body at home, and they bring it to the table when they eat, for example, Jeffrey Dahmer and Dennis Nilsen. In several cases, the smell of the bodies was so overwhelming that police officers had to wear gas masks when entering the serial killer's home. It can be difficult to understand how serial killers can live with those bodies. But if they have an impaired or no sense of smell, it makes sense. In other situations, neighbors have moved away because of the extreme smell that comes from the serial killer's home. Losing the sense of smell means a lot to people, as it is associated with strong emotions. It also seems that extreme rapists lack smell.

Looking at various serial killer cases, only a few are declared insane. This doesn't necessarily mean they are normal. Perhaps more serial killers suffer from mental illness than people want to admit. But more research is needed to determine if this is the case.

Although I believe there are more psychotic serial killers than the FBI and the American legal system would like to acknowledge, few serial killers are clinically psychotic. Serial killers know what they are doing. They control the situation. They often spend a long time preparing for the crime, and they often kill for years. They manage to cover their tracks, avoid law enforcement, and they know what they are doing is legally and socially unacceptable.

Could serial killers experience psychosis or disturbed reality testing? Reality testing is the testing of one's perception of what is real and unreal. People who are psychotics have problems with reality testing. Reality testing takes place through communication with others, where you can correct your incorrect perceptions. It can be difficult to understand how serial killers could be normal, especially when we hear about the different cases. Most serial killers have such behavior that it is even difficult to believe they are human beings. We can argue about what is normal, but they are not typical in the common understanding of normal, as they deviate in several ways, not only by being serial killers but also through many of their other behaviors. However, from a psychological perspective, they are often not psychotic. This may be the reason why serial killers are normal in literature.

However, several circumstances indicate that more serial killers than previously thought are psychotic. In Liebert's (2000) theory, serial killers commit murder while being latently psychotic. In this state, they probably do not have sufficient personal integrity and reality testing to perceive the victim as a real person, so they may also perceive the victim as the target of their own aggression.

More studies need to be conducted, but I believe there is evidence that more serial killers cannot simply be described as normal with various personality disorders. It would require further study and research in this area to clarify this further.

Some serial killers who have been diagnosed with schizophrenia are Edward Theodore Gein. He was convicted of 2 murders and suspected of 7 other murders and 9 corpses mutilated (obtained from desecrated graves). Gein mutilated his victims, often keeping body parts as trophies in his home. Also, David Gonzalez killed four people in 2004 and claimed he'd been inspired by the movie "A *Nightmare on Elm Street*." And Jared Lee Loughner was convicted of killing 6 people and wounding 13, including US Representative Gabrielle Giffords, in 2011. He was diagnosed with paranoid schizophrenia. And lastly, Richard Trenton Chase, "the vampire of Sacramento," killed 6 people in California and drank their blood, was also diagnosed with paranoid schizophrenia.

# CASE: RICHARD TRENTON CHASE

**Epithets: The vampire of Sacramento**

Richard Trenton Chase was born on May 23, 1950. His early childhood was normal. The first signs that something was wrong appeared at the age of five. For starters, he was cruel to animals. It's not unusual for children to pull a cat by the tail or pull the wings off a fly, but in normal children, their conscience will tell them that their behavior is wrong, and they will stop again. This was not the case for Richard Trenton Chase. He also started setting things on fire and continued to wet the bed for no physical reason. Together, these three behaviors make up the so-called McDonald triad, which they thought could predict serious problems later in life. However, there was nothing to note at school. Chase was doing well, and lots of kids came to his birthday. In his teens, he started smoking large amounts of weed and taking LSD. At the same time, he realized he was impotent.

One of the first examples of his strange behavior was when he insisted at a young age that he was part of the Jesse James gang that operated in the late 1800s. He also started sleeping in the living room, taking off all his clothes and turning up the heat, something which sometimes can be seen in people suffering from schizophrenia. Over the years, he became increasingly disheveled and withdrew from other people. At that time, he developed hypochondria. He often complained that his heart wasn't beating and that someone had stolen his pulmonary artery. From time to time, he placed oranges on his head, believing that he could absorb vitamin C through his skull. He was also convinced that his skull bones were loose and moving, and he firmly believed that his blood periodically stopped flowing in his veins.

His condition was exacerbated by drug abuse. He found it increasingly difficult to hold down a job, so his parents began to help him financially.

Periodically, he lived with his divorced mother or father, but they found it difficult to tolerate his strange behavior. He began to fear for his life because he thought there was something wrong with his blood. So, he bought many rabbits, whose blood he began to drink.

Things went wrong when one day he injected rabbit blood directly into his own veins, which led to hospitalization in a psychiatric ward, where he was diagnosed with paranoid schizophrenia. During his hospitalization, he caught birds and mice and drank their blood, earning him the nickname "Dracula." They managed to get his symptoms under control with medication, but when he was discharged, his mother weaned him off the pills, which she believed turned him into a zombie, and he went back to killing animals and consuming their blood. Shortly after that, he started killing humans.

It didn't take long for the police to track down Richard Trenton Chase. He refused to let them in, so the officers loudly told them to leave, and when he believed them and came out, he was arrested. His apartment looked like a scene from a slasher movie. The walls, floor, ceiling, and all the crockery were covered in blood. All around were dog collars and organs in various stages of decomposition, some animal, some human body parts and they also found the full body of one of the victims. Robert Trenten Chase had beheaded him and eaten his brains. "I had gotten hungry," he stated as if it were the most natural thing in the world.

His statements were no less bizarre. He said that he had killed dogs because they were involved in a conspiracy against him by the Italians. When a psychiatrist asked him what was running on the "screen" in his head, he described an exploding jumbo jet. He also said he could see lights in the sky that came from UFOs with Nazis on board.

Bipolar disorder, which is a psychiatric mood disorder characterized by cycles of extreme shifts in mood, energy, and activity levels, ranging from periods of intense highs, which are either mania or hypomania and then shifting to periods of depression. This has also been seen in some killers who have committed multiple murders. The cycle of a serial killer with murder, then a cooling-down period, replaced with symptoms of depression, which is released when they begin to plan a new murder, could be described as a reaction to bipolar disorder.

Source: McLean, 2025.

Multiple killers with the bipolar disorder are for example Austin Harrouff (The College Cannibal), Marjorie Diehl-Armstrong (pizza bomber case), Anthony John Hardy (English serial killer/Camden Ripper), Tommy Lynn Sells (American serial killer/the Coast-to-Coast Killer) and Joel David Rifkin, the next case we will look closer in to.

## CASE: JOEL DAVID RIFKIN

**Epithets: No epithets when he was an active serial killer, but after his capture, he was named Joel the Ripper and The Ripper.**

Joel David Rifkin was born January 20, 1959, and is an American serial killer who was sentenced to 203 years in prison for the murders of 9 women between 1989 and 1993, though he confessed to murdering 17 females.

Rifkin was adopted by Bernard and Jeanne Rifkin on February 14, 1959, when he was three weeks old. The Rifkin's were an upper-middle-class couple living on Long Island, and they later settled in East Meadow, New York, where Rifkin would spend most of his years until he was incarcerated. Rifkin's biological parents were both young teens; his mother was a college student, and his biological father was an army veteran.

Rifkin had an IQ of 128 but struggled in school due to severe dyslexia and difficulty with coordination. Rifkin was described as an awkward, shy, skinny boy with a narrow face, and he wore big spectacles. Rifkin was a target of massive bullying, and he was tormented. They called him Joel the turtle. The terrorizing went on every day, and there were several incidents where the other boys held his head in the toilet and urinated on him. His own view on it was, "I just happen to bring out the bully in people."

Sometimes, when he was just walking by himself, his classmate would walk behind him and pull his pants down, hide his books and food, and call him names. They also isolated him and did everything to make his life a hell on earth. Isolated, he had no one to be with and slowly withdrew from others. Rifkin escaped to a fantasy world.

Rifkin dived deeper into his fantasies when he was about 11 years old. He started fantasizing about dominating women; he had gladiator fantasies where women were fighting over him, which sometimes ended in the death of one of them.

When he was 13, he was afraid to go to school, and the bullying also spread to his home. He stayed late after school before he went home to avoid the bullying, but when he came home, his tormentor was waiting for him and continued the bullying. Rifkin walked with his eyes on the ground, and his shoulders slumped to try to avoid the viciousness, but for that, he was dubbed "The Turtle."

Rifkin asked his parents for permission to leave school, but they didn't quite understand how bad it really was. He started getting worse in school despite his high IQ. He tried to make his father happy but never succeeded; his dad was very disappointed and yelled at him to try to get him to perform, which only made life worse for Rifkin.

The bullying and loneliness followed Rifkind through East Meadow High School. Bill Trofatter, who knew him from the track and cross-country teams told in an interview about Rifkin that he was very withdrawn, and you could not get him to talk, you had to force him to speak, and that he really did not have any friends who were close to him.

Rifkin graduated from East Meadow High School in 1977 and then attended classes at Nassau Community College, the State University of New York at Brockport, and the State University of New York at Farmingdale. He was particularly interested in horticulture and photojournalism, where he worked for a time as a photographer for the school newspaper, *The Stylus*.

But he left before earning a degree.

In 1977, when Rifkin was 17 years old, he searched for a sex worker to try sex because he couldn't find a girlfriend. And before he knew of it, he was addicted to being with them. He spent up to 8 hours straight beaming at them from his car, where he was sitting and watching them on the boulevard where they walked the streets. He spent all his money on them; it made him feel less alone and less tense, but he didn't feel he was in control. He had no friends or social life, he was just by himself and the sex workers, whom he often paid to be with him for many hours, up to 11 hours. At that time, Rifkin moved into his parents' home because he did not have enough money to support himself. All his money went to pay for sex workers. He held various odd jobs and spent much of the little money he earned on sex workers.

On February 20, 1987, his father, Bernard, committed suicide by overdosing after suffering from prostate cancer for several months. That deepened Rifkin's depression. At this time, he became increasingly obsessed with violence, murder, and sex workers. On August 22, 1987, he was arrested in Hempstead, Long Island, for soliciting an undercover police officer he thought was a sex worker. He did not tell his family about this arrest.

Joel Rifkin's first murder was on February 20, 1989, exactly 2 years after his father died. The victim, Heidi Balch, was killed in his home in East Meadow. He then dismembered her body, removing her teeth and fingertips and placing her head in a paint can, which he left in the woods on a golf course in Hopewell, New Jersey. He disposed of her legs further north and dumped her remaining torso and arms into the East River around New York City. He took a great length to dismember her body and scattered the remains in different places in both New York and New Jersey. On March 5, 1989, the severed head of Balch was discovered on the seventh hole of the golf course. The lower limbs of Balch were found on April 8, 1989, in Pequonnock Creek near Jefferson Township, New Jersey. The remains of Balch were not identified until 2013.

Rifkin: "If, you know, make everything as small as possible, that makes it all disappear, that was the overwhelming thought I had."

After the first murder, he panicked, and he thought that it would never happen again and woe to himself not to do it again.

Rifkin: "...that whole night would just keep repeating, some nights it was terrifying, other nights it was pleasant, it was exhilarating, there were moments of terror, you know it ran its course ... oh I was still in denial that I even did it at times."

After the first murder, there was an 18-month cooling-off period. Then suddenly, he started killing again, and over the next four years, he killed a further 16 women. He got increasingly exuberant and felt untouchable. Sometimes, he took his victims back to East Meadow, the house where he lived with his sister and elderly mother. Other times, the victims were killed in his car.

Police finally caught up with Rifkin in June 1993 when state troopers spotted his pickup truck with no license plates on the Southern State Parkway. A high-speed chase ended in Mineola, where he crashed into a utility pole in front of the courthouse, where he would eventually stand trial. Troopers smelled an odor coming from the back of the truck. It came from the body of Tiffany Bresciani, 22, his latest victim.

Rifkin was found guilty of 9 murders in 1994 and sentenced to 203 years to life in prison. He will not be eligible for parole until 2197, at the age of 238.

Rifkin is one of the serial killers with whom I have been in contact for a considerable period. There are periods of extended duration between his letters, during which he informs me of experiencing episodes of depression. In periods of heightened mania, he becomes more communicative and outgoing.

I try to understand what impact his fantasy has on him and his killings. Rifkin describes a recurrent fantasy in which he engages in the act of killing a sex worker during his interaction with them. However, these fantasies rarely result in Rifkin acting out the fantasy, because it is only a fantasy. However, on occasion, these fantasies do materialize, and Rifkin provides an explanation for this occurrence to Safarik (2010).

Rifkin: "and I remember... sitting in the living room for a while debating if I should just fantasize or if I should actually strangle her... and I remember debating it for a while... there comes a point where... well, I can get the first videotape (red... fantasy in his head) to stop... if there is a second one (red... fantasy) if there is a third little bundle together and it won't make sense anymore and I can make it stop."

Rifkin explains that it is possible for him to stop the fantasy to an end at any time by choosing to continue the fantasy and replacing fantasy Scene 1 with fantasy Scene 2 and then continue to fantasy Scene 3, and that way he will avoid the murder which take place in fantasy Scene 2. So, he asserts that if he were to reach fantasy 3, he would not kill his victim for sure. He elucidates that at a certain juncture, he possesses the capacity to persist in his fantasy and that if he does not transition from fantasy to reality and act out, the fantasy will persist in its state as a mere fantasy. There is a juncture at which it becomes illogical to act out the killing. This process of deliberation entails a choice: to either halt the fantasy and act or to permit the fantasy to persist within the mind. The decision to either act or refrain from doing so is entirely within his control, and although he may not be aware of this possibility beforehand, he is constantly aware of its potentiality. He possesses the capacity and authority to either halt or act out his fantasies.

He was trialed in Nassau County Court before Judge Ira. H. Wexner for the murder of Ms. Bresciani. He also faces murder charges in Suffolk County, Brooklyn, Queens, and the Bronx. The defense strategy first tried to argue an insanity defense and pointed to adopted child syndrome (see chapter 4), but that was dropped. Rifkin confessed to 17 murders in total. The defense claimed that Joel Rifkin suffered from paranoid schizophrenia and had difficulty separating fantasy from reality. But Dr. Park Dietz, in his second full day of testimony, rejected this claim, arguing that if Rifkin were schizophrenic, he would also be delusional and suffer from hallucinations and thought disorders.

Dr. Dietz: "It is my experience that Mr. Rifkin has not expressed any of these things ... He has his problems, but he has none of the problems associated with schizophrenia."

As for his own diagnosis, Dr. Dietz gave Joel Rifkin the diagnosis of bipolar disorder, which caused him to have periods of prolonged depression and hypomania, or emotional highs when he was mentally and physically active and drove around a lot in his car, a trait Dr. Dietz said was common among serial killers. Dr. Dietz also said Joel Rifkin was a sexual sadist in that he repeatedly experienced sexual fantasies of inflicting pain on women and necrophilia.

Dr. Dietz: "He acted on such a desire, particularly when strangling, humiliating and dominating his victims ... Mr. Rifkin did not torture his victims before killing them. His primary focus was the killing, the strangulation itself. Mr. Rifkin spoke of tenderly caressing his dead victims, as if stroking and soothing a girlfriend. ... However, Mr. Rifkin said he did not have intercourse with any of the dead. He said, 'It didn't feel right.'"

Dr. Dietz: "It's also important to note the pattern of how long Mr. Rifkin used each body for forms of erotic contact." He said that Mr. Rifkin, like most necrophiliacs, kept the bodies of his victims as long as possible "until it was uncomfortable to do so." He noted that Joel Rifkin kept the body of his 17th victim, Tiffany Bresciani, 22, of Manhattan, in his East Meadow home and garage for 4 days. When he left his home in the early hours of June 28 to dispose of the body, he smeared skin cream under his nose to mask the smell.

We could argue that Rifkin has traits of psychopathy, which could have made it easier for him to commit murder because of the disturbed empathy, but it is not the reason he became a serial killer; the reason is multifactional and is about power and control and the psychological issues that he is reliving through the torment and bullying and I think he resent the sex worker he had to pay for company so he was conflicted in the interaction and he was special triggered if the victim only wanted to forefeel their own need, chasing to get high or sleeping. For Rifkin, it was his only company, and he did not realize that he had not bought a girlfriend and was disappointed repeatedly. Of course, that is the concept for sex workers; it is a job, and johns does not buy the person as a girlfriend, but I think Rifkin hoped that was the case, and that reality, when it dawns on him, triggered him. Rifkin had to buy the company, but it is important that he was together with over 100 sex workers, but most of them he did not kill; but according to himself, the triggers were different. But what all the murders had in common was that Rifkin's psychological needs were not met.

Source: Mladinich, 2002, McQuiston, 1994, Rifkin, in Safarik, 2010, Kasindorf, 1993 and Safarik, 2022a, 2022b, 2022c.

## SOCIOPATH, PSYCHOPATHY, AND ANTISOCIAL PERSONALITY DISORDER

Most criminologists deal with psychopathy, sociopathy, and antisocial personality disorder (ASPD). Since Freud's time, antisocial personality type has been linked to criminal behavior. The relationship that many researchers have studied is the MacDonald triad. The triad is named after MacDonald (1963), who, in the 1960s, believed that children having three behavioral factors, involuntary urination (enuresis), arson, violent animal cruelty, and animal killing, tended to become criminals and specific murderers (Mitchell, 1996). I will discuss in detail the MacDonald triad in chapter 6.

ASPD is often linked to serial killers, probably because most serial killers do not show signs of conscience when dealing with their victims, which can be a symptom of ASPD. The terms ASPD, psychopathy, and sociopath are often used synonymously. However, sociopathy indicates that the cause of the disorder is rooted in social maladjustment (Gabbard, 1994, p. 528). Sociopaths, which some claim is the same as ASPD, but in my opinion, it is not, are egocentric, callous, and impulsive. They have no conscience, can be extremely sexually active, boast a lot, often take significant risks, and have difficulty resisting temptation. They often have an aversion to the opposite sex and struggle to form intimate bonds with others (Hare, 1999). Sociopathy does not appear in ICD-11 or DSM-5 diagnostic systems (APA, 2022; WHO, 1998).

People diagnosed with ASPD are not psychotic but often have other psychiatric disorders. It is estimated that 4% of the population has ASPD. According to the American Psychiatric Association, of the 4% with ASPD, approximately 3% are men and 1% are women. It is even more difficult to distinguish between the types because DSM-TR proposes an alternative DSM-5 Model for ASPD and other personality disorders (APA, 2022).

In DSM-TR 5, it is stated: "The DSM-5 Manual provides an alternative model for personality disorders with a view to overcoming the shortfalls of the more conventional model. While Criterion A involves the level of self and interpersonal functioning that deals with core psychological functioning areas, including identity and self-direction, empathy, and intimacy, Criterion B is concerned with pathological personality traits and includes negative affectivity, detachment, antagonism, disinhibition, and psychoticism, which is defined by Eysenck (2024) as a personality type that is prone to risk-taking, antisocial behavior, impulsivity, or nonconformity. Extraversion includes outgoing or highly social behavior.

These five broad trait domains have 25 distinct trait components. The Level of Personality Functioning Scale uses each of the components of criterion A to identify five levels of impairment, ranging from little or no impairment (healthy, adaptive outlook- Level 0), some impairment (Level 1), moderate impairment (Level 2), severe impairment (Level 3), and extreme impairment (Level 4) (APA, 2022).

In this proposed diagnosis criteria, they have omitted the part where conduct disorder must be demonstrated before the age of 15 years. Also, the systems are on a continuum, so it looks more like psychopathy and sociopathy.

## ***Proposed diagnosis:***

Antisocial Personality Disorder: Proposed Diagnostic Criteria

| | |
|---|---|
| A. Functional impairment in at least two of the following four categories.<br><br>1. Identity: Egotistic, self-seeking behavior.<br>2. Self-direction: failure to obey law/authority.<br>3. Empathy: Lack of sensitivity to others.<br>4. Intimacy: Incapable of forming reciprocal relationships. | B. Presence of at least 6 of the following pathological personality traits.<br>1. Manipulative (denotes Antagonism).<br>2. Insensitiveness (Antagonism): lack of guilt for wrongful action/behavior, violence, or sadism.<br>3. Dishonesty (Antagonism).<br>4. Aggression (Antagonism).<br>5. Risk-prone behavior (denoting Disinhibition).<br>6. Rashness.<br>7. Irresponsible behavior<br>(APA, 2022). |

So, to try to understand the difference, in ASPD, there must be a consistent pattern of indifference and violation of others' rights.

This must have occurred in relation to three or more of the following aspects. They do not adhere to social norms of law-abidingness by repeatedly breaking the law. They are deceitful by repeatedly lying, using false names, and cheating others to satisfy their own needs.

I see a difference where the sociopath tends to be more impulsive. In addition, they have difficulty planning and executing their future. They are easily irritated and aggressive and have low empathy but can get very emotional. Therefore, they can get into fights and assault others.

They are also reckless. Consistent irresponsibility is indicated by difficulty holding a job or meeting financial obligations. When hurting, mistreating, or stealing from others, they show no or little remorse. They have difficulty rationalizing when they treat others badly, often blaming the victim. This could be rooted in the fact that sociopathy stems more from the environment than heredity. Because of trauma, they develop this pattern, and that makes it look different than psychopathy.

To be diagnosed with ASPD, a person must be at least 18 years old; otherwise, it falls under behavioral disorders like conduct disorder. As mentioned, there must be evidence that antisocial behavior must not be linked to schizophrenia, manic episodes, or other disorders (APA, 2022).

It is agreed that some serial killers suffer from ASPD, but far from all are psychopaths. According to Hickey (2023e), most serial killers are sociopaths and do not have ASPD. I observe the same in my research that more serial killers are sociopaths than psychopaths or have ASPD.

We often use ASPD, psychopath and sociopath interchangeably, which can be confusing. I think if we need to get a good understanding of the criteria, we need to be more specific.

Below is an attempt to differentiate ASPD, sociopathy, and psychopathy from each other:

| ASPD | Psychopath | Sociopath |
|---|---|---|
| Cannot adhere to legal social norms, which can lead to repeated arrest.<br>Deceptive behavior.<br>Capriciousness.<br>Irritable and aggressive behavior.<br>Risk-prone behavior.<br>Irresponsible behavior.<br>Unemotional.<br>Conduct disorder before 15. years old. | Insincere charm<br>Being easily bored<br>Compulsive lying<br>Manipulation of others No remorse or guilt Little emotional reaction<br>Cruelty without feeling bad about it<br>Taking advantage of others<br>Behavioral problems that start in childhood<br>Failure to take responsibility Many sexual relationships | Seeking power and dominance<br>Tendency to be devious or deceptive<br>Ruthlessness in pursuing goals Hostile or aggressive to others Easily angered or irritated Irresponsible decision-making<br>Superficial Charm & Persuasion Limited conscience or low moral<br>Few strong bonds or relationships<br>Manipulative tendency<br>Entitlement and impunity Societal Deviancy<br>Thrill-seeking tendencies<br>Opportunistic in the wrong sense<br>Emotionally detached |
| Diagnosis system: In DSM-5-TR | Diagnosis system:<br>Hara's system | Diagnosis system:<br>No confirmed diagnosis |

(McLean, 2026)

# CASE: RODNEY JAMES ALCALA

**Epithets: The Dating Game Killer**

Rodney James Alcala (born Rodrigo Jacques Alcala Buquor; August 23, 1943 – July 24, 2021) was an American serial killer and sex offender who was sentenced to death in California for five murders committed between 1977 and 1979. He also pleaded guilty and received a sentence of 25 years to life for two additional murders committed in New York and was also charged with murder in Wyoming; the charges were dropped because of a technicality. While he has been conclusively linked to eight murders, Alcala's true number of victims is still unknown and could be much higher, as high as 130.

Alcala collected more than 1,000 photographs of women, teenage girls, and boys, many in sexually explicit poses. In 2016, he was charged with the 1977 murder of a woman identified in one of his images. He is known to have assaulted more persons whom he had picture of, and the police did speculate if more of the persons in the photographs could have been rape or murder victims.

Prosecutors have alleged that Alcala would "play" with his victims, strangling them until they lost consciousness and then waiting until they regained their senses, sometimes repeating this process several times before finally killing them. One police detective described Alcala as "a killing machine," and others have compared him to Ted Bundy. Alcala is frequently referred to as the Dating Game Killer because he appeared on the television show The Dating Game during his killing spree in 1978.

Rodney Alcala was born in San Antonio, Texas, as the third of four children born to a Mexican American couple, Raul Alcala Buquor and Anna Maria Gutierrez. In 1951, his father relocated the family to Mexico and departed three years later. In 1954, when Alcala was 11 years old, his mother moved him and his two sisters to suburban Los Angeles. Alcala was good academically, maintained a moderate social standing among his peers, and received support from his family. He attended various private schools during his youth before graduating from Montebello High School. He was a member of the yearbook committee and participated in "track and cross country."

In 1961, at the age of 17, Alcala enlisted in the US Army with the intention of becoming a paratrooper. During his service, he was noted by his commanding officer for his manipulative, vindictive, and rude behavior. At his military time, he was diagnosed with antisocial personality disorder and estimated to have an IQ of 135 by a military psychiatrist Alcala was disciplined on several occasions for assaulting young women. In 1964, following an episode where he had a nervous breakdown, and during which he did not showed up for his duties and hitchhiked from Fort Bragg, North Carolina, to his mother's house in California. He was then discharged from the Army for medical reasons. After leaving the Army, Alcala graduated from the UCLA School of Fine Arts and later studied film under Roman Polanski at New York University (NYU).

On September 25, 1968, a passing motorist named Donald Haines contacted the authorities after observing Alcala forcing the 8-year-old Tali Shapiro into his Hollywood apartment. Shapiro, who resided at Chateau Marmont with her family, was approached by Alcala on her way to school when he stopped his car next to her and asked her to take a ride with him. Shapiro initially declined, but upon hearing Alcala mention that he was acquainted with her parents, she accepted it and entered his vehicle. He drove her to his apartment, where he claimed to have a photograph to show her. Upon the arrival of the police, Shapiro was found to be alive; however, she had been sexually assaulted and beaten fiercely with a steel rod. Alcala had fled the scene. She remained in a coma for 32 days and required months of recovery. After the recovery, she relocated to New York.

To evade the arrest warrant stemming from the Shapiro assault, Alcala left California and enrolled at NYU using the name "John Berger." In 1971, he secured a consulting job at a New Hampshire art camp for children using a slightly different alias, "John Burger." During this time, he began working for the Blue Cross Blue Shield Association, where he worked at an office with serial killer Richard Cottingham. Neither man has claimed to have been acquainted with the other, nor is there any evidence that they were familiar with each other prior to their arrests.

Cornelia Crilley, a 23-year-old flight attendant for Trans World Airlines, was found raped and murdered in her Manhattan apartment on June 12, 1971. Alcala had strangled her with her nylon stockings and left her dead in her apartment at 427 East 83rd. Street. It is believed that Crilley met him when she moved into her new apartment and that she might have accepted his help in moving some furniture. Her murder remained unsolved until 2011.

The FBI added Alcala to its list of Ten Most Wanted Fugitives in early 1971. A few months later, two children attending an art camp noticed his picture on an FBI poster at the post office. He was arrested and extradited to California. By that time, Shapiro's parents had moved their entire family to Mexico and refused to allow her to testify at the trial. Authorities were unwilling to charge him with rape and attempted murder without their primary witness, so he was convicted of child abuse and sentenced to three years in prison. Alcala was paroled in 1974 after seventeen months. Less than two months after his release, he was arrested again for assaulting a 13-year-old girl, identified in court records as "Julie J." who had accepted what she thought would be a ride to school. He was again paroled in 1976 after serving two years.

After his second release in 1977, Alcala's parole officer in Los Angeles took the unusual step of allowing a repeat offender to travel to New York City. NYPD investigators now believe that a week after returning to Manhattan, Alcala killed Ellen Jane Hover, the 23-year-old daughter of nightclub owner Herman Hover and goddaughter of Dean Martin and Sammy Davis Jr. Hover was last seen in her New York City apartment on July 15, 1977. Her datebook showed that she had an appointment to meet a "John Berger" that day.

Later, in 1977, a tip was given to the FBI about how Alcala had been arrested by police for the Shapiro case in New Hampshire a few years earlier. Alcala admitted to knowing Hover during questioning, but investigators could not arrest him as they had not found her body. Her remains were eventually discovered buried under heavy rocks on a hillside overlooking at the Hudson River.

In 1978, Alcala briefly worked at the *Los Angeles Times* as a typesetter and was interviewed by members of the Hillside Strangler task force as part of their investigation of known sex offenders. Although Alcala was ruled out as the strangler, he was arrested and served a short sentence for possession of marijuana. During this period, he convinced hundreds of young men and women that he was a professional fashion photographer and took their pictures for his "portfolio."

An example was a woman who allowed Alcala to photograph her in 1979, she stated: "He said he was a professional, so in my mind, I was modeling for him," said a woman who allowed Alcala to photograph her in 1979. The portfolio also included "...spread after spread of nude teenage boys," she said. Most of the images were sexually explicit.

In 1978, Alcala was a contestant on the popular game show The Dating Game. Host Jim Lange introduced him as a "successful photographer.

Between shots, you might find him skydiving or motorcycling." Another Bachelor contestant later described Alcala as a "very strange guy" with "bizarre opinions."

Alcala won the competition and a date with the episode's bachelorette, Cheryl Bradshaw, who did refuse to go out with him because she found him "creepy."

November 9, 1977, Alcala murdered Jill Terry Barcomb, an 18-year-old girl from Oneida, New York, and dumped her body on a dirt path near

Mulholland Drive in Los Angeles. Barcomb was found in a knee-to-chest position and naked from the waist down. There were signs of sexual assault, and she had been strangled with a pair of blue zip ties and batons. She also had three bite marks on her right breast. Initially, authorities believed that Barcomb had been a victim of the Hillside Strangler, but her case was ultimately ruled by authorities to have been unrelated after the arrests of perpetrators Kenneth Bianchi and Angelo Buono, who neither confessed nor were ever convicted of the murder.

December 16, 1977, 27-year-old nurse Georgia Marie Wixted was discovered dead in her Malibu apartment. She was last seen driving another nurse, Barbara Gale, home from a bar. When she didn't show up for work the next day, Gale and their colleagues reported her missing. Police arrived at her apartment to find signs of forced entry. Wixted was found naked on her bedroom floor, strangled with her nylon thongs. She had been sexually assaulted; her skull had been bashed in, and her genitals had been mutilated. Later, prosecutors used DNA evidence and a handprint found at the scene to convict Alcala.

June 24, 1978, Charlotte Lee Lamb, a 31-year-old legal secretary from Santa Monica, was found dead in the laundry room of the apartment complex where she lived in El Segundo. She had been sexually assaulted, beaten, and strangled with shoelaces and was posed with her hands behind her back. DNA at the scene matched that of Alcala's, DNA and the DNA on a pair of earrings found in his storage locker after Sam's murder would eventually prove to match Lamb's DNA.

February 14, 1979, Alcala picked up 15-year-old hitchhiker Monique Hoyt in Riverside County. He drove her to his apartment, where he raped her. Then he took her to a secluded mountain area near Banning, California, where he took pictures of her in her underwear as well as pictures of him raping her once more. He then bound and gagged her, began a sustained assault that included further rape and sodomy, and then threw a rock at her head. She escaped when he entered a gas station bathroom on the drive back to Riverside County.

June 13, 1979, Jill Marie Parenteau, a 21-year-old computer keyboardist, left work early to go to a baseball game. When she didn't make it to work the following morning, police went to her Burbank apartment and found signs of forced entry. Parenteau was dead, naked on her bathroom floor. She was posed with pillows under her shoulders. She had been sexually assaulted, beaten, and strangled. Her killer cut himself crawling through a window; blood evidence would later identify Alcala as the perpetrator. Parenteau's friend, Katharine Bryant, testified that she and Parenteau had met Alcala at a club several times before.

Robin Christine Samsoe, a 12-year-old Huntington Beach girl, disappeared while riding a borrowed bicycle from her Huntington Beach home to her ballet class on June 20, 1979. Her decomposing body was found twelve days later in the foothills of Los Angeles, dumped off Santa Anita Canyon Road. She had been beaten, raped, and stabbed with a knife. Sam's friends told police that a stranger had approached them on the beach and asked to take their pictures. Detectives circulated a sketch of the photographer, and Alcala's parole officer recognized him. During a search of Alcala's mother's house in Monterey Park, police found a rental receipt for a storage locker in Seattle; in the locker, they found Sam's earrings.

Alcala was arrested in July 1979 and held without bail. He was charged with Samsoe's murder, found guilty in May 1980 and sentenced to death in June. However, the conviction was overturned by the California Supreme Court in 1984 because jurors had been improperly informed of his prior sex offenses. In May 1986, after a second trial that was virtually identical to the first, except for the omission of the prior record, he was again convicted and then sentenced to death in August.

In connection with the trial, Alcala was diagnosed by various psychiatric experts at his trial, including narcissistic personality disorder, borderline personality disorder, and malignant narcissism with psychopathy and sexual sadism comorbidities.

In 1992, the California Supreme Court upheld the conviction, but Alcala filed a federal habeas corpus petition. In 2001, a US district judge granted it, overturning Alcala's second conviction. The ruling was upheld in 2003 by a Ninth Circuit Court of Appeals panel, in part because a witness was not allowed to support Alcala's claim that the park ranger who found Sam's body had been "hypnotized by police investigators."

While preparing for their third prosecution in 2003, Orange County investigators found that Alcala's DNA, taken under a new state law over his objections, matched semen left at the rape-murder scenes of two women in Los Angeles. Additional evidence, including a second cold case DNA match in 2004, led to Alcala's indictment for the murders of four more women: Jill Barcomb, 18, a runaway from New York found "rolled up like a ball" in a ravine in Los Angeles in 1977 and initially believed to have been a victim of the Hillside Strangler: Georgia Wixted, 27, banged in her Malibu apartment in 1977; Charlotte Lamb, 31, raped, strangled, and left in the laundry room of an El Segundo apartment complex in 1978; and Jill Parenteau, 21, killed in her Burbank apartment in 1979.

Another pair of earrings found in Alcala's Seattle storage locker had residue that matched Lamb's DNA. During his incarceration between the second and third trials, Alcala wrote and self-published a book, *You, the Jury*, in which he claimed innocence in the Samsoe case and suggested another suspect. He also filed two lawsuits against the California criminal justice system for a slip-and-fall incident and for refusing to provide him with a low-fat diet.

In 2003, prosecutors filed a motion to join the Samsoe charges with the charges of the four newly discovered victims. Alcala's lawyers contested it; as one of them explained: "If you're a juror hearing a murder case, you may have reasonable doubt, but it's very hard to say you have reasonable doubt about all five, especially when four of the five are not alleged by eyewitnesses but are proven by DNA matches."

In 2006, the California Supreme Court ruled in favor of the prosecution, and in February 2010, Alcala stood trial on the five unified charges. For the third trial, Alcala chose to be his own attorney. He took the stand in his own defense and, for five hours, played the role of both interrogator and witness, asking himself questions, addressing himself as "Mr. Alcala" in a deeper-than-normal voice, and then answering them. During this self-question and answer session, he told jurors, often in a monotone voice, that he was at Knott's Berry Farm looking for a job as a photographer at the time Sam was kidnapped. He showed the jury a portion of his 1978 performance on The Dating Game to prove that the earrings found in his closet in Seattle were his, not Sam's. Jed Mills, the actor who competed against Alcala on the show, told a reporter that earrings were not yet a socially acceptable item of clothing for men in 1978. "I had never seen a man with an earring in his ear," he said. "I would have noticed them on him."

Alcala made no attempt to dispute the four added charges, other than to claim that he could not remember killing any of the women. As part of his closing argument, he played the Arlo Guthrie song "*Alice's Restaurant*," in which the main character tells a psychiatrist that he wants to "kill."

Jurors heard the following play in court: "I wanna kill, I wanna kill, I wanna see blood and gore and guts and veins in my teeth. Eat dead burnt bodies. I mean, kill, kill, kill, kill, kill."

After less than two days of deliberation, the jury convicted him of all five counts of first-degree murder. Alcala died of unspecified natural causes in Corcoran, California, on July 24, 2021, on the anniversary of his 1979 capture, at the age of 77.

Source: Falcon, 2010, McLean, 2025; People v. Alcala, 1992, Sands, 2011, Van Sant, 2024 and Santi, 2023.

# FRACTURED IDENTITY DISORDER

"I forgot about it.... I was not seeing so many prostitutes at that time" (Arthur Shawcross, Case 10 in McLean, 2004).

*Fractured Identity Syndrome,* which I have chosen to call *Fractured Identity Disorder (FID)* is not an official diagnosis, neither in the American DSM system nor in the WHO system. The reason I use the term disorder rather than syndrome is that it is more a disturbance than a syndrome. I will argue that the way FID is developed in a person from trauma is like a personality disorder, which we have and is more accurate in my opinion, because FID is a result of trauma and therefore more of a disorder than a syndrome.

"Fractured Identity Syndrome" (FIS) is a merging of Charles Cooley's "looking glass self" and Erving Goffman's "virtual" and "actual social identity" theories. The FIS suggests that a social event, or series of events, during one's childhood or adolescence, results in a fracturing of the personality of the serial killer. The term "fracture" is defined as a small breakage of the personality, which is often not visible to the outside world and is only felt by the killer. The research concerning the basic etiology and behavior of the serial killer is still in its infancy with this concept. In the time we have been aware of the concept of serial killers, a significant amount of research and writing has been produced regarding case histories of known serial killers, demographic and behavioral profiles of offenders, and attempts to locate patterns within the characteristics and traits of victims.

However, what has remained essentially absent from this work has been a serious attempt at developing a theoretical understanding of how and why such offenses occur. The "theories" of serial murder that have been previously offered have primarily cataloged traits or characteristics of the murderers is limited. The only other "explanations" for serial killing have suggested that offenders suffer from sociopathic or psychotic personality disorders and/or are sexual sadism (Holmes et al. 1999).

The first move toward serious theoretical development appeared with Holmes and DeBurger's (1985, 1988) examination of motives, anticipated gains, and victim selection patterns. However, as has become clear since the appearance of those works, an integral component was missing: the way the basic identity structure of the serial killer develops or emerges.

So, it is a basic theoretical construct that they suggested was at the core of serial killing, relying on a micro-level social conception. Specifically, they have suggested that those persons in significant relationships with individuals who can influence personality and identity constructions have a significant influence on the developmental health of future multiple killers. So, they aim to identify those social events that influence and contribute to the fracturing of the serial killer's identity structure; the first step could be taken in the early identification (and perhaps intervention) of the serial killer's identity.

The term is used to describe a situation where a person's sense of identity is split or fragmented because of trauma. This can happen, especially if the person is struggling to deal with conflicting parts of their personality or parts that they cannot confront. As is clear from the various cases, many murderers and serial killers have experienced terrible trauma growing up, and the idea is that some of them manage to separate the parts of their lives that deal with physical violence, sexual abuse, or severe bullying and humiliation from themselves. It's a way of protecting themselves, escaping the trauma, by fragmenting it away from their inner core. According to the theory, some children who are victims of sexual, physical or emotional abuse perceive that the abuse is happening to someone else, even though they are physically aware that it's happening to them. In this way, fractured identity disorder differs from dissociative identity disorder, which used to be called multiple personality disorder and even earlier, split personality, where the person is not necessarily aware that they have created multiple identities to defend themselves from the trauma.

The idea is that a fractured identity disorder can continue into adulthood, where, in its most extreme form, it can enable serial killers to live a normal family life alongside the horrific crimes they commit. For serial killers with an antisocial or narcissistic personality disorder, or both for that matter, it makes sense that they can live with their crimes because they are often severely challenged to feel empathy or remorse. But as this book shows, not all serial killers are diagnosed with these two disorders.

John Eric Armstrong, who is one of the serial killers I have been communicating with since my thesis in 2004. Armstrong is an example of this. Even after strangling a woman, he managed to go straight home and be a loving father and a good husband. In one of my letters, I asked him if he knew about the phenomenon FID. He didn't. So, I explained it to him, and he immediately recognized it in himself.

"I just killed them and went on with my life. I didn't think about the murders but lived my life as if nothing had happened. I went to work, visited family and friends and spent time with my wife," he wrote (case: Armstrong, in McLean, 2025).

## CASE: JOHN ERIC ARMSTRONG

### Epithets: Babyface Killer and baby doll killer

John Eric Armstrong was born on November 23, 1973, in New Bern, North Carolina. His father, John, was abusive toward Armstrong and his mother. He sexually abused Armstrong when he was a child. In 1978, Armstrong's younger brother, Michael, died two months old from sudden infant death syndrome. Because of the grief caused by Michael's death, Armstrong attempted to commit suicide. Shortly thereafter, his father left him and his mother. Armstrong did not receive treatment for his grief until 1989, a year after he was hospitalized for locking himself in a bathroom.

Armstrong joined the United States Navy in 1992. His colleagues described him as "moody." He allegedly killed his first victim in 1991, although this is not confirmed.

Between 1992 and 1999, the police estimated that Armstrong murdered 11 women, all sex workers. Armstrong himself has confessed to having killed in Seattle, Washington, Hawaii, Hong Kong, China, North Carolina, Virginia, Thailand and Singapore.

Armstrong was honorably discharged from the Navy in 1999 and enrolled at Schoolcraft College in Livonia, Michigan.

On January 2, 2000, Armstrong was questioned by police in Dearborn Heights, Michigan, after he reported finding a body in a river. He claimed he felt nauseated and attempted to vomit in the river when he discovered the body of Wendy Jordan, but he was not arrested at that time.

Armstrong attempted to murder Wilhelminia Drane on April 2, 2000, after she got into his Jeep, but she sprayed him with Mace and was able to flee.

On April 10, police found three bodies in a railroad yard in southwest Detroit. All the victims had been sex workers. They were all strangled to death and left in sexually provocative positions. They were later identified as Robbin Brown, Rose Marie Felt and Kelly Jean Hood.

On April 12, police arrested Armstrong for the murder of Wendy Jordan after DNA evidence found on the body matched Armstrong's DNA. In March 2001, Armstrong was found guilty of first-degree murder in the death of Wendy Jordan and sentenced to life imprisonment.

On June 18, 2001, he was additionally convicted of killing Kelly Jean Hood, Robbin Brown, Rose Marie Felt, and Monica Johnson. He would later explain that the reason he had left Brown, Felt, and Hood in sexually provocative positions after killing them was "so he could always go back and have sex…knew that they would always be there."

***

John Eric Armstrong emphasized that he understood he had killed women, but that he just managed to keep it out of his head and family life.

Something similar has been seen in some of history's most notorious serial killers. Ted Bundy was well-liked, went to law school, was at one point pursuing a career in politics and always had girlfriends.

Even more contrast is seen in Dennis Rader's life. On the one hand, he stalked his victims for days and weeks, torturing and murdering them, and on the other, he was married to the same woman for 30 years, had two children, was involved in their schooling, took them and their friends camping, was a scout leader, and chairman of the local church council. He later described his ability to live such an extreme double life as *compartmentalization*. He managed to divide his life into two spaces that had nothing to do with each other mentally, with watertight bulkheads in between.

The watertight compartmentalization may also explain how some serial killers manage to behave so effortlessly, even in situations where they risk being exposed. Take Zodiac, for example, who was stopped by police as he was walking away from a crime scene. The officers asked if he had seen anything suspicious, and he was able to tell them without being suspected that he had seen a Black man running away. Such killers go under the radar because they seem so credible. They have fragmented the crime away from the rest of themselves and their lives.

When interrogating suspects, law enforcement often looks for so-called *micro-expressions*, which are small and usually unconscious signs that the person is lying to them. These signs are not usually observed in criminals with a fractured identity disorder, so it cannot be assumed that they react as anyone else would.

It is important to emphasize that fractured identity disorder is not necessarily a permanent condition. Major life changes or severe stress can cause the watertight walls to crumble. As mentioned, John Eric Armstrong called the police after he strangled a woman and threw her off a bridge. He did not initially admit anything during interrogations but didn't contradict the investigators when they confronted him with their evidence.

There is little evidence to suggest that he did this because he wanted attention, in which case he could have sent letters or made anonymous calls. He also agreed without protest to give the police access to his car and agreed to give a blood sample. My hypothesis is that he found it increasingly difficult to keep his two lives from each other. I think that after getting married and having a son, he was met with love from the young child he had never known before, and he gave it back to his son. It made it harder for him to carry on as before. The contact with the police may have been a skewed way of trying to be stopped because the fragmentation was becoming decreasingly effective. The ability had not completely disappeared because he killed again after both attempts, but it is clear to me that it had started to crack.

As I mentioned, I have chosen to call fractured identity syndrome a disorder, as it is still a theory, although it is often used among those who research serial killers. Personally, I think it's well-founded, but it clearly needs more research. Whether it is a personality disorder is not yet known, but however you choose to describe the phenomenon, it may help explain something that the official personality disorders do not consider.

Source: McLean, 2004, case: Armstrong, in McLean, 2025, and Bates & Gerald, 2021.

# 4. THE ETIOLOGY OF SERIAL KILLERS

Serial killers have been extensively studied psychologically and physiologically to find a cause for their behavior. They have also been studied to see if factors distinguish serial killers from others. These factors, among others, may include brain damage and genes, e.g., monoamine oxidase A genes (MAOA). Known as the warrior gene, monoamine oxidase A is a variant of the monoamine oxidase (MAOA) gene that is associated with aggression and risk-taking behavior.

Brain tumors, early brain damage, psychological and socio-cultural factors have also been searched for as an explanation for serial killer behavior and often bizarre actions (Baker, 2020; Hickey, 2016; Raine, 2003). No clear-cut answer has been found. Some serial killers have brain damage, some do not; some suffer from physiological disorders, some do not. So far, no single cause has been identified that leads to serial killing. What has been found are several interrelated causal explanations that can result in serial killer behavior.

I have chosen to explain the vulnerability-stress model (see Table 7), the importance of frontal lobe damage, biological factors, and psychological factors as possible explanations for why some people become serial killers. Furthermore, I will discuss the link between emotional pain and violence. Finally, I will review social and environmental factors as a possible explanation for why some people become serial killers.

## THE VULNERABILITY-STRESS MODEL

There are many reasons why people become serial killers. Therefore, it is relevant to look at the vulnerability-stress model. This applies both to psychological disease and ASPD development (APA, 2022).

The different factors that influence the development of personality disorders and personality types must interact in a way that results in vulnerability to mental disorders. These factors are called predisposing factors. If a person has this vulnerability, the risk of disorder increases. But it takes more than that. This vulnerability must be exposed to a stressor, which causes the disorder to occur at a given point in time. But along with the triggering factor, there may also be protective factors that prevent personality disorder from developing. So, for example, to develop ASPD, a particular vulnerability is required, along with triggering events (the so-called stressors).

According to the vulnerability-stress model, vulnerability combined with stress results in the activation of current causal mechanisms (Dahl & Dalsegg, 2002). Causes can be biological, psychological, or social. These causes can occur in different degrees and combinations. It is assumed that the factors affect each other in close interaction, making it difficult to determine whether these factors are primary or secondary (Cullberg, 1996). The next section accounts for the biological, psychological, and social factors that influence the vulnerability-stress model.

Table 7: Integration of disease levels or vulnerability-stress model

| | | | | |
|---|---|---|---|---|
| | | | | Psychological symptoms |
| Biological etiology | -> | Biological | | |
| | Vulnerability | Stress | Diseases | |
| Psychological etiology | -> | Psychological | | |
| | | | | Psychological + biological disease processes |

Source: Bechgaard, Jensen & Nielsen, 2001, p. 17

The vulnerability-stress model is a tool that tells us how and why mental health ailments develop. It was developed in 1977 by Zubin and Spring to explain the development of schizophrenia. After its initial introduction to the mental health world, the model extended to include a broad range of psychiatric diagnoses (Bechgaard et al., 2001).

## BIOLOGICAL AND GENETIC FACTORS

Some argue that genetics determines whether someone becomes a serial killer. They believe there are biological or genetic reasons that explain why certain individuals become serial killers. Other researchers, including me, believes that there is a genetic predisposition to become a serial killer, which must then be triggered by other factors.

Over time, there have been several attempts to find the exact factor that creates a serial killer. In the 1960s, researchers found a double Y chromosome in some men. It has been debated whether this extra Y chromosome may be responsible for some people becoming serial killers. It has been suggested that a double male Y chromosome causes aggression and criminality. Some serial killers, such as Arthur John Shawcross had a double male Y chromosome, even he told me that later examinations, did not reveal the extra Y chromosome (case: Shawcross, 2003).

Another genetic factor could be Robert Joe Long who had an extra X chromosome.

## CASE: ROBERT JOE LONG

### Epithets: The Classified Ad Rapist, The Adman Rapist

Robert Joe Long was born on October 14, 1953, in West Virginia. He was born with an extra X chromosome, a condition known as Klinefelter's syndrome. This condition, among other things, leads to an elevated level of the female sex hormone estrogen in the body. Consequently, Robert Joe Long developed breasts, which led to severe bullying in his school years. When he reached adolescence, he underwent a surgical procedure to remove a portion of his breast tissue. The bullying could have led to a profound anger toward females, an anger that persisted despite experiences with an abusive mother.

At the age of two, Robert Joe Long's parents divorced, and his mother abruptly relocated him to Florida. During the day, the two were inseparable; however, in the evenings and at night, she worked as a bartender and waitress, while he was left in the care of strangers. She insisted he sleep in her bed until he was well into his teens, even when she was there herself. He also witnessed how she started bringing strange men home at night and having sex with them while he was in the same room.

When she secured employment at a bar that mandated wearing revealing attire, Robert Joe Long began to verbal abuse of an extremely obscene nature, despite her attempts to explain to him that the attire would result in more money. His resentment and anger initially manifested in his treatment of animals, and he also discovered early on how masturbation could alleviate his frustrations. Longs academic performance suffered, prompting him to engage in a series of minor criminal activities, including theft and burglary. His physical development, marked by his imposing stature and strength, also led to frequent altercations.

However, at the age of 19, Robert Joe Long enlisted in the army, where he was trained as a highly specialized electrician. Meanwhile, he entered a marital union with his high school sweetheart, with whom he had two children. However, this union proved to be short-lived. One day, he was struck by a vehicle while driving his motorcycle, resulting in severe injuries to his leg and head. Afterward, his wife observed a marked change in his behavior, characterized by an uncharacteristic desire for sexual activity and compulsive masturbating, which happened four to five times daily. Additionally, his anger outbursts became more frequent and intense. Long was forced to leave the army and embark on a series of professional endeavors. However, his conduct, marked by instances of inappropriate behavior toward the children's babysitter and others, ultimately led to his wife's decision to initiate a divorce in 1980.

It is noteworthy that during this period, she had also been subjected to several acts of violence, including being choked and having her head forcefully pressed against a wall. Robert Joe Long later threatened her with death should she disclose the incident to the hospital.

In less than a year, Long is believed to have perpetrated his first rape, which would be one of at least 50 in a series of attacks. He gained notoriety under the nickname "The Classified Ad Rapist" because he found his rape victims through "Craigslist" or "Yellow & Free," which are classified advertisements websites. Long sought out ads from women who wanted to sell things and showed up at their addresses after convincing them that he was a potential buyer. Once inside, he would request to use the restroom, at which point he would retrieve his equipment, a knife and a rope. He would then immobilize his victims, proceed to sexually assault them, and, in some cases, rob them of their valuables. In one instance, a single assault led to a criminal trial, resulting in an initial conviction. However, this conviction was overturned on appeal. Following this, Long moved from the area to Tampa, where he kidnapped Lisa McVey.

It is noteworthy that at the time, law enforcement officials were unaware of the presence of a serial killer operating within the Tampa area. However, given the nature of the crimes committed, it was evident to the officers that this was not an "ordinary" murder case. Consequently, they sought the assistance of the FBI at an early stage in the investigation. Fortunately, the investigators had some key pieces of evidence. Most notably, they found a tire print and a red textile fiber that matched the carpeting commonly found in automobiles.

By November of that year, the police had identified at least eight victims of the serial killer, though they had not yet identified the killer's identity. While there were some discrepancies in the modus operandi most of the women were strangled, while Robert Joe Long also used a firearm and knife it was relatively straightforward for investigators to link the crimes. Not only were there technical clues, such as the tire tracks and red fibers that appeared repeatedly at the crime scenes, but they also recognized the killer's behavior. The bodies were discovered in isolated locations where they had been left for an extended period before being discovered, and many of them exhibited the same posture as at the initial crime scene. I think that Robert Joe Long posed the deceased was an attempt to provoke a strong emotional response in those who might discover the bodies. His actions were driven by his personal desires and the symbolic representation of the women involved. The women themselves are of particular significance, as they exhibited a commonality despite their differences in terms of age, ethnicity, and appearance. Most of these women were marginalized, with five being sex

workers, two strippers, and the remainder grappling with substance abuse. They had endured challenging circumstances. They resided in the same economically disadvantaged area of Tampa, and their lives were intricately intertwined with the city's unsavory nightlife. This indicated to investigators that the perpetrator likely operated within this specific district. However, one victim emerged as particularly noteworthy: the third victim. This 23-year-old factory worker stood out due to her unique circumstances. She resided in a trailer park with her family, but she also frequently ventured out alone on foot to escape the overcrowded mobile home environment. Witnesses characterized her as a trusting individual who frequently accepted rides from strangers when she was out and needed to return home.

Victimology constitutes is a pivotal instrument for both investigators and profilers, aiding in the establishment of connections between crimes and the profiling of perpetrators. However, as with other components of the methodology, victimology cannot be regarded as an independent tool. The victims of serial killers or serial rapists can offer significant insights into the perpetrator. The perpetrator's actions are intrinsically linked to his personal history and psyche, and when he encounters his victim, he projects aspects of himself onto them. The nature of Robert Joe Long's murders exemplifies this phenomenon. The victims were vulnerable women who resided in a locale conducive to victimization. The murders did not necessitate extensive planning, as the victims is willing to follow and unknown "Johns" to do their business.

It is noteworthy that three of the victims were not sex workers or strippers, yet they were perceived as vulnerable by their family and friends. This perception was attributed to their nocturnal activities, which often involved walking alone in deserted areas. This observation offers insight into the mindset of the perpetrator. In my professional experience, I have encountered both male and female perpetrators of violence and the partner affected by their aggression. It is evident that some individuals with these tendencies possess a particular skill in identifying persons who may face challenges in resisting their advances.

Controlling behavior, violence, and stalking are not sudden occurrences within a relationship; rather, they are the result of a gradual and meticulous manipulation by the perpetrator. This manipulation often begins with the development of a sense of togetherness, gradually intensifying until it culminates in the isolation of the victim from their social circle. In instances where a person attempts to resist, the perpetrator may resort to violence, and even if the person manages to leave the abusive relationship, they are often susceptible to entering a new abusive relationship. In the field of psychology, this phenomenon is referred to as repetition compulsion, which suggests that individuals who have experienced violence, mental, physical, sexual or other traumatic events during childhood are at risk of repeating that pattern in their own lives.

The signals that violent persons are adept at picking up on are commonly observed in serial rape and murder cases, offering insights into the perpetrators' motivations and potential psychological profiles. In some of the case where Robert Joe Long, did managed to lure women who did not usually go with strange men in three separate incidents, it would be pertinent to consider whether we are dealing with an individual who possesses the capacity to target women who are already in a state of vulnerability. Furthermore, it would be worthwhile to explore whether the perpetrator can sustain a relationship characterized by control and violence as a central dynamic.

While not all cases involve serial killing, such knowledge can be advantageous in law enforcement investigations, as it allows for the identification of potential patterns of domestic violence or previous convictions. The analysis of victim appearance, background, and behavior provides crucial insights, as it can reveal why a particular individual was targeted and the potential connection, often perceived but not objectively present, between the victim and the perpetrator. This process aids in the development of a profile of the individual sought by investigators. In the case of Robert Joe Long, the application of victimology may not have been fully realized, yet its role in facilitating the apprehension of the perpetrator was crucial.

Long was sentenced to death for one of the murders and life imprisonment for seven others and was executed by lethal injection on May 23, 2019.

Source: McLean, case RJL, 2004, McLean, 2023, Long vs State, 1988, 1992.

***

Even though some serial killers have an extra X or Y chromosome, it is not enough to make someone a serial killer. It cannot be ruled out that some serial killers have biological and/or genetic factors that may play a role in the development of their behavior patterns. I will outline some of these factors in the next sections.

## EARLY INJURIES

Injuries can occur to the fetus that affect the child's development later. Studies have shown that cocaine abuse affects the genetic code of sperm in men. Alcohol and drugs can damage the fetus to the extent that later developmental disorders can be seen (Raine, 2003). Children with developmental disorders may have brain or nervous system damage. This can result in difficulty with controlling violent and impulsive behavior as an adult. Researchers have also tried to examine whether serial killers have a different genetic code than normal people. However, as mentioned, there is no clear evidence to suggest that this is the sole reason or even the case for someone becoming a serial killer (Bahn et al., 1995).

## BRAIN INJURIES

Money (1990), a forensic sexologist, explains sexual sadism as a major symptom of brain damage. Robert Joe Long engaged in compulsive masturbation and sexual activities so much after a motorcycle accident that he damaged his penis.

Money (1990) specifically points out the limbic system, which deals with sexual arousal and mating behavior, as well as anticipatory and defensive behavior. Sexual sadism is explained this way:

"...the brain becomes pathologically activated to transmit messages of attack simultaneously with messages of sexual arousal and mating behavior..."

People with brain injuries or brain dysfunction have confused messages activated in their brains. The problem is not continuous but episodic, as seen in epilepsy. This is not the cause of sexual sadism, but together with other contributing factors, sexual sadism can develop. Five factors influence its development:

1. Hereditary predisposition
2. Hormonal disturbances
3. Pathological contexts
4. Childhood sexual abuse
5. Symptom overlaps include, among others, temporal lobe epilepsy, manic depression, and schizoid personality disorder.

## TRAUMATIC BRAIN INJURIES

Williams et al., (2018) have examine traumatic brain injury as a potential crucial cause of violent crime.

Traumatic brain injury (TBI) is the biggest cause of death and disability in children and young people, but is it also a potential cause of violent crime? TBI compromises important neurological functions for self-regulation and social behavior and increases the risk of behavioral disorders and psychiatric morbidity. Crime among young people is a major social issue. So called early starters often continue for a lifetime. A substantial majority of young offenders are reconvicted soon after release. Multiple factors play a role in crime. Williams et al., (2018) argue in their research that TBI is a risk factor for earlier, more violent offending. TBI is linked to poor engagement in treatment, in-custody infractions, and reconviction. There are some schemes on the way that can assess and manage TBI. Williams et al., (2018) hope that it can improve the engagement of offenders in forensic psychotherapeutic rehabilitation, and it can be a factor in reducing crime.

TBI appears to be associated with earlier age of incarceration, increased risk of violence, and more convictions. Neurological abnormalities are common in offenders. Brain functions, in areas important for social functioning, such as impulse control and empathy, appear compromised. They estimate that people in custody are estimated to have complicated mild TBI or moderate to severe head injury, which is prevalent in 5 out of 10 people, and three-quarters of 10 people could have a milder form of TBI. We know that neuropsychological dysfunction (poor judgment, impulsivity, and mentalization problems) is linked to violence, infractions in prison, poorer treatment gains, and reconviction. But they also argue that we see histories of abuse, neglect, and trauma appear particularly elevated in those with TBI versus those without TBI histories, as are ongoing mental health and drug and alcohol problems.

Young offenders with TBI are particularly at risk of self-harm and suicidal behavior. TBI could amplify any neurocognitive issues due to adverse life events. People with TBI have an elevated in facilities and might not be placed the right place that can address their needs. There has been an assumption that TBI was just a coincidental occurrence in the lives of risk takers: people who were premorbid, set to be on a trajectory toward crime. But Williams et al. (2018) argue that the research evidence suggests otherwise. Addressing TBI offers a means not only to improve the lives of those who offend, but also, crucially, to reduce crime.

Williams et al., (2018) argue that when we see interpersonal violence and impulsivity with TBI, it is predominantly seen in males but is also related to trauma in 30% of offenders. There are few studies on the severity of TBI, comorbid conditions, and patterns of offending. Williams and colleagues studied 197 young male offenders in prison (average age 16 years), and 60% had a reported head injury. Most had a history of abuse (sexual, violent, or emotional), and 44% of the females had TBI.

As we have seen, TBI occurs within a constellation of socio-adverse factors. This is particularly evident when looking at studies of girls and women. Of 113 female prisoners in the USA, Brewer-Smyth & Burgess (2019) found that 42% had a history of TBI. Those who had committed violent crimes had an average of two TBIs. History of domestic violence, previous suicide attempts, and TBI with loss of consciousness were all associated with current violent convictions. Similarly, Colantonio et al., 2014 in Williams et all., (2018) found that women with TBI who had offended had suffered earlier physical and sexual abuse than women without TBI. Abuse may be associated with concussive blows or TBI in a variety of ways. Such injuries may complicate the experience of post-traumatic stress disorder (PTSD). Survivors may have inconsistent memories of events.

Future studies must be completed to characterize the nature and severity of neurotrauma in perpetrators and controls. Ideally, in addition to measures of chronic TBI biomarkers such as tau, neuroimaging, such as diffusion tensor imaging, should also be used. Such analyses would provide a better understanding of the underlying pathology of TBI in offenders. They would provide windows for the design of novel therapies.

## CASE: PETER WILLIAM SUTCLIFFE

**Epithets: The Yorkshire Ripper**

Might Peter William Sutcliffe's inherent killer instinct have been sparked by the brain damage he suffered while in an incubator as a newborn baby? Let us look at it.

The lack of oxygen certainly wasn't the sole cause of his temperament or actions, but scientists have found a link between these kinds of brain injuries and violent crime.

Peter William Sutcliffe was born on June 2, 1946, in Shipley, West Riding of Yorkshire, to a working-class family lived in Bingley. His parents were John William Sutcliffe and his Irish wife, Kathleen Frances Coonan, a native of Connemara. Sutcliffe's mother was Catholic, and his father was a member of the choir at the local Anglican church of St. Wilfred's. Sutcliffe and his siblings were raised in their mother's Catholic faith, and Sutcliffe briefly served as an altar boy. His mother endured domestic abuse from Sutcliffe's father, a likely factor in the emotional distress his mother experienced during her pregnancy. Sutcliffe's preterm birth resulted in a two-week hospital stay.

His father was an alcoholic, and during a Christmas dinner dispute, he violently struck Sutcliffe with a beer glass. Additionally, he harbored animosity toward Sutcliffe's mother. He was known to express his hatred for her, stating, "She was a bitch, and the less said about her, the better." Sutcliffe's father frequently belittled his slightly built son, dismissing him as "a wimp, always hanging from his mother's apron, a mummy's boy." Sutcliffe's father was known to physically discipline his children, using a belt as a punishment. Sutcliffe's siblings later described their father as "a monster." According to Sutcliffe's younger brother, "the atmosphere in our house would change as soon as he [father] walked in. His life revolved around playing football, cricket, singing in a choir, and womanizing."

Sutcliffe's mother, in contrast, showered her son with attention, fostering a sense of perfection in him.

In 1970, Sutcliffe's father made a ruse in which he posed as his wife's lover, thereby luring her to a local hotel. Accompanying him were Sutcliffe and two of his siblings. The purpose of their presence was to witness the expose of his wife's infidelity. When Sutcliffe's mother arrived at the hotel, her husband pulled a negligee, which was in fact her own, out of her purse. This incident unfolded before the eyes of her children. In his late adolescence, Sutcliffe developed an obsession with voyeurism, which led him to engage in frequent spying on and stalking, targeting sex workers and their male clients.

Sutcliffe's behavior indicated a tendency towards solitude, as evidenced by his decision to leave school at the age of 15. This decision was followed by a series of menial jobs, including two stints as a gravedigger at Bingley Cemetery in the 1960s. This occupation, while seemingly unremarkable, was indicative of a macabre sense of humor that would persist throughout Sutcliffe's life. Co-workers reported that Sutcliffe derived a considerable amount of enjoyment from his work, even volunteering for overtime shifts that involved the cleansing of corpses. From November 1971 to April 1973, Sutcliffe was employed at the Baird Television factory, working on a packaging line. He left this position to pursue a career as a salesman, a decision that would ultimately contribute to his eventual involvement in criminality.

February 14, 1967, Sutcliffe met Sonia Szurma, a 16-year-old of Ukrainian and Polish heritage born to refugee parents from Czechoslovakia, at the Royal Standard pub on Manningham Lane, located in a red-light district within Bradford. The couple got married on August 10, 1974. Sonia was pursuing her dream of becoming a teacher when she was formally diagnosed with paranoid schizophrenia.

Sutcliffe secured employment at the Britannia Works of Anderton International, where he worked night shifts from April 1973. However, in February 1975, he took redundancy and utilized half of the £400 payout to pursue training as a heavy goods vehicle (HGV) driver. On March 05, 1976, his employment was terminated due to allegations of theft of used tires. He remained unemployed until October 1976, when he secured a position as an HGV driver for T. & W.H. Clark Holdings Ltd. on the Canal Road Industrial Estate in Bradford.

According to reports, Sutcliffe engaged in sexual acts with sex workers during his early years. It has been speculated that he experienced a negative encounter, possibly involving financial fraud by a sex worker and her pimp. However, analysis has not identified definitive evidence that he actively pursued the services of sex workers. Nonetheless, it has been observed that he developed a strong fascination with sex workers, engaging in behaviors such as observing their solicitation in public spaces in Leeds and Bradford.

The relationship between Sonia Szurma and Sutcliffe was characterized, as "domineering," with Sonia exhibiting a tendency to physically restrain her husband during episodes of unprovoked rage. Barbara Jones, a journalist who engaged in numerous conversations with Sonia, characterized her as "the most irritating, strangest, and coldest person I've ever met. She's so incredibly prickly and demanding."

Sonia experienced several miscarriages in her marriage to Sutcliffe, and the couple was informed that she would be unable to conceive. She resumed her teacher training course, during which time she engaged in an extramarital affair with an ice-cream van driver. After the completion of her teacher training course in 1977, she resumed her position as a teacher, and the pair used her earnings to purchase a house at 6 Garden Lane in Heaton, into which they moved on September 26, 1977. This house was where the two remained at the time of Sutcliffe's arrest in 1980.

Sutcliffe was charged on January 5, 1981. At his trial that May, he said he was not guilty of thirteen charges of murder, but guilty of manslaughter because he was not acting in the fullest sense of responsibility. He said that he was just doing God's will. He said he heard voices telling him to kill sex workers while working as a gravedigger. He said the voices came from the headstone of a Polish man, Bronisław Zapolski. He also said the voices were from God. Sutcliffe admitted he was guilty of trying to murder seven people. The prosecution was ready to accept his plea after four psychiatrists said he had paranoid schizophrenia. The trial judge, Justice Sir Leslie Boreham, asked for a very detailed explanation of why the prosecution thought this was the right decision. After the Attorney-General, Sir Michael Havers, speaking for two hours, a ninety-minute lunch break, and another forty minutes of legal discussion, Justice Boreham rejected the plea of diminished responsibility and the expert opinions of the psychiatrists. He insisted that the case should be dealt with by a jury. The trial was set to begin on May 5, 1981.

Sutcliffe's trial lasted two weeks. Despite the efforts of his lawyer, James Chadwin, Sutcliffe was found guilty of all counts of murder and was sentenced to twenty life sentences. The jury did not accept the testimony of four psychiatrists who said that Sutcliffe had paranoid schizophrenia. One of the psychiatrists was influenced by the testimony of a prison officer who heard Sutcliffe say to his wife that if he could convince people he was crazy, he might get ten years in prison. The judge said that Sutcliffe could not be redeemed and hoped he would never leave prison. He said that Sutcliffe would have to serve at least 30 years before he could be considered for parole. This meant that he would not be able to leave prison until at least 2011. On July 16, 2010, the High Court sentenced Sutcliffe to life in prison without the possibility of parole. After his trial, Sutcliffe admitted to two more murders, but he was not prosecuted for these murders.

Peter Sutcliffe passed away at the age of 74 on November 13, 2020, at the University Hospital of North Durham. The cause of death was documented as a combination of complications from diabetes and the novel coronavirus (SARS-CoV-2). He returns to HM Prison Frankland two weeks prior for treatment of a suspected heart attack, which was initially diagnosed at the same hospital. Prior to his death, he had a history of significant health complications, including obesity. The funeral arrangements were private, and Sutcliffe's body was cremated.

Source: Cook, 2024 and Jomes, 1996.

## FRONTAL LOBE DAMAGE

Adrian Raine, a professor of neuropsychology at the University of Southern California, and Monte Buchsbaum, a psychiatrist at Mount Sinai Medical School in New York, with others, have researched frontal lobe damage and violent criminals. Raine, along with Buchsbaum, conducted brain scans of 25 murderers (Bihrle et al., 1998). They found that many killers had frontal lobe abnormalities. Their research indicates that criminally violent men often damage the frontal lobes. The frontal lobes are the most active part of the brain. In the scans of the mothers, they found that several had reduced frontal lobes, which could be because of traumatizing life (PTSD) (Schechter et al., 2011). This part of the brain is vital because the frontal lobes are involved in planning and organization. Understanding violent crime requires the frontal lobes involved in impulse control. Furthermore, in their study, Raine and Buchsbaum found a malfunction in the prefrontal cortex, which is the area related to control and behavior.

Buchsbaum (in Potter, 2002) believes that we should not read too much into the results they come up with. In his opinion, research has moved away from brain research because researchers don't want to give the impression that they are looking for an excuse for extremely violent individuals. Buchsbaum writes:

*"I can't specifically say, this person will be a sniper and at age 30 will carry out violent and aggressive crimes...That is fundamentally impossible...What I can do is understand the underlying dimensions of impulse control, how the brain stops behavior, and perhaps I can learn to strengthen this, with educational strategies, or with drugs" - (Potter, 2002, p.1).*

Raine believes that these changes in the brain are congenital and predispose the child to behavioral disorders, which can manifest in lying, cheating, stealing, and/or being cruel at an early age. He believes that children who are exposed to risk factors such as smoking, birth complications, or other indicators such as a low heart rate may benefit from intervention as early as possible. He further states that initiating attempts to reach children and adolescents is often too late.

But despite Raine and Buchsbaum's findings, neuroscientists agree that brain damage is not the only reason why someone becomes a serial killer. Research shows that people with poor impulse control, disorganization, and social incompetence are at risk. Raine says:

*"It is possible, for example, that prefrontal dysfunction does not cause violence; instead, living a violent life (including substance abuse and fights) may cause the*

*brain dysfunction I observed. No previous study, however, has shown that substance abuse and head injuries produce the specific profile of brain deficits that I observed. Finally, although I controlled for schizophrenia, other psychiatric disorders in the control group could have contributed to the findings. But again, this specific pattern of brain deficits has never been reported in any psychiatric group" (Raine, 1999).*

However, other factors must be present for someone to kill. Jonathan Pincus, a psychiatrist at Georgetown University in Washington, has studied more than 100 murderers. He said in an interview with ABC News:

*"Frontal lobes are the part of the brain that brake impulses and drives. It's the part of the brain that allows us to say, 'Don't do that! Don't say that! It's not appropriate! There will be consequences!" (Potter, 2002, p. 1).*

Pincus suggests that children who have experienced severe abuse may have pent-up anger waiting to be released. If the person also has a frontal lobe injury, they may have difficulty controlling their anger and aggression. This creates a dangerous combination of impulses and drives that a damaged frontal lobe cannot control. This combination can trigger serial killings (Pincus, 2002).

As mentioned, some serial killers suffer from various brain injuries or other physiological disorders. However, not all brain injury victims become serial killers. Nor do all serial killers have brain injuries. This was also the case with Jeffrey Dahmer, who, at the time of his death, had no brain injuries or other physiological disorders that could explain his behavior (Lane, 1996).

We also know that if an infant is under stimulated or abused, certain centers in the brain, such as those related to empathy and compassion, can negatively affect development. In this way, the changes seen on brain scans may be changes in the brain triggered by under stimulation of certain centers in the brain. Perry (2003) suggests that physical, psychological, and sexual abuse affect brain development.

## PSYCHOLOGICAL FACTORS

Psychological factors that can cause someone to become a serial killer can, as mentioned, be events in the person's life. These events can include abuse, maltreatment, trauma or crises. In addition, temperament, personality, emotions, and cognition can influence development. Psychological factors impact motivation, self-esteem, developing meaningful social roles, and maintaining relationships with significant others. I will review some significant psychological factors related to serial killer development.

## EMOTIONAL PAIN AND VIOLENCE

Martens (2002) studied psychopaths and found that social isolation, loneliness, and similar emotional pain precede violent criminal behavior. Psychopaths perceive that the whole world is against them and convince themselves that they can satisfy their own needs. They therefore demand special privileges. Jeffrey Dahmer and Dennis Nilsen both had emotional problems that became more difficult after they killed. Their actions accelerated from murder to serial killing and bizarre interactions with victims, dead or alive. Dahmer and Nilsen both explained that they started murdering because they wanted company. They had difficulty relating and interacting with other people, including their families. Nilsen talked to the dead for hours while watching television. Dahmer consumed parts of his victims because he wanted them to be a part of him. He was convinced that his victims lived inside him.

Serial killers describe loneliness and social failure as agonizing and unbearable. Dahmer and Nilsen experienced personal rejection, abuse, humiliation, and emotional suffering. They created their own sadistic universe where they could avenge their social failures. Some serial killers explained that killing was not enjoyable. Dahmer wanted 100% control over his victims. Therefore, he tried to turn his victims into zombies by first sedating them with sleeping pills and then injecting acid into their brains. When this failed, he killed his victims. Nilsen was more comfortable with corpses than with living people. He read poetry to the dead and lived with them for as long as possible. He enjoyed spending time with corpses. Other serial killers reported feelings for their victims. Their problem is that they don't know how to interact with real people (Bahn et al., 1995). But loneliness is not enough to explain why some people become serial killers; it may be one of the reasons serial killers commit murder. Most lonely people don't kill to make friends. Jeffrey Dahmer was diagnosed with a personality disorder known as schizotypal personality disorder, among others. I hypothesize that today; he would have been given another diagnosis, which is based mostly on Lionel Dahmer's description of his son's behavior in childhood.

There are other examples of emotional pain resulting in violence. Martens (2002) found that emotional pain underlies domestic violence. Men who use this type of violence often have difficulty managing human relationships themselves.

## SOCIOCULTURAL AND ENVIRONMENTAL FACTORS

In the following sections, I will discuss psychological, physical, and sexual abuse. The role of the mother and father will be discussed, and finally, I will explain Lewis and Pincus' theory.

Vaknin (2003) argues that in most cases, serial killers are constructed.

Serial killers are created by culture and society as they are influenced by their personal circumstances and genetic makeup.

As mentioned, physical and mental abuse, sexual abuse, alcohol abuse, and/or drug abuse are seen in serial killers' family histories. Parents often can see the problems with their children, but they don't have the skills to deal with them. O'Connor (2002b) estimates that some of the signs of problems may be the MacDonald triad, animal cruelty, arson, and enuresis (see chapter 6).

Several studies indicate that children who have experienced maltreatment are at risk of becoming violent killers. Serial killer Carl Panzram said:

*"All of my family are as average human beings are. They are honest and hardworking people. All except me. I have been a human-animal ever since I was born. When I was very young, 5 or 6 years of age, I was a thief, a liar, and a mean, despisable one at that. The older I got, the meaner I got" (Ressler, 1992, pp. 98-105).*

It is difficult to know for sure if someone grew up in a normal family. You also can't be sure it's true when they say they grew up in violence and abuse. You can obtain school reports, medical records, witness statements, and/or hospitalization reports to confirm or deny serial killers' stories. However, it is important to know that these reports may not necessarily reveal sexual and psychological abuse.

Pincus (2002) studied 100 killers and found that although some killers reported a happy and safe childhood and their families outwardly appeared normal, a different picture emerged when he examined the circumstances in detail. Children can learn a Dr. Jekyll and Mr. Hyde routine from their parents, where the parents outside the home are model parents, but when the family comes home, things turn chaotic. It is largely agreed that violence begets violence. Scott (2003) sees violence as circular:

*"Parents who abuse their children, physically and psychologically, instill in them an almost instinctive reliance upon violence as a first resort to any challenge."*

If the child experiences violence or abuse, this can also be turned inwards. Instead of aggressive behavior, the person turns anger toward themselves by engaging in self-mutilation, substance abuse, eating disorder, or contemplating suicide. Serial killers exhibit externalizing and internalizing behaviors. There are examples of serial killers who have attempted to castrate themselves and have attempted suicide numerous times. Many abuse drugs and alcohol. The cause of the behavior can be physical, psychological, and sexual abuse, which I will discuss in the next section.

## TRAUMA - PSYCHOLOGICAL, PHYSICAL, AND SEXUAL ABUSE

For many serial killers, the attachment between them and their family is problematic. This lack of connection affects peers and later relationships, resulting in difficulty making friends and forming relationships with others. They have problems with interpersonal relationships in general.

It is not only physical violence, but also psychological violence that affects the child. Prentky et al. (1989) believe that psychological violence affects the child more than physical violence. Brown (1984) found in his study that psychological violence correlates with criminal behavior, whereas physical abuse does not correlate to the same degree. This was also observed in the FBI's study of 36 serial killers. It was found that 42% had been exposed to physical violence, whereas 74% had been exposed to psychological violence

(Ressler, 1992, p. 19). This indicates that psychological violence can affect children more than physical violence, depending on the child. At the same time, it is more difficult to detect and stop psychological violence than physical violence. This is because you do not have the same opportunity to determine if the child is subjected to psychological violence as you can with physical violence.

In sexual abuse, the child may withdraw from themselves and withdraw into a fantasy world to protect themselves. The child imagines that abuse is not happening to them, but to another person. Virtually all serial killers experienced this withdrawal as children. But for serial killers, fantasies continue even as they age. Serial killers are preceded by fantasy. The fantasies of these children may contain a power/dominant aspect, something not normally present in children. Retvitch (1980) argues that the mother's ambivalent relationship, characterized by overprotection, treating older children as infants, or by pursuing their child or rejecting the child completely, may also contribute to the child's withdrawal into a fantasy world:

*"The paternal relationship may be particularly cold, distinct, authoritarian and (often physically) punitive" (Brittain, 1967, p. 38).*

Ressler (1992) and Scott (2003) believe that the cause of someone developing into a serial killer can be found in a dominant, distant, promiscuous mother or a mother who is oppressed and abuses herself. The promiscuous mothers exposed their children to inappropriate sexual behavior. However, various studies (Hickey, 2016) suggest that it is not only the mother's fault. The father is often absent in one way or another. In situations where the father is present, he is often sadistic, disciplinarian, alcoholic, and overly aggressive toward women.

Serial killers experience abuse that they inflict on their victims as well.

This is repetition compulsion, which is significant as serial killers often represent aspects of what they were exposed to as children. They try to escape their own traumatic experiences and thus inflict the horror and terror they have experienced on others.

## THE FAMILY - MOTHER

Serial killers often have an unusual and unnatural relationship with their mothers; some even kill their mothers (Hickey, 2023). Serial killers often blamed their mothers, but it has become a cliché. In movies for example, Norman Bates in Hitchcock's *Psycho* (1960) and *Manhunter* (1986) with Hannibal Lecter, where mothers are portrayed as the primary cause of serial killing.

Examining the parenting methods used by the serial killers' mothers in raising their sons, there is a link between becoming a serial killer and problems growing up. However, this is not the only reason why some become serial killers, as the father has just as much influence on the child's upbringing as the mother has (see next section on father influence).

Some mothers link sexuality with violence when raising their children, believing it keeps them away from sexuality. Serial killer Edward Theodore Gein's mother convinced him that women were sinful. She told him that women only gave him disease. Later, he used his victims' skulls to make bowls and other objects. Women were objects to him.

## CASE: EDWARD THEODORE GEIN

### *Epithets: The Mad Butcher, The Plainfield Ghoul*

Edward Theodore Gein was born on August 27, 1906. He was an American murderer, suspected serial killer, and body snatcher who gained notoriety for his crimes committed around his hometown of Plainfield,

Wisconsin. These crimes garnered significant notoriety following the 1957 discovery that Gein had stolen corpses from local graveyards and had made mementos from their bones and skin. Furthermore, he confessed to the killings of Mary Hogan, a tavern owner, murdered in 1954 and Bernice Worden, a hardware store proprietor, murdered in 1957.

Edward Theodore Gein was the second of two sons to George Philip Gein and Augusta Wilhelmine Gein. Gein had an older brother named Henry. Augusta, a devout Lutheran, instilled in her sons a fervent belief in the inherent moral corruption of the world, the evils of alcohol, and the natural promiscuity of women as instruments of the devil. She allocated time every afternoon to read to them from the Bible, selecting verses from the Old Testament and the Book of Revelation concerning death, murder, and divine retribution. She played a significant role in Gein's upbringing, shaping his character and influencing his future behavior.

George Gein's professional engagements encompassed roles in carpentry, tanning, and the municipal fire department. At the same time, he also operated a local grocery business, which he relinquished to pursue agricultural endeavors in Plainfield, Wisconsin, with his family. Augusta strategically utilized the seclusion offered by their farm to shield her sons from external influences.

Edward Gein left the farm only to attend school. Outside of school, he spent most of his time engaged in farm-related chores. He was known for his shyness and was remembered by his classmates and teachers as having peculiar mannerisms, such as laughing in seemingly random moments, as if he were laughing at his own jokes. Augusta punished Edward Gein whenever he attempted to make friends, according to family acquaintances. Despite his poor social development, Edward Gein demonstrated notable academic aptitude, particularly in reading.

April 1, 1940, Gein's father passed away from heart failure at the age of 66. Gein and his brother Henry took on them miscellaneous small jobs within the community to generate revenue sufficient to cover their living expenses. The community generally regarded the brothers as reliable and honest. While both individuals engaged in similar occupations as handymen, Edward Gein also engaged in childcare services for neighbors on a frequent basis. He derived pleasure from the act of babysitting, exhibiting a proclivity to establish stronger connections with children in comparison to adults. Henry initiated a romantic relationship with a divorced mother of two and expressed his intention to cohabitate with her. He expressed concern regarding his brother's emotional bond with their mother and frequently voiced negative remarks about her in Gein's presence, who reacted with astonishment and emotional distress.

May 16, 1944, Gein burned marsh vegetation on the property. The fire escalated beyond his control, prompting the intervention of the local fire department. When the conflagration had been extinguished, and the firefighters had departed, Gein reported Henry as missing. Equipped with lanterns and flashlights, a search party commenced the endeavor of locating 43-year-old Henry, whose lifeless body was discovered in a prone position. It was evident that Henry had been deceased for a considerable time, and the underlying cause of death was attributed to heart failure, as no external signs of burn injuries or other trauma were observed.

Reports by biographer Harold Schechter indicated the presence of contusions on Henry's cranium. Law enforcement officials dismissed the possibility of foul play, and the county coroner later officially listed asphyxiation as the cause of death. The authorities accepted the accident theory, yet no official investigation was conducted, and no autopsy was performed.

In questioning Gein about the death of Bernice Worden in 1957, state investigator Joe Wilimovsky raised questions concerning Henry's death. George Arndt, who conducted an exhaustive study of the case, posited that, in retrospect, it was "possible and likely" that Henry's death constituted the

"Cain and Abel" aspect of the case.

Following Henry's death, Augusta suffered a debilitating stroke, and Edward Gein took the role of primary caregiver. In 1945, he and his mother paid a visit to a man named Smith, who resided in proximity, with the intention of procuring straw. According to Gein, Augusta witnessed Smith beating a dog. A woman inside the Smith residence came outside and yelled for him to stop, but Smith proceeded to physically subdue the dog, resulting in its death. Augusta was visibly distressed by this scene; however, her discomfort did not appear to stem from the brutality toward the dog, but rather from the presence of the woman. She informed Gein that the woman was not married to Smith and therefore had no right to be present. In a state of anger, she referred to the woman as "Smith's harlot." After this event, Augusta suffered a second stroke, which precipitated a swift and precipitous decline in her health. She passed away on December 29, 1945, at the age of Gein experienced profound devastation upon her death. He was now entirely isolated from all other people.

November 16, 1957, Bernice Worden, a 58-year-old proprietor of a hardware store in Plainfield, disappeared. According to the available sources, the vehicle belonging to the hardware store was observed departing from the rear of the building. The hardware store recorded a notable absence of customers throughout the day, a circumstance that some residents attributed to the ongoing deer hunting season. Deputy Sheriff Frank Worden, son of Bernice Worden, entered the store to locate the cash register, which was found open and with blood stains on the floor. He informed investigators that on the evening prior to his mother's disappearance, Gein had been in the store and was expected to have returned the next morning for a gallon of antifreeze. The final transaction involving the antifreeze was documented on the morning prior to Worden's disappearance, as indicated by the receipt.

In the evening, Gein was apprehended at a West Plainfield grocery establishment, and the Waushara County Sheriff's Department searched

Gein's farm. A sheriff's deputy found Worden's decapitated body in a shed on Gein's property, hanging upside down by her legs with a crossbar at her ankles and ropes at her wrists. The torso was "dressed out like a deer." The victim had been shot with a .22-caliber rifle, and the mutilations were made after her death. A search of the residence by authorities yielded the following findings: whole human bones and fragments, a wastebasket made of human skin, human skin covering several chairs, skulls on his bedposts, female skulls, some with the tops sawn off, bowls made from human skulls, a corset made from a female torso skinned from shoulders to waist, leggings made from human leg skin, masks made from the skin of female heads, victim Mary Hogan's face mask in a paper bag, Mary Hogan's skull in a box, victim Bernice Worden's entire head in a burlap sack, Bernice Worden's heart "in a plastic bag in front of Gein's potbelly stove," nine vulvas in a shoe box, a young girl's dress and "the vulvas of two females judged to have been about fifteen years old," a belt made from female human nipples, four noses, a pair of lips on a window shade drawstring, a lampshade made from the skin of a human face, and fingernails from female fingers.

Initially deemed unfit to stand trial due to mental health concerns, Gein was committed to a mental health facility. By 1968, his legal status had changed, and he was found competent to stand trial. He was found guilty of Worden's murder and was declared legally insane. Consequently, he was remanded to a psychiatric institution.

Edward Gein passed away on July 26, 1984, at the age of 77, due to respiratory failure resulting from lung cancer at the Mendota Mental Health Institute. He is interred in a now-unmarked grave in the Plainfield Cemetery, alongside his family.

Source: McLean, 2004, 2023, Ramsland, 2013 and Noe, 2007.

***

Another serial killer, Joseph Kallinger, was adopted and molested by sadistic Catholic parents. After undergoing hernia surgery at six, his mother told him that the surgery was done to stop his penis from growing. Kallinger believed God told him to kill men and cut off their penises. His mother punished him by forcing him to hold his hand over a flame. If he cried, his mother would beat him. Kallinger grew up and enjoyed torturing others. He became a sadistic father of 7 children himself and murdered his own 13-year-old son. He got his other son, Michael, 12 years old, to help him commit more crimes.

Another case is Edmund Emil Kemper, whose mother was described as tyrannical. She locked Kemper in their basement because he scared her sister. As he grew up, he and his mother fought constantly. The mother placed him with his grandparents, whom he murdered as a young teen, where the same abuse continued. When he was out again, he went to live with his mother afterward because his father rejected him.

## CASE: EDMUND EMIL KEMPER

***Epithets: The Co-ed killer, Co-ed Butcher, Ogre of Aptos, The Mad Titan***

Edmund Emil Kemper III, born December 18, 1948, is an American serial killer who was convicted of murdering 10 people in total, including six women and one girl, between May 1972 and April 1973. Years earlier, at the age of 15, Kemper had murdered his grandparents. Most of his victims were female college students. These students were typically found hitchhiking in the vicinity of Santa Cruz County, California, at the time of their murders. The nature of the murders included necrophilia, decapitation, and dismemberment. At his trial in 1973, the court found Kemper sane and guilty, and the prosecutor requested that capital punishment be imposed on him. However, the court had suspended the death penalty in the state of California at the time. As a result, Kemper received eight concurrent life sentences. Since that time, he has been detained at the California Medical Facility in Vacaville.

Edmund Emil Kemper III was born in Burbank, California. He was the middle child of three children and the only son born to Clarnell Elizabeth Kemper, a native of Montana, and Edmund Emil Kemper Jr. Edmund Jr., a World War II veteran, participated in the testing of nuclear weapons at the Pacific Proving Grounds following the war. He returned to California, where he pursued a career as an electrician. Clarnell often expressed dissatisfaction with her husband's occupation, characterizing it as "menial." In later years, he remarked that his experiences in wartime, including atomic bomb testing, were eclipsed by the challenges he faced in his personal life with Clarnell.

Kemper's physical differences were pronounced from an early age; he weighed 13 pounds (5.9 kilograms) at birth and grew to exceed his peers in height by the age of four. His early behavioral tendencies exhibited signs of antisocial tendencies, including animal cruelty. At the age of 10, Kemper buried a pet cat alive, then dug it up, decapitated it, and mounted its head on a spike, all to the delight he derived from misleading his family about the cat's dead. At the age of 13, he killed another family cat when he perceived it to be favoring his younger sister, Allyn Lee Kemper, over him; he kept pieces of it in his closet until his mother found it.

Kemper was known to harbor dark fantasies and have a morbid imagination. In his youth, he performed rites with his younger sister's dolls that culminated in his removing their heads and hands. In one incident, when his elder sister, Susan Hughey Kemper, teased him and asked why he did not attempt to kiss his teacher, he responded with a statement that implied a sense of fatalism, stating, "If I kiss her, I'd have to kill her first."

Kemper also recounted how, during his early years, he would often sneak out of his house, armed with his father's bayonet, to his second-grade teacher's house and observe her through the windows. In later interviews, he stated that his favorite childish games included "Gas Chamber" and "Electric Chair." In these games, he would request that his younger sister restrain him and flip an imaginary switch. He would then roll over and around on the floor, pretending to be executed by gas inhalation or electric shock.

Kemper also reported having several near-death experiences during his childhood. On one occasion, his elder sister attempted to place him in the path of a train, and on another occasion, she pushed him into the deep end of a swimming pool, where he almost drowned. Kemper's relationship with his father was particularly close; he was devastated when his parents separated in 1957 and divorced in 1961. He was sent to live with his mother, Clarnell, in Helena, Montana. The relationship between Kemper and his mother, Clarnell, was characterized by significant dysfunction. Clarnell exhibited narcissistic tendencies. She had a history of alcoholism and a domineering personality. She frequently engaged in behaviors that were intended to belittle and humiliate Kemper, including physical abuse with a belt. It has been documented that Clarnell would often sequester her son in a locked basement, driven by the concern that he might inflict harm upon his sisters.

It is also noteworthy that she routinely subjected him to mockery and derision concerning his physical stature, which by the age of 15 had reached an imposing height of 6 feet 4 inches (1.93 meters). In a telephone conversation with Kemper's father, Clarnell went as far as to label her son as "a real weirdo," unaware that her son had been eavesdropping on the conversation. She also refrained from expressing affection toward him, citing concerns that it might "turn him gay." She further elaborated that Kemper's behavior and appearance resembled that of his father and asserted that no woman would ever be attracted to him. Kemper described his mother as a "sick, angry woman."

At the age of 14, Kemper tried to reconcile with his father in Van Nuys, California, by running away from home. Upon arriving, he discovered that his father had remarried and had a stepson. Following a brief period of residence with his father, Kemper was dispatched to live with his grandparents, who lived on a ranch situated in the foothills of the Sierra Nevada mountains, approximately two miles west of the town of North Fork, at a location known as Road 224. Kemper expressed profound displeasure with his living situation in North Fork, characterizing his grandfather as "senile" and his grandmother as persistently "emasculating both myself and my grandfather."

On August 27, 1964, Kemper fatally shot his grandmother, Maude Matilda Hughey Kemper, once in the head and twice in the back with a rifle after an argument. He then stabbed her several times. When Kemper's grandfather, Edmund Emil Kemper Sr., came home, Kemper fatally shot him in the driveway. He then phoned his mother, who told him to call the police. He did so and waited for the police to arrive.

He told the police that he "just wanted to see what it felt like to kill Grandma" and later said that he had killed his grandfather because the latter would have been angry with him. His crimes were deemed incomprehensible for someone his age to commit, and court psychiatrists diagnosed him with paranoid schizophrenia. Kemper was sent to Atascadero State Hospital, a maximum-security facility in San Luis Obispo County that houses mentally ill convicts.

At the California Youth Authority in Atascadero, psychiatrists and social workers disagreed with the court-appointed psychiatrists' diagnoses. According to their reports, Kemper showed "no flight of ideas, no interference with thought, no expression of delusions or hallucinations, and no evidence of bizarre thinking." They also observed him to be intelligent and introspective. Initial testing measured his IQ at 136, which is more than two standard deviations above average. Kemper was diagnosed with a less severe condition: a personality trait disturbance of the passive-aggressive type. Later, during his stay at Atascadero, he took another IQ test and scored 145.

Kemper endeared himself to his psychiatrists by being a model prisoner; he was even trained to administer psychiatric tests to other inmates. A psychiatrist later said, "He was a very good worker, and this is not typical of a sociopath. He really took pride in his work."

Kemper also became a member of the Jaycees while in Atascadero. He claimed to have developed new tests and scales for the Minnesota Multiphasic Personality Inventory, including an Overt Hostility Scale, while working with Atascadero psychiatrists.

After his second arrest, Kemper said that understanding how these tests worked allowed him to manipulate his psychiatrists. He admitted that he learned a lot from the sex offenders to whom he administered tests.

On December 18, 1969, Kemper's 21 birthday, he was released on parole from Atascadero. Contrary to the recommendations of the hospital psychiatrists, he was released into the custody of his mother, Clarnell, who had remarried and taken the surname Strandberg. She then resided in Aptos, California, a short drive from where she worked as an administrative assistant at the University of California, Santa Cruz (UCSC). Kemper later showed his psychiatrists that he had been rehabilitated.

On November 29, 1972, his juvenile records were permanently expunged. The last report from his probation psychiatrists read:

*"If I were to see this patient without having any history available or getting any history from him, I would think that we're dealing with a very well-adjusted young man who has initiative and intelligence and is free of any psychiatric illnesses. In my opinion, he has responded very well to years of treatment and rehabilitation, and I see no psychiatric reason to consider him a danger to himself or to society. Since it may allow him more freedom as an adult to develop his potential, I would consider it reasonable to permanently expunge his juvenile records."*

Six months before the report, during the period spanning from May 1972 to April 1973, Kemper would select female students who were hitchhiking as his victims, leading them to isolated areas where he would shoot, stabbed, smother, or strangle them. Thereafter, he sometimes would transport the bodies to his residence, where he would decapitate and dismember them, and engage in sexual intercourse with their corpses and their severed heads.

In interviews, Kemper has stated that he frequently sought out victims in the aftermath of contentious interactions with his mother. Additionally, he has indicated that she declined to facilitate his introductions to women affiliated with the university where she was employed. Kemper said she claimed that his resemblance to his father was the reason he wasn't a suitable candidate for the females from her university. The prevailing hypothesis among psychiatrists and Kemper himself is that the young women were surrogates for his ultimate target, his mother.

April 20, 1973, Kemper was awoken by his mother, who had returned home from a social gathering. While in a seated position in her bed, she observed Kemper entering her room and stated to him, "It is likely you will wish to remain upright throughout the night and converse." His response was a refusal, accompanied by a remark that indicated an imminent cessation of communication. After this, he proceeded to await the onset of sleep in the mothers rom. Thereafter, he returned to his mother's room and proceeded to assaulted her with a claw hammer, resulting in severe lacerations to her throat.

According to a 1984 interview, Kemper said that he decapitated the corpse and subjected it to further humiliation. He "placed her head on a shelf and screamed at it for a duration of one hour, threw darts at it," and ultimately, "smashed her face in." Additionally, he proceeded to excise her tongue and larynx, disposing of them in the garbage disposal unit. However, the apparatus designed for the disintegration of solid waste was unable to adequately destroy the resilient vocal cords, resulting in the tissue being expelled back into the sink. "That seemed appropriate, given the significant number of years during which she had expressed her discontent through vocalized protest," Kemper stated.

Kemper concealed his mother's corpse within a closet and proceeded to a nearby bar to consume alcohol. Upon his return, he extended an invitation to his mother's closest companion, 59-year-old Sara Taylor Hallett, to visit his residence for dinner and the viewing of a film. Upon Hallett's arrival, Kemper strangled her. He placed her corpse in a closet, took measures to conceal any obvious indications of a disturbance, and left a note addressed to the police. The following text was presented:

"Appx. 5:15 A.M. Saturday. No need for her to suffer any more at the hands of this horrible 'murderous Butcher.' It was quick, asleep, the way I wanted it. Not sloppy and incomplete, gents. Just a 'lack of time.' I got things to do!!!"

Kemper fled from the scene. He embarked on a non-stop journey to Pueblo, Colorado, ingesting caffeine pills to maintain alertness throughout the over 1,000-mile (approximately 1,600 km) expedition. He had three firearms and a considerable amount of ammunition in his vehicle. He believed that there was an active manhunt. Upon arriving in Pueblo, he observed that there had been no reports on the radio regarding the murders of his mother and Hallett.

Kemper located a phone booth and contacted the authorities. He admitted to the murders of his mother and Hallett; however, the police disregarded his call and instructed him to call back later. Several hours later, he called again, requesting to speak to an officer with whom he had a personal connection. He admitted to the officer that he had killed his mother and Hallett and then awaited the arrival of the police to take him into custody. Following his apprehension, he also admitted to the slayings of the six students.

At his trial in 1973, the court found Kemper sane and guilty, and he requested that capital punishment be imposed on him. However, the court suspended the death penalty in the state of California at the time. As a result, Kemper received eight concurrent life sentences.

In an interview, Kemper provided the following rationale for his decision to turn himself in.

He stated that the original cause of the murders had been lost. It's clear to him that the murders provided no tangible physical, real, or emotional benefits. The murdering of female students was now pointless. I reached my breaking point. As the attempt reached its conclusion, I felt the futility of the whole endeavor. I made the decision to abandon the task when I was at the point of imminent exhaustion and collapse.

Since that time, Kempher has been detained at the California Medical Facility in Vacaville.

Source: McLean, 2004, 2023, Smith, 2019, Kemper, 1998, Case 20, 2001 and Vronsky, 2004.

***

Despite the outrageous crimes, many serial killers are characterized by living ordinary lives. I regularly meet people who think you can tell they are murderers, but they don't run around with hunchbacks and black circles under their eyes like in the silent era. Take Edmund Kemper, for example. Due to problems at home, he came to live with his grandmother and grandfather on their farm in the mountains of California at the age of 14 in 1963. One day, he was sitting at the kitchen table with his grandmother when an argument broke out. He was so angry that he got a shotgun and shot his grandmother in the head. When the grandfather came home from the grocery store, he too was shot and killed.

In court, Kemper was sent to a hospital for the criminally insane, but when he turned 21, he was paroled and moved in with his mother, who worked at the University of California at Santa Cruz. It was here that Kemper found the young women who became his victims. During the murders, he went to counselor, a requirement of his parole, but none of them realized what was going on, not even when Kemper had two bodies lying down in his car while he told one of them how good he felt. Many later described him as friendly, charming, and intelligent.

***

Kenneth Bianchi (The Hillside Strangler) also had issues with his mother, who authorities describe as:

*"...deeply disturbed, socially ambitious, dissatisfied, unsure, opinionated and overly protective...had smothered this adopted son in medical attention and maternal concern from the moment of adoption" (Scott, 2003, p. 6).*

As a child, Bianchi was both dependent on his mother and hated her. He projected this hatred onto other women, especially after being betrayed by his girlfriend.

Serial killer Robert Joe Long killed sex workers, which reminded him of his own mother. Long shared a bed with his mother until he was 13 years old.

There are several accounts of mothers who were sadistic and exploited and humiliated their sons. But the father is just as significant to the serial killer's upbringing.

## THE FAMILY - FATHER

Several studies (Bahn et al., 1995; Hickey, 2016; Ressler et al., 1988) indicate that serial killers' fathers were not present, or if present, were often sadistic and disciplinary. John Wayne Gacy (The Clown Killer) (see next case) was beaten by his father, called a wimp, gay, and a failure. His father was a violent alcoholic who also abused his mother. At one point, his father shot and killed Gacy's dog as punishment for a minor incident. Later, as Gacy strangled his victims, he encouraged them to be brave and face their deaths with courage. Norris (1989) suggests that through these rituals, Gacy strengthened his masculine identity, which had been eroded by his father.

Albert DeSalvo's (The Boston Strangler) father brought home sex workers and violently abused his mother. He broke his mother's fingers one by one as DeSalvo watched helplessly. When DeSalvo grew up and had children of his own, he sold his own son to a farmer in Maine, unbeknownst to his wife. She desperately searched for her son for six months. This story has been corroborated by social services and family members.

Hickey (2016) found that fathers who abuse their children were often abused by their own fathers. Serial killer Ricky Lee Green was abused by his father and grandfather for many years. Green's father had also been abused by his father. When he was six years old, his father forced him to run around on the porch while beating him with a gun. He clearly remembered his father telling him from a very young age that he wasn't good enough and couldn't ever be good enough. Later, Green sexually assaulted his victims as they fought for their lives, then killed them.

## CASE: JOHN WAYNE GACY

***Epithets: The Killer Clown***

John Wayne Gacy (March 17, 1942 – May 10, 1994) was an American serial killer and sex offender who committed rape, torture, and murder against at least 33 young men and boys in Norwood Park Township, near Chicago, Illinois. He was given the moniker "the Killer Clown" due to his previous employment as a clown, a profession he continued unbeknownst to the public until the discovery of his crimes.

Many of the homicides were committed inside the confines of the ranch-style house he owned. The modus operandi that he employed involved luring a victim into the house under the pretext of performing a magic trick and restraining the person with handcuffs. The victim would then be raped and tortured before he proceeded to kill the victim either by asphyxiation or strangulation. A total of twenty-six victims were buried in the crawl space of his residence, while three others were buried in other areas of his property. Four victims were disposed of in the *Des Plaines River*.

Prior to the crimes under investigation, Gacy had been convicted in 1968 in Waterloo, Iowa, for sodomy of a teenage boy. He was sentenced to ten years' imprisonment but served only eighteen months. The investigation revealed that Gacy murdered his first victim in 1972 and then murdered two more by the end of 1975. He murdered at least thirty victims after his divorce from his second wife in 1976. The investigation into the disappearance of Robert Piest led to Gacy's arrest on December 21, 1978.

John Wayne Gacy was born at Edgewater Hospital in Chicago, Illinois, on March 17, 1942, the second of three children and only son of John Stanley Gacy and Marion Elaine Robison. His father was an auto repair machinist and World War I veteran, and his mother was a homemaker. Gacy was of Polish and Danish ancestry, and his family was Catholic.

Gacy's relationship with his parents was characterized by tensions, particularly with his father, who exhibited both verbal and physical abuse. His childhood was marred by the frequent mistreatment by his father, who would belittle him verbally and compare him unfavorably to his sisters. One of Gacy's earliest memories was of his father assaulting him at age four for accidentally damaging car engine components. His mother tried to shield her son from her abusive husband, but this resulted in accusations that he was a "sissy" and a "mama's boy" who would "probably grow up queer."

In 1949, Gacy's father physically disciplined him after he and another boy were caught sexually fondling a young girl, and in that same year, a family friend began to molest him on occasion. Gacy refrained from disclosing these incidents to his father, fearful of being blamed for them. Despite their challenging relationship, Gacy held a strong affection for his father, yet he perceived himself as "never good enough" in his father's eyes. He was an overweight child and below-average athleticism. Due to a heart condition, he was advised to avoid from participating in sports. In the fourth grade, he began experiencing intermittent blackouts. He was hospitalized on occasion because of these episodes. In 1957, he was hospitalized again for a ruptured appendix. Gacy later estimated that between the ages of 14 and 18, he had spent almost a year in the hospital; he attributed the decline of his grades to missing school. His medical condition was never conclusively diagnosed; his father suspected he was malingering. On one occasion, he openly accused his son of faking as he lay in a hospital bed.

In 1960, at age 18, Gacy became involved in politics, working as an assistant precinct captain for a local Democratic Party candidate. This led to more criticism from his father, who called him a "party patsy." The same year, his father bought him a car. He retained the vehicle's title in his own name until Gacy had paid for it, a process that took several years. His father would confiscate the keys if Gacy did not comply with his demands.

In April 1962, Gacy procured an additional set of keys, which prompted his father to remove the distributor cap, retaining the component for a period of three days. Shortly thereafter, Gacy departed from his home with his parents, embarking on a journey to Las Vegas, Nevada, with a total of $136 and moved in with a cousin. He secured employment in the Las Vegas ambulance service prior to being transferred to Palm Mortuary. He worked as a mortuary attendant for a period of three months, during which time he observed morticians embalming bodies and occasionally served as a pallbearer. Gacy slept on a cot located behind the embalming room. He later confessed that on one evening, while alone, he climbed into the coffin of a teenage male, embraced and caressed the body before experiencing a sense of shock. This experience prompted him to return home.

Shortly thereafter, Gacy enrolled at Northwestern Business College, despite having failed to complete high school. He graduated in 1963 and took a management trainee position with the Nunn-Bush Shoe Company. In 1964, the company transferred him to Springfield, Illinois, to work as a salesman, and eventually promoted him to department manager. In March of that year, he became engaged to Marlynn Myers, a co-worker.

During this period, Gacy became involved with the local chapter of the *Jaycees*, an organization dedicated to the development of business leaders. It was during this time that Gacy had his second homosexual experience, which he described in detail. According to his account, a colleague from the Jaycees persuaded him to consume alcohol and then invited him to spend the evening on his sofa. The colleague then performed oral sex on Gacy while he was intoxicated.

By 1965, Gacy had risen to the position of vice-president of the Springfield Jaycees and was named the third most outstanding Jaycee in Illinois.

According to Gacy's confession to the police, he would pick up Caucasian male runaways or male sex workers in their mid-teens to their early twenties from the Chicago Greyhound Bus station or from the streets. Afterward, he would take them back to his house by either promising them money for sex, offering them a job with his construction company, simply grabbing them by force, or forcing them into his car at gunpoint. Once they got back to his house, he would handcuff them or tie them up in another way after intoxicating them with alcohol or knocking them out with chloroform. He would torture them in various ways, such as using a fire poker on them, dripping hot, melted candle wax on their bodies, repeatedly drowning them in his bathtub, and then revive them, or by placing them in a homemade "rack." As a show of dominance, he would urinate on his victims. He would rape his victims both before and after killing them, keeping the bodies around for a day or so.

One of his most infamous ways of capturing his victims was convincing them to allow him to handcuff them under the pretense that it was part of a magic trick. He would often stick paper towels or clothing, such as a sock or even their own underwear, in their mouths to muffle their screams, causing them to asphyxiate. He would also kill his victims by strangling them with a rope or a board as he sexually assaulted them with sex toys, then bury the bodies in his crawlspace. Periodically, Gacy would pour lime in the crawlspace to hasten the decomposition of the bodies. Three victims were disposed of the property by being dropped into the Des Plaines River. When he killed his first victim, Timothy McCoy, he stabbed him in the chest with a kitchen knife instead of asphyxiating him.

The defense lawyer tried to make an insanity defense, sane or evil. Gacy's mother testified and talked about John's abusive father, a mean drunk.

Gacy was convicted for thirty-three murders on March 13, 1980, he was sentenced to death. He was executed by lethal injection at Stateville Correctional Center on May 10, 1994.

Source: McLean, 2004, 2023, 2021, MMP, 2022 and Hermann et al., 1983.

## ADOPTED CHILD SYNDROME

Adopted child syndrome is a term that has been used to explain behaviors in adopted children that are claimed to be related to their adoptive status. Specifically, these include problems in bonding, attachment disorders, lying, stealing, defiance of authority, and acts of violence. The term has never achieved acceptance in the professional community. The term is not found in the American Psychiatric Association's Diagnostic and Statistical Manual (3+3TR) and 4th edition, TR; the syndrome is not in the DSM-5.

The condition can be found at the end of the lengthy section on diagnostic criteria in DSM-5. On page 715, there is a brief section called "Other Conditions That May Be a Focus of Clinical Attention." These conditions merely affect mental disorders; they are not mental disorders themselves, and, per DSM-5, they cannot be treated as mental disorders. In the DSM-5 coding system, they receive a "V code" designation and, in general, are non-reimbursable by insurance companies.

It is important to note that research suggests that adoptee parricide (the killing of adoptive parents by their adoptive children) may be linked to psychopathology. For example, a study by Hubbell, Heide, and Wagers (2021) found that law enforcement records indicate that adoptees are 15 times more likely to commit parricide than biologically raised children. While only 2-3% of the population in the USA, roughly 5-10 million people, are adopted, adoptees are overrepresented in the juvenile criminal system, prison system, psychiatric institutions, and substance abuse rehabilitation settings. They are also prone to learning disabilities and organic brain syndromes and are more likely to have difficulties with drugs and alcohol, eating disorders, and suicide.

The first studies on the topic were by Jean Paton (1953), who studied adoption psychopathology. Later, Betty Jean Lifton (1975), a psychologist, studied the detrimental effects of sealing adoption records, which cut adoptees off from their biological parents and caused undue psychological stress, grief, and aberrant behavior. Nancy Newton Verrier (2003) revolutionized the way we understand the complex trauma experienced by the adopted individual. She was able to identify the primal loss and the resultant lifelong primal wound. She gave adoptees, whose pain had long been unacknowledged, validation for their feelings and explanations for their behaviors. While most adoptees resolve, to one degree or another, the issues surrounding being adopted, there are some at the far end of the spectrum who have developed severe psychopathology.

David Kirschner (1995) first used the term "Adopted Child Syndrome" (ACS) to describe an underlying dissociative disorder, and he found that a small clinical subgroup of adoptees at the far end of the spectrum react to the traumatic effects of adoption with identified anti-social behaviors. These individuals may experience a range of challenges, including feelings of grief and loss, difficulties with identity and belonging, and a sense of being left alone and unloved. These challenges can potentially contribute to difficulties in forming secure and intimate relationships, leaving individuals vulnerable to intense and destructive outbursts of anger when confronted with perceived or actual abandonment.

It has been suggested that particularly those who have experienced adoption as a closely guarded secret within their family or have not been able to engage in open dialogue about it. Without an appropriate outlet for expression, these feelings may become dissociated, potentially leading to a fragile ego and a heightened sensitivity to further rejection. It has been observed that once an individual has learned to dissociate parts of themselves, it becomes a natural tendency. As emotions begin to accumulate, they are contained until something triggers their release.

Although the American Psychological Association does not officially endorse it, the concept of Adopted Child Syndrome (ACS) has been employed as a successful defense in capital murder cases where the accused has been adopted. ACS describes a set of behaviors that have been used to explain problems with bonding, attachment, lying, stealing, defiance of authority, and acts of violence, often directed at those closest to them. This theory is supported by psychologists specializing in adoption. However, the psychopathology of adoption has historically been overlooked in forensic mental health evaluations.

In a report in the journal *"Psychology and Law," "Adoption & Murder"* suggests that although adopted children commit murders more often than is commonly believed, there is resistance to acknowledging it. This may be because of the secrecy associated with many adoptions, or because of the failure of criminal justice agencies to record or acknowledge the nature of an offender's family background. From a legal perspective, an adopted child is simply the child of their adoptive parents. The most extreme cases of pathological behavior are seen in acts of mass murder and serial killing. According to Kirschner, (2009) in "Adoption Forensics: The Connection Between Adoption and Murder," of the 500 estimated serial killers in USA history, 16 percent were adopted as children. These individuals have been profiled in terms of having suffered intolerable childhood emotional abuse, severe neglect, multiple placements, and unresolved, conflicted mother/father relationships. While a troubled childhood is not an excuse for committing heinous crimes, these are the most troubled children because of adoption. They are the ones who need the most attention, as symptoms of ACS begin to be seen in childhood, such as oppositional defiant behaviors. If these behaviors are not treated by a therapist with expertise in adoption issues, there is a risk that they may develop into pathological behaviors.

It is important to clarify that adoption itself is not the cause of the syndrome. Often, but not all the time, adopted children have an underlying problem with attachment, and some have been neglected and abused, physically, mentally, and sexually by their biological parents before they are adopted. Still, the abuse can also be from the adoptive parents.

O'Connor (2002b) estimates that if the parents are stepparents or the child is a foster child, there is a risk of antisocial personality disorder. It is not clear from the article where O'Connor got his assumption, but there is some evidence to suggest that he may be right. There are several serial killers who are adopted and suffer from adoption syndrome, which is a hatred of their biological parents. FBI found that out of approximately 500 serial killers, 30 are adopted (16%). Only about 2% to 3% of the total population is adopted. Therefore, 16% is a relatively large number (Carangelo, 2003).

Some of the serial killers who have been adopted are Joseph Ernest Atkins, Charles Albright, Matthew Heikkila, Joshua Jenkins, Joseph Kallinger, Patrick Niiranen, Ritchard Ramirez, David Burkowitz, Hillside strangler Kenneth Bianchi /Bono, Ted Bundy, Joel Rafkin, Lawrence Bittaker, and Aileen Wuornos.

Kirschner & Nagel (1988) explain why adoptees are more vulnerable to becoming serial killers:

*"What then is the adopted child syndrome? On the behavioral level, it is an antisocial pattern that usually includes pathological lying, stealing, and manipulativeness. Fire setting is sometimes seen, and promiscuous behavior is common."*

Adoptees can face the following problems:

*"The senior author has observed extreme, provocative, aggressive, antisocial, and delinquent conduct much more consistently among adoptees than their non-adopted counterparts. Behind the recurrent behavioral and personality patterns, there have emerged emotional and psychodynamic issues specifically linked to adoption."*

It is unclear whether adoptee problems are caused by rejection from their biological parents in early childhood. It is also unclear whether they have developed an inadequate attachment to their adoptive parents. One could also imagine that problems arise because of a perpetual search for their identity.

## PINCUS AND LEWIS THEORY

I have discussed a few different theories about why people become serial killers. As mentioned, there is no single reason, but there are multiple factors involved. Therefore, Pincus and Lewis's work on serial killers is extremely interesting. Pincus and Lewis argue that three key factors influence serial killer development. They write:

*"This case [Louis Culpepper] and cases like it led me and my colleague, Dr. Dorothy Lewis, to develop a new theory, one that can explain violent crime ... it is the interaction of childhood abuse with neurologic disturbances and psychiatric illnesses that explains murder. Abuse generates violence. Neurologic and psychiatric diseases of the brain damage the capacity to check that urge" - (Pincus, 2002, p. 19).*

Pincus & Lewis (2002, p. 29) thus conclude that abuse, psychiatric disorders involving paranoid thinking or paranoid personality type, and brain damage are the root causes of some people becoming serial killers. Interestingly, among the 100 killers studied by Pincus and Lewis, the above three factors were present in all of them. However, more studies are needed to be certain.

# 5. CRIMINAL PROFILING

The criminal profiler has been portrayed, in some criminal profiling literature, as a person who needs to look inside Evil to understand Evil (the serial killer). The criminal profiler must have insights beyond the ordinary. He/she is portrayed more as a clairvoyant. They see images in their minds that show the different murders serial killers have committed, and sometimes also future murders. Some criminal profilers say they need to get inside the serial killer's mind and be like him to understand his actions. I have heard that it has been stated that there is a risk of becoming the perpetrator once you peer into the abyss, and that every time he peers into a serial killer's abyss, he loses a piece of his humanity.

That is not reality. You do not have to be like a serial killer to understand them, just as you do not have to be schizophrenic to understand the schizophrenic. It is not possible to become a serial killer by being a criminal profiler. We have seen it go the other way, that criminal people work with criminality or in law enforcement. I do think that the reason is that they want to be a better criminal to examine the felt, not the other way around.

Such statements, unfortunately, push criminal profiling away from science and towards an intuitive, clairvoyant-like, frivolous method.

The FBI states that it is not a scientific method, and the profile produced by criminal profiling does not give us a clear picture of the perpetrator. The method cannot replace investigative work. Criminal profiling is an investigative tool used in investigations by the FBI, law enforcement and private Criminal Profiler. Fundamental to profiling is an understanding of behavioral science, which includes aspects of psychology, sociology, criminology, and forensic science. Criminal profiling is the result of psychological factors and police expertise.

Behavioral science has different terms for normal and abnormal behavior. From different aspects of behavior (symptoms), various disorders are identified, as can be seen in DSM-5 and ICD-11. Together, these symptoms indicate specific behaviors. Symptoms can be seen in the perpetrator's behavior regarding the crime(s). By examining a crime scene, you can determine the offender's behavioral type (Safarik, 2022a). A crime scene can reflect the personality traits of the offender in the same way, that the way we decorate our homes, reflect something about our personality.

I can sum Criminal profiling up to roughly having three main steps to review. The first step is to investigate what happened and what the behavior is on the crime scene. Here, you need to learn as much as possible about the crime scene. Secondly, the person's behavior must be analyzed, and as a criminal profiler, you must ask yourself why and how the crime happened. Thirdly, you need to ask yourself what type of person can commit this type of crime.

Criminal profiling is also called offender profiling, criminal personality profiling, psychological profiling, or simply profiling (Turvey, 2015).

There are several definitions of criminal profiling, but the most used is Burgess & Hazelwood's (1999, p.1):

*"...methods of classifying and predicting criminal behavior derived from similar techniques in the fields of Criminology, Psychology, and Forensic Science..."*

Howard Teten, a former FBI agent from the Behavioral Science Unit, helped create the FBI's criminal profiling methodology. Teten defines criminal profiling simply as a method to identify a person who commits a crime (Ainsworth, 2002).

Based on the offender's behavior before, during and after the crime, aspects of the offender's behavior and personality can be determined. The profile is based on the evidence seen at the crime scene, along with the physical evidence left behind by the offender. This gives the criminal profiler a picture of the personality type they should look for. However, it also determines other aspects of the perpetrator, like how to interview the person and where they might strike next. Behavior can provide insight into personality. Similarly, crime scene and profiling can be used to analyze offender personality (Keppel & Birnes, 2003).

Before I explain the different types of criminal profiling, I will outline a historical overview of how criminal profiling started.

## HISTORICAL OVERVIEW OF CRIMINAL PROFILING

Criminal profiling methods can be traced back to the early 1800s, when anthropologists linked criminological psychology to criminal physical characteristics. It was believed that you could tell by a person's appearance if they were a criminal. It was considered that people with a low forehead were dangerous. Fries (1821) studied criminal appearance. These findings helped understand criminals in the 20th century. The psychiatrist Kretschmer had a major influence on the perception of possible perpetrators based on body type analysis. It was believed that a person's body type indicated whether they were a criminal or not. This phenomenon can be seen if you watch old crime movies where all the criminals have the same appearance. They're dull and dark-skinned, black around the eyes and look angry and evil. There was no doubt who the criminal was then.

Despite our knowledge today, this continues to follow us. One FBI agent said that he was involved in Theodore Robert Bundy's arrest. Serial killer Theodore Robert Bundy murdered 15 women and girls. Bundy admitted to murdering between 20 and 30 women (depending on which report you read), but some believe he may have killed more than 100 people, starting as a teenager. He was caught in 1978, at the age of 32. The earliest murder he confessed to was in 1973. He was surprised that Bundy looked normal and was well-behaved and intelligent. The FBI agent explained that he expected an ugly and scary man with a hunchback. Not a handsome, articulate and seemingly normal man. Another FBI agent said he was surprised when he helped arrest Berkowitz (Son of Sam). He saw a small man who seemed harmless (Discovery Channel, 2003a).

Furthermore, Turvey (2012) writes that when interviewing serial killers, he sometimes had to read their files to be sure that they had committed the murders they were charged with. I also had a hard time imagining that the people in my study who had insight, knowledge, and clarity about serial killers could be the same people who were charged with the murders in their cases. When FBI agents and police officers think this way, you can't blame anyone for thinking that they can see by just looking at a person whether they are serial killers. This indicates that humans have an internal image of criminals. Even though reason tells us that we can't tell if people are criminals, we are surprised that a given killer doesn't look like our stereotypical image of a murderer.

Thomas Bond was chiefly a Police Surgeon with the Met's A-Division in the 1880s. Bond performed an autopsy on Mary Kelly, who was the last victim of Jack the Ripper. He could be described as the world's first criminal profiler. Bond reconstructs the crime committed by analyzing the perpetrator's behavior and his personal signature. A personal signature is the way the perpetrator performs the act repeatedly, for example, strangling the victim with a stocking, tying the victim in a certain way, or cutting out the victim's eyes. In this way, Bond created a profile of the perpetrator. Bond's observations in the Jack the Ripper case were summarized by the interpretation of the perpetrator's behavior at the crime scene, along with interpretations of the autopsy.

The way the victim is murdered can tell a criminal profiler something about the perpetrator.

Through this, you can calculate the probability of whether the perpetrator was male or female. You can also estimate whether the person was strong or weak or had some surgery and anatomy knowledge. Or whether the perpetrator had plenty of time or had to leave quickly and wanted the person to spend time with the body afterwards. Mutilating the body or practicing necrophilia can also tell us something about the perpetrator.

In 1943, the Office of Strategic Services sought psychiatrist Walter Langer's help to profile Adolph Hitler. This work resulted in a psychodynamic personality profile. It clarified Hitler's Oedipus complex and his need to prove himself as a man to his mother. But Langer also found that Hitler was interested in sexual proclivities. Hitler, according to his profile, was interested in Coprophilia (urine/feces in sexual acts). The profile also predicted Hitler's suicide when the war ended (Harrison, 1993).

Between 1957 and 1972, the FBI used psychiatrist James A. Brussel to create profiles. Among others, he profiled George Metsky (Mad Bomber) and Albert DeSalvo (Boston Strangler) (Jackson & Bekerian, 2001, p. 3). Brussel worked closely with Teten.

In 1978, Teten left the Behavioral Sciences Unit. After Teten left the unit, Douglas and Ressler joined and changed the FBI's methodology. This method is highly inductive, but the FBI also used deductive profiling, where inductive profiling is one strategy of criminal profiling that is particularly effective for comparing criminals with similar backgrounds and motives. Deductive is best used when you want to know something specific about the serial killer. The information is based on criminal interviews, profiler experience and computerized databases as it uses the findings from the study of serial killers, along with findings such as common general traits and behavioral patterns of serial killers (Teten, 1995).

In the 1980s and early 1990s, academic criminologists became interested in serial killers and criminal profiling. One of the first was Philip Jenkins, who in 1988 wrote an article on serial killers (Jenkins, 1994).

Around 1992, psychologist David Canter led a series of studies at the Investigative Psychology Research Group at the University of Surrey. From these studies, Canter and his colleagues created a profiling method. Canter's method has changed over the years (Canter, 2022). The method is based on crime scene evidence, along with the behaviors identified in the offender from victimology.

Turvey advocates for a deductive profiling method. He believes that it is problem to only make inferences from FBI scientific studies.

Around 1997, several freelance criminal profilers appeared. Some were more serious than others. One of the first and more serious was Brent Turvey (1995), who has a Master of Science in Forensic Science from the University of New Haven, Connecticut, whose approach is Behavioral Evidence Analysis. I will describe his approach later in this chapter.

I will first review the FBI's study of the 36 serial killers and some general considerations about criminal profiling. Afterwards, I will review three types of criminal profiling methods, and finally, profiling effectiveness will be discussed.

## METHOD OF CRIMINAL PROFILING

In the following section, I will look at the FBI's study of 36 serial killers. However, the method is applied differently today, where the Behavioral Science Unit in the FBI unit, has developed the criminal profiling methodology (Safarik, 2022a).

Douglas, Ressler & Burgess from Behavioral Science Unit (BSU) studied and interviewed 36 serial killers from 1979 to 1983. Some of the serial killers included in this study were: Edmund Emil Kemper, William Heirens, Richard Speck, Jerry Burdos, Monte Rissell and David Berkowitz.

Burgess et al. (1997) formalized the interviews and developed the profiling methodology. This work is called the Criminal Personality Research Project.

The 36 serial killers included in the study murdered 118 known individuals but are believed to have murdered more. The victims were predominantly women. The murders were bizarre and violent, with subsequent mutilation and abuse of the bodies.

The serial killers received a 57-page questionnaire (Burgess et al., 1997). They also assisted them through follow-up questions. In addition, official records were used to collect information about both the perpetrator and the victims.

They enumerated the different factors present in various serial killers based on the collected 36-questionnaire material. The results of this study were used to identify different factors in perpetrators who committed serial murders.

The study found that all 36 serial killers were male, whites made up the majority (92%), and they had normal to above normal intelligence (80%). More than half were the oldest sons (56%), and 57% had both parents at birth. Furthermore, 86% lived a stable and self-supporting economic life.

Apparently, the families were on the surface well-functioning, but on closer inspection, many had problems such as substance abuse (alcohol 70%, drugs 33%), psychiatric problems (53%), criminality (50%), physical

violence (42%), psychological violence (74%), sexual abuse (46%), unstable housing situation (68%), loss of the father before the age of 12 (47%), problems with the mother (44%), and problems with a father figure (72%) (Markunas, 2000). In other words, a troubled family pattern.

The FBI's study found that the 36 serial killers experienced negativity, abuse, and instability in their childhood. When examining serial killers' childhood and adolescence, they often found the MacDonald triad: animal abuse, enuresis, and arson. These three aspects are significant predictors of developing an extreme homicidal nature and/or becoming a sexual offender.

The study also showed that despite their intelligence, many performed poorly in school. They often failed to graduate and were given menial jobs, and they often did not do well in the military.

The FBI's study further showed that fantasies impact serial killers. Many had extremely violent sexual fantasies that started at an early age. At the same time, it was estimated that serial killers murder when stressed. The typical stressors were conflicts with women or their parents. But there can also be financial or work-related stressors.

Serial killers' age was also significant. Almost all of them were under 40 when they committed their first murder. However, their criminal history often dates back much further, starting with various criminal and behavioral problems in early childhood.

The FBI's study further showed that serial killers can be divided into two types. There is a type of murderer (50%) who spends a lot of time planning. Serial killers identify their victims in advance and stalk them. At the same time, this type of serial killer spent time strategizing how the murder would happen. They found out as much as they could about the victim's movements and habits. Everything was organized down to the smallest detail, time and place were precisely chosen. This type was called the organized serial killer (see Table 8).

The second type of serial killer finds victims randomly. Their approach was to search for areas that were easily accessible and where they could kidnap the victim or carry out the crime at the place they were. They waited until they felt the urge to kill. When that urge arose, they would seek out places where they thought there was a high chance of finding a victim. They drove around at night, often looking for victims among sex workers, often in deserted areas because they were easy to lure into their cars under the assumption that the serial killer wanted to make a deal with them. This type was called the disorganized serial killer (see Table 8).

The FBI's study also found that serial killers differ in other ways. The first type of serial killer stalks his victims. He is charming and finds it easy to get close to his victims. They may do this by pretending to be tradesmen, policemen, or any other profession with authority. The second type of serial killer, who has looks or speaking skills against them, surprises the victim with a blitz attack.

The study also showed that the way the offender disposes of the body says something about the offender. There is a difference between the offender randomly dumping the body in a ditch or staging the crime scene. Serial killers can stage their bodies in a way that means something to them, or they can send a message to those who find them. There are many examples of this, but the classic ones could be where serial killers display the severed head of the victim so that it is the first thing you see when you walk in the front door, for example, Danny Rolling. Another example is where the body sits on a chair, undressed and in an embarrassing position. Serial killers often humiliate their victims. The victim may be placed with their legs spread apart in a position that humiliates both those who find the victim and the victim themselves. How the body is positioned says something about the way that serial killers' thinking, they either want to punish the victim or the society or both, but you need to look at the hole case to be sure what the meaning is for the killer, the underlaying motive is pawer and control and some psychologically issue they are reliving.

The behavior the offender exhibits after the murder also impacts understanding of the offender's personality. Often, the offender will return to the location where he has placed his victim (see Shawcross in the case study in chapter 9) or to the crime scene itself. Serial killers may also participate in victim discovery or investigation. This makes them feel in control of the situation and shows that serial killers want control. They may also give law enforcement anonymous tips or leave clues at the crime scene. Some serial killers are in close contact with the media, such as TV, radio, or newspapers. Some serial killers collect souvenirs. Examples of souvenirs can be jewelry, pictures, small items from the victims or their homes, or it can even be body parts, which include eyes, genitals, fingers, heads, and breasts. Some also take or make trophies. Holmes and Holmes (2002) distinguish between souvenirs and trophies. A trophy represents what a person has achieved, whereas a souvenir represents the crime committed by the serial killer, from their victims. These can be jewelry, clothing, ID cards, or even body parts. Serial killers collect information about their murders, and scrapbooks are frequently found at their residences. Serial killers often videotape, draw or photograph the murderers themselves or take pictures of themselves with their victims just before the murder. Often, the killers are in the pictures, and in some investigations, this has helped solve the murder (Burgess et al., 1997). When serial murderers have souvenirs, trophies, films, drawings or pictures, they can relive the murder continuously.

I have only reviewed a small portion of all the behavioral patterns and personality traits the FBI's study of 36 serial killers found. In the next section, I will discuss three types of profiling that have made the most impact over the years. The FBI applied criminology, Canter's Investigative Psychology, and Turvey's Behavioral Evidence Analysis.

## THE FBI'S APPLIED CRIMINOLOGY

The FBI's Profiling Unit within the Behavioral Science Unit (now the Investigative Support Unit) started in 1974. The unit was headed by Howard Teten and Pat Mullany. They were both criminologists and negotiation guides at Quantico, which is the FBI Academy in Virginia, USA (Burgess et al., 1997). Between 1975-1977, Robert Ressler, Dick Ault, and John Douglas joined the unit and became instructors in the profiling methodology: Applied criminology. Other members of the unit included a sociologist and an expert in stress-related disorders. When Teten left the unit in 1978, Ann Wolbert Burgess joint the team and Ressler and Douglas changed the profiling methodology to divide offenders into organized and disorganized types (see Table 8).

In 1983, the Violent Crime Apprehension Program (VICAP) was created, which is an American data information center built to collect, compare, and analyze violent crime, especially homicide (Burgess et al., 1997, pp. 331-350). In VICAP, you can search for a specific type of crime scene, and several of the most likely features will appear, which can then be combined into a profile. In other words, VICAP can determine and identify the traits of perpetrators who commit a certain type of serial murder. VICAP has its limitations and cannot replace police work, but it is a database of all crimes committed, both unsolved and solved.

FBI's criminal profilers start out as FBI agents and are later trained through the FBI's Profiling Unit. Applied criminology is inductive, as it assumes that a certain type of crime committed by different offenders has similarities. From this, it is believed that the perpetrators also have some personality traits in common.

The FBI profiling methodology consists of six steps: Profiling inputs, Decision Process Models, Crime Assessment, The Criminal Profile, The Investigation, and The Apprehension.

<u>Profiling inputs.</u> In this step, all material related to the case is collected and assessed. This may include crime scene photos, pictures of the victim, background information on the victim, autopsy reports, and other forensic investigations relevant to the crime in question. This includes aspects before, during, and after the crime is committed. This is critical and the foundation for all subsequent profile work.

<u>Decision Process Models</u>. This is where you take the information from the previous step and put it into a logical and coherent pattern. This also involves collecting and obtaining information about how many victims are involved

in the case; that is, whether you are dealing with serial crimes or a single crime.

Crime Assessment. This reconstructs crime sequences. The behavior of both the perpetrator and the victim is clarified at this stage. This helps the criminal profiler to understand the role of those involved in the crime and later shape the profile of the offender.

The criminal profile. It is in this process that the actual offender profile is created. The profile includes information about the offender's background, physical appearance, and behavioral characteristics. Law enforcement can identify an offender with the help of the profile. They can exclude or include suspects in their investigation materials based on this. The profile provides information on how law enforcement can interview a potential perpetrator. The right way to interview the perpetrator can help to get the most information. The way the interview is organized varies according to the type of personality they are dealing with.

The investigation. This is when the profile is handed over to law enforcement or the unit working on the case. It is brought into the investigation as one of many tools. If relevant evidence emerges along the way, the profile is revised.

The apprehension. This step investigates whether the profile information fits the perpetrator. This can only be done if you have the offender. Geberth (1996) estimates that in less than 50% of criminal cases where profiling is used, the perpetrator is found, because of the cases where profiling is used often is the most complex and difficult cold cases. Therefore, it is not always possible to verify whether the profile fits the perpetrator in all cases (Safarik,

2022a).

# ORGANIZED/DISORGANIZED SERIAL KILLERS

The FBI distinguishes between organized, disorganized, and mixed groups of killers (see Table 8). The division into organized and disorganized killers was made to make criminal profiling training easier for those with little or no psychological background. Organized and disorganized refer to if the perpetrator has psychopathy or is mental ill, which can be seen in how chaotic or controlled a crime scene is.

The term organized type was synonymous with a psychopathic serial killer. This particular modus operandi involves meticulous planning, with the perpetrator employing deceptive tactics to manipulate their victims. The second category of serial killers is characterized by a lack of organization, which corresponds with the serial killer being psychotic. These individuals are typically diagnosed with schizophrenia, paranoia, or delusions (FBI, 2005).

The organized killer has above-average intelligence, is socially competent, plans the murder carefully, murders strangers, and wants the victim to be submissive and humble. They spend a lot of time researching the potential victims.

A disorganized killer has normal or average intelligence, is socially immature, inflicts sudden violence, and commit murder spontaneously. Furthermore, they may kill people they know casually, but they do also kill acquaintances or family members.

Douglas & Olshaker (1995, 1998) and Ressler et al. (1988) argue that it is critical to distinguish between the two types of killers. This makes it easier for law enforcement to work with, and it can give a general picture of the suspected perpetrator.

Turvey (2015) and Canter (1995) argue that this division is illogical and can lead to confusion and problems finding the killer. The characteristics of organized and disorganized killers provide a standard or boilerplate, which is a description that can be used continuously without changing over time; this is the profile of the killer, without referring to unique characters based on the crime committed. This is one of the criticisms of the FBI's profiling method. The FBI does have a mixed group today, where a killer can be both organized and disorganized, called mixed crime scene/serial killer, but it was not the case when the method was formed, and the method is called "Criminal Investigation Analysis" (Safarik, 2022a).

Table 8: "Organized vs. disorganized offender"

| **Profile Characteristics** | |
|---|---|
| Organized | Disorganized |
| Good intelligence socially competent Skilled work preferred Sexually competent High birth order Fathers work stabile Inconsistent disciple controlled mood Use of alcohol in crime Precipitating stress living with a partner Mobile, good car Follows crime in media Change job, leaves town | Average intelligence Socially immature Poor work history Sexually incompetent Minimal birth order Fathers work unstable Harsh discipline Anxious mood Minimal alcohol use Minimal stress Living alone Poor mobility, lives near Minimal interest Minimal lifestyle change |
| **Crime Scene difference** | |
| Organized offender | Disorganized offender |
| Offence planned t argets a stranger Personalizes victim Controlled conversation scene reflects control Demands submissive victims Restraints used Aggressive acts before death Boddy hidden Weapon/evidence absent Transports body | Spontaneous offence Victim/location known Depersonalizes victim Minimal conversation Scene random/sloppy Sudden violence Minimal restraint Sexual acts Body in view Evidence present Body at scene |
| ***Source: Ressler et. Al., 1988*** ***OBS: A mixed organized/disorganized group was added in.*** | |

# CANTER'S INVESTIGATIVE PSYCHOLOGY

David Canter was a psychology professor at the University of Liverpool, England. Canter's profiling method, like the FBI's method, is also based on statistical material. The statistical basis is a database where you enter all information about all crimes (typologies) committed in the UK. The information you have about a given crime is compared with the information in the database. This means that it is assumed that the same type of person commits the same type of crime.

Canter (1995) writes that the database is far from sufficient to create a profile, as the statistical material is too narrow to create a profile of. Canter's method includes geographical profiling, which is a method of identifying where criminals commit crimes based on location.

Geographic profiling has, through research, shown that murderers, arsonists, and rapists commit crimes within an area they know in one way or another. This could be where they live, near their work, or at acquaintances' homes. Canter and his associates' studies show that most serial offenders repeat their crimes in the same area.

Environmental psychology, which is the study of the transaction and interaction between human behavior and the environment uses circle theory. The method deals with criminals' geographical behavior in relation to their crimes. Circle theory is used in the sense that a map is made of the series of crimes a given offender has committed. A mark is then placed at the two outermost points on the map, and a line is drawn from one point to the other. In the center of this line, a compass is placed. Here, you make a circle that goes from one outer point to another outer point, making a circle. Within this circle, there is a high probability that the offender has his anchor point, whether it is his home, where he works, or it is a known area (Canter, 1995).

Today, we have computer programs that can make this calculation, like QGIS (2025) and ArcGIS (2025).

There are two types of circle Models: marauder and commuter. In the Marauder Model, it is assumed that the offender commits his crimes in known environments. While the commuter Model assumes that the offender travels away from their local environment and commits the crime. The Models are made retrospectively, and it is difficult to know which model the offender operates after before the offender can be linked to the murders, and the offender can also switch back and forth from marauder to commuter (Canter & Larkin, 1993). According to Hickey's (1991) study of 200 serial killers, 66% fell into the marauder Model.

Even that many serial killers' first murders are committed close to their home (workplace or other known location for them) when you look at older cases, but because of the effectiveness in DNA and other forensic technique that law enforcement have today serial killer is declining and the estimate is there is around 50 serial killer (42 in the 2010's) active in a given time (Mello-Klein, 2023).

My hypothesis is that many serial killers try to find victims away from their known locations, and it might be more difficult to locate today than before the DNA and Investigative genetic genealogy, also known as forensic genetic genealogy, because they choose victims who are not even known to be missing.

Investigative psychology started around 1985 when Canter was called to Scotland Yard to discuss the possibility of linking investigative techniques with psychological principles. Canter's focus was to investigate which basic ideas could be used to develop a method to solve criminal cases.

Canter's method is based on five principles that center around the interaction between the victim and offender. These principles include interpersonal relationships, the importance of time and place, the nature of the crime, criminal history, and forensic information (Canter, 1995).

Interpersonal context. Interpersonal context should be seen as the way the perpetrator treats and relates to people in his or her social circle. It is assumed that there is a similarity between the way the perpetrator relates to his victim and the way he speaks to others. Furthermore, it is assumed that the victim represents significant people for the perpetrator. An example of this would be Theodore Robert Bundy, who allegedly murdered women who resembled his ex-girlfriend. She ended their relationship shortly before he murdered women.

The importance of time and place. Time and place are very crucial, as they can give the criminal profiler information about the offender's mobility and where he may be staying. It also says something about the offender's daily movements, working hours, and interests.

The nature of the crime. The perpetrator is classified into different subgroups according to the nature of the crime. This can be used by the criminal profiler to come up with characteristics the offender is most likely to have. Such systems include the FBI's organized and disorganized killers. However, Canter is skeptical of this division because there is so much overlap between the two types of killers. Many offenders alternate between being disorganized and organized in their criminal careers.

Criminal history. What is the offender's criminal history? This looks at the likelihood of the offender having committed a crime earlier in his life and the type of crime he may have committed.

Forensic information. The forensic awareness that the offender may have refers to the knowledge or awareness that the offender displays in relation to the crime he commits. It may be that he spends time to be sure not to set fingerprints on the crime scene, cleaning the body for biological clues, or he may spend time making it challenging for law enforcement to identify the body. This can make law enforcement work more challenging. Without the person's identity, it is difficult to determine where they were at the time of the murder. It is also difficult to determine their movements prior to the murder. This may indicate to what extent the perpetrator knows how police work forensically, or whether the perpetrator has a history of burglary or has a police or military background.

Canter's profiling method generates hypotheses. It is imperative not to have a fixed conclusion, but to be willing to change your hypotheses and profile when new relevant information is discovered.

## TURVEY'S BEHAVIORAL EVIDENCE ANALYSIS

Behavioral Evidence Analysis (BEA) is a method developed by Brent Turvey, a criminal profiler and profiling educator. Turvey's motivation for working with criminal profiling was his interest in human behavior and the justice system. Turvey started by investigating sex offenders. But in 1991, he interviewed serial killer Jerome Brudos. Before the meeting, Turvey spent months reviewing court records and other reports related to the crime Brudos committed (Esparza & Turvey, 2016).

This was critical to getting accurate information about the individual. It turned out that much of the information Turvey got from Brudos conflicted with the other material he had access to. Turvey wrote:

*"...It was after my first interview with incarcerated serial murderer Jerome H. Brudos that I realized how truly naive my understanding of sex offenders was. I spent the first five hours with him, and he lied to me almost the entire time. He lied about almost everything he had ever done (or rather, he claimed, everything he hadn't done) ..." (Petherick, 1999a, p. 15).*

Turvey's profiling methodology points out the importance of considering that the perpetrators are lying. At the same time, it is critical to know that what happened at the crime scene is a reconstruction of the perpetrator's behavior. BEA was developed because many profiling methods emphasize the intuition of the individual criminal profiler rather than looking at the offender's behavior before, during, and after the crime was committed.

BEA was built around four main steps: equivocal forensic analysis, victimology, crime Scene characteristics, and offender characteristics:

Equivocal Forensic Analysis. This analysis is the first step. Here, the evidence is thoroughly examined. In this step, the most likely interpretation of the evidence is determined. Turvey believes that this step is imperative because you cannot create a truthful profile without analyzing all the physical evidence.

Victimology. The second step is victimology, where you find out as much as you can about the victim. Turvey prescribes that a victim profile be created like an offender profile. Turvey says victimology receives too little attention. This is an area that is often overlooked in some criminal profiling methods. By examining the victim, you can learn more about the perpetrator. Victimology examines why the offender chose this victim. Furthermore, the location of the body can tell you something about the offender's physique and build. If the victim has been transported a long distance or carried a long distance, it may indicate that the perpetrator is physically strong. In addition, there may be multiple perpetrators. Gender, physical appearance, or whether the person was right-handed, or whether the victim knew the perpetrator. Victimology can also tell the criminal profiler whether the perpetrator has shown authority by acting as a police officer, for example, so he could get the victim to let the perpetrator into their home or follow them to the perpetrator's car.

Crime Scene Characteristics. This step involves identifying various factors relevant to the crime scene and comparing different crime scenes to each other in serial crimes. You look at how the offender approached his victim. This may indicate that if the crime scene is without many forensic clues, the offender has committed crimes before because he is aware of the risk of getting revealed as the offender.

Offender Characteristics. The final step in the BEA is offender characteristics. In this step, the criminal profiler puts together the offender's behavioral characteristics and personality profile that came out of the previous three steps. This profile is not final and is constantly changed and reshaped as relevant information is added to the case. The characteristics may include information about gender, marital status, physical build, mental state, work situation, work habits, remorse or guilt, the offender's mode of transportation, his education, level of aggression, his residence and relationship to the crime, and possibly his medical history.

All the above information provides the criminal profiler with an offender profile, which is then given to law enforcement to use in their investigation. This profile can help law enforcement rule out suspects and include others in the investigation that they have suspected before but have excluded due to lack of evidence.

The profile is used in two phases. The first phase is the investigation phase. This is where the offender may commit multiple murders if they are a serial killer, and the investigation is still ongoing. In this phase, you have an unknown perpetrator that you need to link to a known crime. In the second phase, the testing phase, you have a suspected offender that you are trying to link to a known crime. Turvey points out the importance of criminal profiling being a process that can change many times depending on the stage of law enforcement investigation. It is an ongoing process of expanding, adding, and subtracting (Turvey, 2012).

## CRIMINAL PROFILING, ART, OR SCIENCE?

Douglas stated in the beginning of the development of criminal profiling that it was more an art than a science. Canter (1995) and Turvey (2012) argue that criminal profiling should be transformed into a science and moved away from an undefinable process. It is important to note that Douglas has become more scientific and, as a result, he does not state that profiling is an art anymore.

Canter, as mentioned, criticizes the FBI's methods. In particular, he opposes intuition. Douglas & Olshaker (1995, 1998), on the other hand, assess that intuition is a large part of profiling work. Canter points out that intuition means that the profile may risk being incorrect, and he compares it to clairvoyants who use empathy and intuition. Furthermore, Canter argues that what FBI agents describe as intuition often turns out to be based on observations they have gained through their training and experience and not intuition.

We often misunderstand what intuition is, it is a survivor skill that is important and all human have it, we can interpretate the world from our knowledge and experience and that way make good choices in our life and we often can avoid accident or bad things that can happen, because we know what we have to do next to survive, it is not some spooky or weird thing. We all have intuition, just in different scales, some have little, and some have a lot. If you can see other people more than you see yourself, you often have a good and solid intuition.

## HOW EFFECTIVE IS CRIMINAL PROFILING?

Criminal profiling is often portrayed in the media as an effective tool with high clearance rates. However, opinions differ on criminal profiling effectiveness.

Ressler & Burgess (1985) estimate a clearance rate of 93%. Other argue that the clearance rate is only 2.7%. The disagreement is complicated by the fact that it can be difficult to determine what is behind criminal profiling studies. But how to measure profiling success? What should the criteria be for success in a case?

Keppel & Birnes (2003) agree that criminal profiling is not the successful method that some make it out to be. There are many examples of inaccurate profiles. An example of how badly it can go was the DC Beltway snipers in Washington, D.C., who in October 2002 killed 10 and wounded 3 people within a month. The FBI profile was of a white male, lonely, living a normal life with a wife and children, and probably right-wing. But there were two perpetrators. They were blacks, and the older one was active in the Nation of Islam. Both lived near the shootings and lived in a homeless shelter.

There are more examples where the profile can be completely wrong. Criminal profiling was widely criticized after this. As a result, several criminal profilers said that profiling was only one tool out of many. They also said that it was difficult to estimate ethnicity when you create a profile. It can be difficult when you want to profile ethnicity because you cannot distinguish between races unless you find the perpetrator's hair at the crime scene. There is no specific behavioral pattern or personality type that distinguishes one race from another.

A misconception is that most serial killers are white. However, if the percentage of black serial killers is calculated in relation to the number of blacks in the United States, it turns out that there are as many black as white serial killers. Hickey (1991) writes that with urbanization, as more blacks move to cities, there will be an increase in black serial killers. It is not that there are racial differences in serial killers; there are just more whites in the US than blacks.

In an English study that used criminal profiling on 184 cases, the result was that five cases out of the 184 (2.7%) were solved (Gudjonsson & Copson,

1997, p. 90). However, law enforcement reported back that they had gained a greater understanding of the cases in 61% of the 184 cases. In 52% of cases, law enforcement became more confident in their own conclusions. But in 32% of cases, law enforcement concluded that the profile was completely irrelevant.

Teten (1995), on the other hand, estimated that in 77% of cases, the FBI's applied criminology helps solve cases. That is, criminal profiling has helped them rule out perpetrators and clarify which suspects to investigate further. If the profile they get of the offender tells them that the offender is most likely to be a person with a medical background, they can prioritize the list of suspects by first examining people with a medical history. In this way, the list of suspects can be reduced until only a small group remains to concentrate on.

Ressler, Burgess & Douglas (1988) claim that criminal profiling is a reliable method that is effective in 76-93% of the cases in which they use it. Saferstein (1998) and Ainsworth (2002) argue that criminal profiling is not as effective a tool as it is portrayed by those who use it. They argue that when reviewing crime cases, the perpetrator is often apprehended by law enforcement. This is not because of the profile. It may be that the offender is caught for a minor offense, and further investigation can link the person to the unsolved crime he has committed.

However, if the offender is compared to the profile, the similarity is often striking. Even if law enforcement knows the offender's personality type, behavior, work area, and characteristics, they cannot arrest an offender with that information alone. The profile is only one tool of many tools.

I have not been able to find out what is behind the clear-up rate numbers when using criminal profiling. It is therefore difficult to say how effective criminal profiling really is. Furthermore, there is no information on how high a clearance rate law enforcement normally has in the same type of crime case without criminal profiling. As mentioned, Geberth (1996) estimates that less than 50% of criminal profiling cases are solved, because it is often the most difficult cases to work with. Therefore, the clearance rate is generally low. Furthermore, it can be difficult to say anything about the effectiveness of criminal profiling, only that these are cases that are difficult to solve in general.

The difficulties begin before you begin the profiling investigation. In evaluation studies where criminal cases are divided into two groups, one group using criminal profiling and the other group not applying profiling, it will be difficult to conclude that criminal profiling is beneficial, even if the group using profiling has solved more cases than the group not applying profiling. The reason is that there will be crucial differences between the two clearance rates. People who work as criminal profilers are often trained FBI agents who excel at their jobs. This can be a reason for their success. Despite the poor profile, law enforcement may be so effective that they are the reason a case is solved, and not that the profile was the reason for the case to be solved. Furthermore, criminal profiling is used for extreme crimes such as serial murders or multiple rapes. Therefore, the environment always pressures them to solve crimes quickly. This may mean that profiling is beneficial for law enforcement, as profiling requires them to work more efficiently. Coupled with the fact that local police often do not have experience with violent criminal cases such as serial murders, the criminal profiler, on the other hand, has worked with this type of extreme crime for many years (Howitt, 2002). All these aspects make it difficult to determine profiling effectiveness.

It's a myth that a criminal profiler solves crimes. The strongest thing a criminal profiler can do is point to a specific type of person with several behavioral and personality traits. The criminal profiler can also indicate the person's psychiatric history, physical appearance, work, work rhythm, marital status, and where they are likely to live and stay.

In other words, it is law enforcement who solves the given cases through their investigative work and not the profile or the criminal profiler.

Criminal profiling can be an effective tool for reducing possible suspects in crime cases. Furthermore, profiling can be valuable to law enforcement in understanding the behavior, dynamics, and motivation of a given offender. It is debated whether criminal profiling is a science or an art form. Turvey and Canter advocate that criminal profiling should be a scientific method, requiring criminal profilers to be trained in psychology, psychiatry, forensics, and sociology (Esparza & Turvey, 2016).

A study by Kocsis, Orwin & Hayes (2000) indicates that the profession of the criminal profiler differs in relation to the profile outcome. The researchers divided the criminal profilers into five groups: professional criminal profilers, police officers, psychologists, students, and self-proclaimed psychics. Professional criminal profilers were the best at solving murder mysteries by using profiling, while psychologists came second. Holmes & Holmes (2002) suggest that this may be due to psychologists' insight into human behavior.

More research is needed in this area, but this indicates that the most effective criminal profiler could be a trained psychologist who has investigative experience, like in law enforcement. In the above study, it is difficult to assess, as it is unclear how the study is structured.

An example is Robert Hansen, the Alaskan baker who kidnapped, raped, and hunted strippers and prostitutes in the wilderness outside Anchorage. Robert Hansen, who was born in 1939 in the USA to Danish immigrants. As a young man, he was skinny, stammering, and suffered from severe acne, which meant that girls at school turned their backs on him. He developed a fierce hatred of girls and women, and over time, he began to fantasize about revenge - fantasies he had plenty of time for as he was almost always alone.

He had a problematic relationship with his domineering father, yet like his father, he chose to become a baker, but he spent his free time hunting and archery, where he didn't need to be with others. John Douglas compiled a fairly accurate profile that triggered a search warrant, but he also advised local police on the interrogation of the serial killer. The crimes were rooted in extremely low self-esteem and a desire for power and revenge over women, and John Douglas believed that the culprit would feel very powerful and in control when arrested. Therefore, he recommended that the investigators fill the interrogation room with maps, pictures, and reports that would give Robert Hansen the impression that they knew even more than they really did. He told them to leave him alone in the room for a while so that the uncertainty that characterized his innermost feelings could grow. Investigators were told that Robert Hansen saw the interrogation as a game and that his goal was to beat the system at its own game. In this context, this meant that he would most likely confess to the murders that the police could link to him with forensic evidence, while he would deny everything else. If they wanted to get the baker to confess to more crimes, they had to avoid condemning him but instead show interest in him and his motives and generally pretend to enjoy hearing him talk. One result was that they pretended to be deeply impressed by his planning and the things he did to avoid getting caught. The combination of listening, asking with interest, and then letting the full weight of the evidence weigh on Robert Hansen had a clear effect, one of the prosecutors, Frank Rothschild, reported much later in an interview in Newsweek in 2020:

"It worked! While we were doing that, I looked at Hansen across the table, and I watched a wild transformation from the mild-mannered baker Bob, who was a small guy. He wasn't physically imposing. And he wore glasses and seemed like such a little nerd. But suddenly his neck turned fire red, and the hairs on the back of his neck stood up, and he turned into the man who had killed all the women. Right before our eyes, he got really angry."

Hansen then demanded to speak to his lawyers and made the deal that resulted in a life sentence in exchange for confessing to four murders and a string of rapes.

## THEORIES BEHIND CRIMINAL PROFILING

It can be difficult to identify references to theories that support and endorse criminal profiling. The reason can be that profiling is a tool or method used by the FBI in investigative work.

The FBI's criminal profiling method was developed using police experience and law enforcement. It was developed to identify likely behavioral structures and personality traits in people who commit the same type of crime.

Despite this, some personality and sociocultural theories can be outlined that could underlie criminal profiling, special when you look at the method retrospective. Some of these theories will be reviewed in the next sections.

## PSYCHOLOGICAL THEORIES

Behind criminal profiling, we can find some personality theories, including psychodynamic, developmental psychological, and attachment theories. It is assumed that the offender had problems in his childhood, and this affects his behavior and personality in adulthood.

Oedipus complex is a theory from psychodynamic and psychoanalytic theory, which is an ostensibly universal phase in the life of a young boy in which, to immediately satisfy basic desires, he unconsciously wishes to have sex with his mother and disdains his father for having sex and being satisfied before him. This theory was introduced by Sigmund Freud in "Die Traumdeutung." This is often indicated to be seen, where there are problems between mother and son (Freud, 1899).

Hickey (2016) and Ressler et al. (1988) found that most serial killers had problems with attachment to their parents, both the mother and father. Furthermore, they have experienced psychological, physical, or sexual abuse. People who grow up with these issues can have psychological problems of various kinds. These may include violent behavior, criminal behavior, depersonalization of others, or personality disorders. These factors can be explained by psychodynamic theories, which I will explain in this section. Holmes & Holmes (2002) claim that Freudian theories are behind most criminal profiling interpretations. It could be conflicts in childhood that result in a weak attachment to their parents. Or it could be unresolved physical or emotional conflicts from childhood.

Freudian psychoanalysis is one of the oldest psychology theories. Psychoanalysis relies on the unconscious, which is rooted in traumatic childhood experiences (Freud, 1899; Hougaard et al., 1998). These traumas affect us in different ways and can cause problems later in life, such as personality disorders.

Psychoanalytic theory divides humans into three components: superego (conscience), ego (self), and id (drives). Conflict can arise between the superego (conscience) and the id (drives) (Freud, 1917, 1995). It can also be difficult to control the id, as the drives only respond to what Freud called the pleasure principle: if it feels right, do it. The ego should be understood as the self in which the person recognizes and sees himself. The ego is dominated by the reality principle: the real world in which the person lives. The superego tries to control and show what the person wants, but also how he wants him to be (ego-ideal). This ego ideal comes from the person's first love attachment, usually to a parent (Freud, 1917).

Freud's psychosexual development theory describes how the child moves through different phases throughout adolescence: oral, anal, and genital. The oral phase is where the person develops a sense of satisfaction and satiety by figuring out how much is enough. This is done through food and fluid intake. This stage can show how adults relate to managing food, drink, and/or smoking. The anal phase is where the person develops their sense of order through, for example, toilet training. The genital phase is the phase where sexuality is formed. The child needs to see if they can have a loving relationship with their parents. Sexual preferences are also clarified during this phase. The oral, anal, and genital phases are experienced the same for both boys and girls, but the subsequent phases are experienced differently. The boy moves through the Oedipus complex, and the female moves through the Electra complex. The name Electra complex was coined after Freud's time and refers to the girl's relationship with her father, like the Oedipus complex, which refers to the son's relationship with his mother. Both complexes involve the child having sexual (romantic) feelings for the parent who represents the opposite sex. Depending on how the individual child resolves this complex will determine how they will later manage their love life (Freud, 1995).

In criminology, the conflicts a person experiences in the different phases are assumed to be psychodynamic conflicts.

Serial killers may be motivated by Oedipal conflicts to displace hatred on their female victims (see Shawcross case chapter 9). In Freudian theory, repressed aggression is acted out on other women who represent the person who previously was the source of the serial killer's conflicts or problems. This displacement, which is when you have problems with a given person, but instead channel the problem to a third person, or it can be time displacement, explains various types of crime, including murder. However, not all serial killers are motivated by hatred of women.

According to O'Connor (2002a), many serial killers hate both their parents, although the relationship with the mother has a special meaning for the boy (Nielsen & Rudberg, 1991). This psychodynamic personality conflict is often used in criminology and forensic psychology as an explanation for crime (Feldman, 1993). This conflict can be seen at the crime scene, and which hypothesis a criminal profiler will make will depend on how the offender acts towards the victim before and after the homicide.

Proponents of both Freudian and Neo-Freudian theories believe criminals dream of being caught. This is explained by the fact that they have been spoiled in the oral phase and punished in the subsequent phases. This allows them to grow up with an underdeveloped superego which can leads to lack of conscience, guilt and dominance to pursue primitive urges. O'Connor (2002a) explains the underdeveloped superego by saying that they have not passed through the genital phase; therefore, their ego is underdeveloped. That is, they have nothing to mediate between the id and the superego, and then the superego, therefore, gets underdeveloped. Therefore, their personality becomes an endless series of aggressive conflicts. This is called delinquent ego. There are some examples of serial killers exhibiting behaviors that indicate they want to be caught. They may leave clues at the crime scene, plea to the FBI to catch them quickly; if not, more people will get killed, or they may volunteer themselves to law enforcement. Edmund Kemper was an example of a serial killer who killed his mother and her friend, and in that way surrenders, because he then knew that they would know he was the killer. His explanation for murdering his mother at the time was that no more women should die because of his mother's cruelty.

Criminal profiling can also predict, from analyzing the crime scene, whether the offender has had difficulty controlling their impulses. If the murder is impulse-driven, there is a high risk of murder again. This inference comes from the perpetrator's difficulty controlling his impulses. Psychoanalysis hypothesized that serial killers do not experience the conflict between the id and the superego because they have a weak superego. When they have a weak superego, they don't see following their urges as a problem. Therefore, they can give in to their murderous impulses.

Lansky (1983) says impulsive actions can be seen retrospectively because impulses can hold emotional equilibrium in adults who suffer from disorders that trace back to that attachment in the pre-oedipal period: the first three years of the child's life. Lansky describes a profound sense of the absence of attachment disturbance, followed by the absence of more normal emotions that follow the impulsive act.

As mentioned earlier, serial killers are likely to have experienced abuse and/or problems with love/hate relationships with their parents. Therefore, the criminal profiler may conclude that it is likely to find the perpetrator within a group of people with a history of abuse and problems with their parents.

In a case where the FBI solved a murder case of a specific victim, they appeared on TV and asked elementary school teachers, based on the serial killer's profile, to recall and list students who had the MacDonald triad and report back to the FBI. It was through these reports that they found the perpetrator (Discovery Channel, Thursday, October 24, 2002).

Lowenstein (1989) also uses Freudian explanations for why some people become serial killers. He advocates the concept that unresolved childhood sexual conflicts, along with maternal overprotection or outright rejection of the child, are significant factors in serial killer development. Gallagher (1987) suggests that abnormal and violent behavior comes from conflicts between the id and superego rooted in unresolved childhood trauma. Sears (1991) suggests that crime is caused by an upbringing where the perpetrator learns that sexual acts are shameful. This shame prevents him from having a satisfying sexual life. This conflict can result in him inflicting blame on his victims as a response to his shame.

An example of this shame around sexuality is William Heirens, who, in an interview, had difficulty deciding which was more heinous: sex, burglary, or murder. In the end, he answered sex and murder. When faced with the choice between sex and murder, he lowers his head and answers murder. This is interpreted by Kennedy et al. (2000) that Heirens found sex to be more horrible than murder, but with his intellect, he knew he should not commit murder. Kennedy et al. (2000) wrote:

*"...I believe that William Heirens nodded his head to indicate that subjectively he felt sex was worse than murder, but in verbalizing stated murder..."*

Levin & Fox (1985) suggest that inferiority complexes play a role in why some people find necrophilia appealing. Corpses cannot reject people, cheat, or make sexual demands. Serial killers have a feeling of inadequacy, along with inferiority, which can be worse than the feeling of not being in control of their lives. This may be what causes serial killers to desire control and power over others by murdering them. When they kill, for a moment, they have total control and power. These relationships can be seen at the crime scene in the way the offender treats their victims.

One example could be the lack of care and help in dealing with chaotic emotions experienced by abused children. In terms of a psychodynamic approach, the child has, through such an upbringing, developed a chaotic inner parental image. This is due to the abuse the parents inflicted on the child. Parents' own emotions they pass on to their victims. You could say that they transfer chaotic emotions to their victims, who experience the same feelings of fear, frustration, and anxiety.

Retvitch (1965) says the build-up of tension triggered by the attack can come from a build-up of tension or a clouding of suddenly evoked negative emotions that can be transferred from the mother or killer surrogate to the victim. In this way, serial killers continuously try to get rid of parental image and abuse. This chaotic feeling can be seen at the crime scene. For example, if the victim has been tortured, if the perpetrator wants the victim to suffer, it can be traced back to their own emotional world.

According to O'Connor (2002b), most incarcerated criminals have 20 points lower intelligence than non-criminals. It is argued that police catch them because of their low intelligence. According to Feldman (1993), intelligence is unlikely to matter when talking about street crime. However, in economic crime, intelligence plays a role. This phenomenon is also seen when dealing with serial killers. Serial killers with higher intelligence take longer to catch. Holmes & Holmes (2002) assume that successful criminals and most serial killers who are not caught quickly have an intelligence about 20 points above normal. The offender's intelligence can be interpreted from the crime scene. One example is that intelligent offenders are difficult to find traces of, as they are cautious about leaving traces. Nevertheless, intelligent serial killers may act in bloodlust if they have been on drugs or prevented from committing murder for a long time. Therefore, the crime scene will be marked by uncontrolled behavior. This can cause an untrained criminal profiler to misinterpret the offender's intelligence.

There is no evidence for the above claims, but according to O'Connor (2002b), psychopaths and people with personality disorders, such as paranoid-narcissistic types, have intelligence that is 10 to 20 percent (or more) above normal. This is not supported by studies. However, serial killers who are on the loose longer have higher intelligence than those caught quickly by law enforcement. But you can't conclude that psychopaths are above normal intelligence. More research is needed in this area.

In this section, some psychological factors were reviewed that can explain how the criminal profiler uses the crime scene, autopsy reports, and victimology to produce a profile that describes the perpetrator.

The psychological factors I have reviewed are not solely theories on which criminal profiling is built. However, I believe that there are factors that explain criminal profiling conclusions. But more research in the field is needed to determine the validity of the above factors with certainty.

In addition to the psychological theories I have just reviewed, in the next section, I will clarify some sociocultural theories that do not necessarily explain criminal profiling. However, they may explain why some people become serial killers. I will examine whether these theories can underpin criminal profiling.

# SOCIOCULTURAL THEORIES

Mitchell (1996) believes that sociocultural theories have been overlooked in the serial killer literature. This is because, according to Mitchell, both academics and professionals have difficulty recognizing that serial killers' actions can be a product of an individual's social and cultural environment. But it is possible to identify some sociocultural theories that may explain why some people become serial killers.

I have outlined strain theory, learning theory, and control theory, all with interesting considerations.

Strain theory. Merton (1968) states that social skills and the ability to develop social skills are learned. We all strive for different goals, and if cultural goals exceed our own capabilities, anomie, Anomie is a lack or weakening of social norms and hence a feeling of insecurity and disintegration, normlessness. Durkheim's theory of anomie (later strain theory) can be overcome through innovation. This innovation can be, for example, the use of illegality to accomplish legitimate goals (Holmes & Holmes, 2002). In some countries, achieving personal goals is considered acceptable. If one cannot achieve personally desired goals in an acceptable way, they can be obtained illegally. For example, rape may be an "illegitimate" way for rapists to obtain a sexual partner. This happens if the person cannot legally find a partner. In this way, the perpetrator takes what he is prevented from getting in a normal way and feels justified.

When you hear serial killers talk about why they kill, there are several examples of them claiming that they are fulfilling their own personal desires by killing. Some do not believe that it is wrong. However, personal desires are not always murder or rape. The propensity to find a way out by using illegal methods to achieve one's own accepted goal can be indicated by the fact that 60% of serial killers have previous criminal convictions (Myers et al.,

1993). If they believe they are entitled to expensive cars, they will steal them if they cannot buy them themselves. In relation to murder and rape, serial killers may feel satisfaction from fulfilling their desired goal. The perpetrator takes what he wants by gaining control and power over his victims. It is mostly not the act itself (rape or murder) that serial killers and perpetrators of rapists want, but total power and control over the victim.

Strain theory should be understood from two perspectives: social processes and personal experiences.

Strain theory says criminals are simply people who want the same thing as everyone else. However, they feel blocked from achieving what they want, so they create creative, inventive ways to achieve it. Criminologists are divided on what creates strain: inward blockages, occupational blockages, educational blockages, or something else entirely.

Strain theory points out the importance of the Western middle class. This causes frustration for those outside the middle class. The type of criminal who rebels against middle-class values such as honesty, politeness, responsibility, etc., then they turn those values on their heads. Those on the outside are drawn to equality. Together, they share their resentment towards outsiders and become habitual offenders. The external expectation that they, as an underclass, will fail drives them to an ingrained perception of injustice, which can result in them collecting alternative status symbols (O'Connor, 2002b).

An example of a serial killer who feels outside the middle and upper classes is Theodore Robert Bundy. Theodore Robert Bundy had what Hickey (2016) called social-class paranoia. Bundy wanted to belong to a higher class in society than he did. The women he murdered were middle or upper class. Leyton (1986), who interviewed Bundy, suggests that by murdering middle- and upper-class women, he found an outlet for his obsession with class differences.

Learning theories. Learning theories focus on the principles of stimuli and control, which are the steps to being Modeled (leading, restraining, telling, and performing) and vicarious learning (people and media influence) (Bandura, 1963, 1973).

According to learning theories, anyone can become a criminal at any time if they learn the techniques, motives, drives, rationalization, and attitudes required. When individuals reach the point where they have more reasons to commit a crime than not, they become criminals. There are different circumstances that make an individual a criminal. Interpersonal relationships are of particular importance in relation to this n importance according to this theory. Behavior is shaped by various individual stimuli, more than reinforcement stimuli. The variables of deprivation and gratification make these stimuli meaningful to the individual (O'Connor, 2002b).

Control theories. Lack of punishment may be the reason some people become, or remain, criminals. Criminals are only active for periods of time. Most of the time, they adapt and stay away from crime, and only sometimes do they engage in criminal acts. Habitual offenders are constructed through various factors. It can be a weak attachment to their family, relationships (obligations), school or work (involvement), or other social institutions (trust in others). It depends on the family they grow up in. If one parent is a criminal, the child is at risk of alcoholism, drug abuse, and/or mental health problems. According to Hirschi's (1990) control theory, people are least likely to become criminals if they have contact with the conventional world, and it emphasizes that there are four dimensions related to connection to society: attachment, commitment, involvement, and conviction.

Attachment is when someone else cares about or loves you. This could be a family, friend, or teacher who is not deviant in behavior or personality. For example, a person is attached to a teacher. The person will not disappoint the teacher by committing a deviant act because of their strong attachment to the teacher. Those with a high attachment level are likely to adapt. Those without a strong attachment will not adapt. Under normal circumstances, the child has a secure attachment to their parents. Commitment is the degree of investment the person has in following the given rules (conformity). Those with a high level of commitment are likely to conform. Those with low conformity will not conform. Involvement is a conventional behavior that limits deviant/criminal behavior. This could be, for example, schoolwork. Some have a greater belief that they must obey the laws and rules of the country, and this belief helps them not to become deviant/criminals (Hirschi, 1990).

The theories I have just reviewed are an excerpt of sociocultural theories that may explain some criminal profiling conclusions. Sociocultural theories used in criminal profiling could be where the crime scene is located. This may indicate that the offender wants to convey a message to law enforcement, society, and the media. There are several examples of serial killers wanting to be known. In the USA, the media tends to focus on serial killers. They are in the media, books are written about them, they get their own websites and become heroes or anti-heroes. Serial killers' desire to be known could be explained by strain theory. If the person has the feeling of not belonging to the elite and being an outsider, being a serial killer can give them a sense of finally being known, having accomplished something, and finally gaining hero status.

Another example of theories that explain criminal profiling conclusions could be when the profile of an offender suggests that the offender is likely to remain with their mother. Some serial killers live with their mother while killing, e.g., Edmund Kemper lived with his mother until he killed her and just waited for to law enforcement to find him. The fact that the person stays with their mother until a later age could indicate unresolved Oedipal conflicts.

However, we must be careful not to overemphasize serial killers residing with their mothers. In many European countries and the USA, many people live with their parents if they can't afford to live alone, studying or saving for their own place. Presumably, it is considered more acceptable in some countries for adult men to stay with their mothers. However, it may also indicate unresolved issues between mother and son.

While it may be possible to link the reason why some people become serial killers because of social class, it is not the only reason. It is possible that the correlation found is due to a third factor, for which Brown (1984) presents evidence. He does this by showing that social class, child abuse, and crime correlate. Therefore, it can be difficult to determine which factors are decisive for criminal development. It may be a combination of the various factors that contribute to serial killer development.

Both sociocultural and psychological theories can be found behind criminal profiling. Therefore, it is critical that one does not exclude the other, so a synthesis of both sociocultural and psychological theories could be the explanation to why criminal profiling can predict behavior and personality from the crime scene and information about the crime.

## SYNTHESIS BETWEEN PSYCHOLOGICAL AND SOCIOCULTURAL THEORIES

In the criminal profiling methodology, theories can be found to support profiling. Psychological and sociocultural theories can be applied to criminal profiling. After reviewing the above theories, it seems that a possible answer to why people become criminals could be found through a synthesis of psychodynamic and sociocultural theories. Furthermore, it is demonstrated that both psychological and sociocultural theories could explain why criminal profiling appears to predict behavior and personality from crime scenes.

The Chicago School (Ainsworth, 2002) contains this kind of synthesis. The basic idea is that through subcultural groupings, criminals receive alternative rewards. Sociocultural theories say criminals gain status by being criminals. This happens regardless of whether they are caught by law enforcement, in which case they must use resources on them, or if they are not caught, in which case they can avoid law enforcement. The psychodynamic aspect is seen in the fact that criminals often have a fatherless upbringing, where the mother bears all responsibility. By committing criminality, the son ensures that the family can survive and thus takes on the role of family/mother protector. Holmes & Holmes (2002) say profiling methods combine psychological and sociocultural theories to understand the offender's personality.

In the next chapter, I will examine whether the theories I have just reviewed, together with the factors I have identified as having an impact on the development of serial killers, can be used to find potential serial killers.

# 6. IDENTIFYING SERIAL KILLERS?

There have been various attempts to create a method to identify potential serial killers before they commit their first murder. This work has been criticized. The criticism has been about the method itself, but also because of the risk of stigmatizing children at an early age by identifying them as potential serial killers.

Even so, I believe that such a method can contribute something valuable when working with children and young people at risk. Therefore, I will examine whether it is possible to establish some factors that may indicate a risk of a person developing into an extremely violent and, in the extreme, a serial killer. Before I do this, I will outline some behavioral characteristics that may indicate you are dealing with potential serial killers.

## THE MACDONALD TRIAD

MacDonald (1963) estimated that if a child or adolescent met three factors, animal cruelty, enuresis after 12 years of age, and arson, there was a high risk of becoming a serial killer.

Retrospective studies (Ressler et al., 1988) indicate that this is the case; many serial killers have had at least two of the three factors in their childhood.

These MacDonald triad findings are retrospective. If one wishes to examine the relationship between the triad and serial killers, one must examine whether children who exhibit the MacDonald triad grow up to become serial killers or extremely violent.

In such a study, I would suggest identifying children who display the triad and following them into adulthood. This way, you can investigate whether children who exhibit the triad grow up to be normal or extremely violent, serial rapists or serial killers. Another research proposal could be re-analyzing studies of children with severe mental health problems of the type seen in the triad. As a result, one could investigate whether it is possible to identify children who exhibit the triad and find out if they have become extremely violent criminals.

## ANIMAL ABUSE

Freud recommended extra attention to cruel children in 1905. Today, there is growing evidence that children who commit animal cruelty have severe problems and are at risk of becoming violent (Ainsworth, 2002).

The FBI, psychologists, and psychiatrists working with murderers in the USA have further found that there is a possible link between animal abuse and both domestic violence and child abuse. Animal cruelty has even been linked to child and adolescent homicide. In 1999, four out of six young mass murderers abused or killed animals in their childhood. Albert DeSalvo, Theodore Robert Bundy, David Berkowitz, Jeffrey Dahmer, Marc Lepine, Carroll Edward Cole, and Martin Bryant are some of the serial killers who committed animal abuse in their childhood. Animal abuse is not only a flaw in the abuser's personality, but it can also be a symptom of coming from a disturbed family. Perpetrators of animal abuse are mostly teenage boys who can come from all walks of life. Comparative studies also show that children who abuse animals have also experienced abuse themselves (Tapia, 1971). Young people repeat the pattern they themselves experienced in their childhood, repetition compulsion, which refers to an unconscious need to reenact early traumas. A person with this condition repeats these traumas in various situations that symbolize the initial trauma. They treat the animal as they observe it in their environment. If children see their parents react with violence when they are frustrated or angry, they themselves often participate in bullying and mistreatment of vulnerable and weak people and animals

(Quinn, 2000).

## ENURESIS AFTER THE AGE OF 12 YEARS OF AGE

In the MacDonald triad, enuresis after 12 years of age is also an indication of a potential serial killer. Ressler et al. (1988) found that 68% of serial killers had enuresis after 12 years of age.

I want to point out that there are some important issues to know about enuresis. Firstly, the physiological causes of enuresis must be ruled out. Furthermore, enuresis can be a symptom of sexual abuse, especially when seen after the age of 12 (Moesgaard, 1999). Therefore, it should be noted that serial killers may suffer from enuresis because they have been sexually assaulted. If the other traits from the MacDonald triad (animal abuse and arson) appear at the same time as enuresis, it is a sign that something is wrong with the child.

One of the 36 killers investigated by the FBI said he humiliated himself and his family by wetting the bed until he was 16 years old. He says that he stopped wetting the bed himself because his family started making fun of him instead of getting angry (Ressler et al., 1988, p: 23). In this case, this indicates that there may be an aspect of rebellion or punishment associated with the action, as he stopped himself when he was made fun of. However, it needs to be researched why the child suffers from enuresis.

## ARSON

The last marker in the MacDonald triad is arson. The American Prosecutors Research Institute suggests that arson may be a sign that the child will later commit extreme acts of violence. Serial killers report their desire and enjoyment of arson as children. Some say that arson gives them an enormous sense of power; others say that it gives them sexual gratification along with a sense of power. Arson can be compared to dramatic destruction when people are murdered. Serial killers see others as objects. Therefore, it can be relatively easy for them to jump from arson to murdering people (Scott, 2003).

Hellman & Blackman (1966) considered enuresis a sadistic and rebellious way of reacting against parents by destroying the bed and causing parental distress. Fire setting is associated with violence, where torturing animals is a form of rebellion against the norm of keeping pets. Enuresis, animal cruelty, or arson, individually, I believe, cannot be used as a sign of a potential serial killer. However, it can be a sign of abuse of the child or that the child has other serious problems, so it is critical to examine what is causing the child to have the various problems. If the child has all three factors, it is imperative to find out whether it has other psychological or behavioral problems, or if the child is being molested, or what cause these issues.

# 7. THE DEVELOPMENT OF THE MULTIFACTOR-MODEL

This book researched whether the theories behind criminal profiling can be used to design a method to find potential serial killers.

I have looked at criminal profiling as a method. The method of criminal profiling has been examined whether is it an art or a science, and what theories the method is based on. According to the hypothesis, I aim to design a method to find serial killers using criminal profiling and psychological theories. In the next part of this book examine if the method can be used.

Lastly, I will outline the advantages and disadvantages of that method.

## DEVELOPING THE MACDONALD TRIAD INTO THE MULTIFACTOR MODEL

Erick W. Hickey (2002a), a criminal psychology professor, also used the MacDonald triad. However, he expands it with other factors that he found can predict how children with these traits will turn out as adults.

Ressler, Burgess, and Douglas created a list in 1988 with 24 behavioral indicators that they believed played a role in serial killers (Ressler et al., 1988, pp. 28-30). The Model is divided into childhood, adolescence, and adulthood.

Another researcher who has tried to create a list is Norris (1992b), who lists some signals to know in early childhood:

- The child feels neglected in childhood.

- The feeling that others are preferred, which breeds guilt, shame, and anger. Children can deal with these feelings by controlling something else. This includes abusing animals or other children by, for example, sexually exploiting them.

- Sexual exploitation as a child.
- Retreat into a fantasy world.
- A secluded life with few or no friends after school.

As I can see from the above, various researchers over the years have researched whether it is possible to find factors that indicate that you are dealing with potential serial killers.

McKenzie (1995) compiled 28 factors for the serial killer development. The 28 factors are divided into 4 categories: Childhood Environmental Incubator, Childhood Dysfunctional Indicators, Adulthood Floodgate Disinhibitory, and Adulthood Dysfunctional Contributors. He then compared his own study with Ressler's 1988 study. McKenzie's study indicates that some of the components of the MacDonald triad are not as strong indicators as suggested in various parts of the literature. For example, arson is significant in Ressler's study (56%), but in McKenzie's (1995) study, only 6% of the 16 serial killers studied practiced arson in childhood. There are several factors that are not consistent with McKenzie's study. The reason for this difference may be that since FBI has access to more information about the serial killers; they include them in their study. McKenzie points out that if we examine serial killers in a different way than we have done so far, namely with qualitative studies, but instead conduct controlled quantitative studies that can be standardized and used to calculate statistics, it is possible that we can understand serial killers in a different way than we do today.

The biographical method has some limitations, although McKenzie finds these studies relevant. Most of the studies done so far have been the work of the FBI to help catch serial killers and not to understand them completely.

Triangulation, which is defined by Denzin (1978) as "a combination of methodologies used in studies of the same phenomenon." This could be interesting in this context, starting with a qualitative study to identify which hypotheses to research. Subsequently, quantitative studies could be conducted based on the qualitative study. Furthermore, comparative studies are desired that could tell something about the relationship between different criminals. McKenzie writes further:

*".. a distinctive differentiation characteristic might emerge from a comparative study of serial murderers, child abusers, and sex offenders, specifically pedophiles and rapists..." (McKenzie, 1995, p. 9).*

The study that McKenzie (1995) refers to as Ressler's 1988 study is the same study that is in this book's reference list.

The above factors are of importance and must be included when assessing whether the child is at risk of growing up with severe problems and, in the extreme, extremely violent criminals. However, there are more critical markers that I will discuss later in the Multifactor Model, but first, I will briefly outline the links between family dysfunction and violent behavior.

## FAMILY DYSFUNCTION AND VIOLENT BEHAVIOR

In the last sections, I outlined some of the reasons why some people can become serial killers. Some factors were reviewed that indicated that family dysfunction could be one of the causes of serial killers' behavior. Therefore, it is critical to examine children with these problems more closely. I believe that it is more important to intervene before their problems become so severe that it becomes difficult to intervene. Ressler points out that much can be done if problems are detected in time. If you discover problems later, you can still make a difference. However, children are unlikely to develop into Model citizens, but you can prevent them from being destructive to themselves and others.

**Ressler (1992) writes:**

*"There are always ways to retard the offending behavior of a potentially dangerous child who has had a bad life... Psychological counseling might get to the heart of the problem and move the child away from the path leading to deviant behavior"*

In chapter 2, about paraphilia, fantasy, and sex pointed out that children living out their fantasies are violent toward others. Therefore, this behavior can indicate major problems. They may copy what they see around them and/or act out their fantasies.

To identify children with the above factors, I will outline a proposal for a Model that contains the significant factors that I found in my thesis from 2004 to have an impact on the development of serial killers.

## PROCEDURE OF THE QUESTIONNAIRE SURVEY

This book examines whether the theories behind criminal profiling can be used to design a method to find potential serial killers.

I have looked at criminal profiling as a method. The method of criminal profiling has been examined whether it is an art or a science, and what theories the method is based on. According to the hypothesis, I aim to design a method to find serial killers using criminal profiling theories. In the next part of this book, walk through this and see if the method can be used. I will also see the advantages and disadvantages of that method.

The study was a survey with open-ended qualitative questions. The survey was designed to send several questionnaires to selected serial killers in the USA, UK, and Australia.

From the responses I received, I selected Arthur Shawcross (Case 7a-b to

10a-b 03-05) as one of my 5 main cases in the thesis (see chapter 9). I have chosen to analyze only one case, as it would be too extensive to go through all the responses I received.

The Shawcross case was chosen because he answered all the questions. From 2002 to 2005, I sent additional questions. The reason I sent the follow-up questions to Shawcross was that I wanted further information about his life.

My interest in criminal profiling began in 1997. I contacted the FBI's training division for information on criminal profiling training. This put me in contact with John E. Douglas, who is a former FBI agent and criminal profiler. He and his team design the FBI's criminal profiling methodology. I joined the Forensic Network, which was a forensic/criminological e-mail list established to provide an information network for academics, students, clinicians and academics and other professionals. John E. Douglas had a bulletin board called "John Douglas Mindhunter Bulletin Board," which John added me to. I got in contact with John Arvidsson, who was a Swedish private profiler, regarding criminal profiling in Denmark. They put me in touch with the serial killers I included in my study.

To participate in the study, the serial killers had to fulfill the following requirements:

1. They had to meet the FBI's definition of a serial killer.

2. They had to be mentally capable of participating in the study.

This study aimed to describe serial killers' own experience of serial killing, self-understanding, and to shed light on their own perspective. People included in the study were in prisons and mental institutions around the world, mainly in the USA, and therefore, interviewing them was slow. It also required approval through an exchange of letters correspondence.

The survey I sent to the selected serial killers was designed as a five-section questionnaire divided into 13 sub-questions. The questions were semi-structured and open. However, I also wanted answers to specific issues, so there were closed questions.

If I were to research serial killers further, I would interview them in conjunction with the survey. By formulating questions based on the answers you receive, you can ask more in-depth questions. This would give the interview a dynamic that you can't get when conducting it through letter correspondence. It is a slow way to communicate, and you miss direct and immediate answers. However, I have asked questions about the answers I have received. You can't manipulate the interviewer when you answer through letters. You don't know what the interviewer is looking for. It can be very difficult to write about yourself. There is a hypothesis that psychopaths and other people who are in trouble have different communication styles when they are interviewed in person and when they answer by writing. In person, they use the cue, they get from the interviewer to answer the questions, and that way they manipulate. I have seen in my clinic over the years that disturbed people have difficulty generating answers from inside themselves. So, they use the interviewer's cue (questions) to generate an answer they think the interviewer wants to hear.

I used the narrative method, and the answers are phenomenological. This contrasts with the quantitative method, where data analysis and statistical calculations are made on the collected data. However, the case circumstances are analyzed afterwards.

I did not have any preconceived ideas about the interviewees and did not look for specific answers. Instead, I asked open questions, even though the questions were about certain areas. However, I pointed out that if they don't want to answer the questions, it's fine to write what they think is significant. This has given them the opportunity to answer in more detail. This does not imply truth. However, since the phenomenological method explores people's perception of the world, not only the immediately experienced meanings emerge, but also the meanings that are not immediately reflected. For example, the person wants to perceive themselves, so the individual's history and what is social accepted in the studies questions, meaning that they will produce what they think the interviewer wants (Giorgi, 1975).

With the phenomenological method, you gain insight into the person's inner life, which is difficult to achieve with a statistical method. This is if you only focused on statistical outcomes. A biographical method extracts the general conclusions from the study.

In the selected case, I used information from other sources from Mike Aamodt, Professor of Psychology at Radford University in Radford, Virginia, has created a timeline of Shawcross' life from his birth in 1945 to 1996, when he married Clara Neal. I got his permission to use his study in my dissertation on October 26, 2003.

There are other problems, besides the lack of dynamism in the survey form, with the questionnaire survey used in the thesis from 2004. It is the person themselves who must answer the questions, so they can choose what they want to say and how much they want to answer. It can be difficult to know whether their own accounts are true or fiction.

But despite these problems, I believe something interesting has emerged. If you don't ask for something specific, the answers will usually reflect the person's wishes about what they want to convey. Furthermore, the positive questions I asked may show a different side of the serial killer. Examining what is normal about serial killers can tell us why they are so difficult to detect. Serial killers are human beings with desires and goals. They can display human emotions such as grief, joy, anger, shame, and remorse. Perhaps we can learn more about serial killers if we recognize their humanity. We should not only focus on how serial killers are different from us but also examine what we have in common. That way, we might better understand why a person develops to be a serial killer.

Through understanding, my hypothesis is that we can prevent serial killing. Few empirical studies have been conducted on serial killers. Therefore, more research is needed in this area to know if studies of normality and abnormality in serial killers can contribute to prevention.

I consider my study from 2004 as a pilot project. There are several areas I would change if I did the same study again. With the knowledge I have today, I would suggest conducting an interview where I spend more time questioning the individual serial killers. I would conduct the study as a personal interview together with the survey, which I think is good and informative, but I might consider changing some sections of the survey.

## PARTICIPANTS: THE QUESTIONNAIRE SURVEY

In February 2002, I sent out questionnaires to some selected serial killers, and Arthur Shawcross was chosen as one of the 5 main cases. Most of the serial killers were on death row. Some had multiple life sentences, and some were in closed psychiatric wards.

Before I started the research, I contacted people who had interviewed serial killers. As mentioned, I received advice and guidance from John E. Douglas and John Arvidson on what to pay special attention to when examining serial killers.

In the questionnaire, I explain the purpose of the study and why I want to include them in the study. I point out that I don't know anything about them in advance, only that they, by definition, are serial killers, though I did know some serial killers from my research. The responses I received to the survey varied in quality. Some refused to participate in the study due to their rehabilitation program, but many did answer the questionnaire, and some of the answering first came after the thesis was finished, so I used them for further research.

I didn't want them to feel that they must live up to a certain reputation, this may have affected the Shawcross case. There has been a lot of discussion about Shawcross because he was featured in a television program about cannibalism. In this program, Shawcross talks about how he ate his victims.

However, Shawcross was not a cannibal. It also turns out that Shawcross was extremely competent at telling what the interviewer wanted to hear. At no point in my communication with him did he talk about cannibalism, but I didn't ask about it either.

I also point out that I was bound by confidentiality so that their answers from the survey would only be used in my thesis from 2004 and maybe a future PhD. Many people sell their letters from serial killers online to the highest bidder, so I assure them that this will not happen if they reply to me. Only a few serial killers have after the thesis was done given me permission to use their answers and communication in other aspects as a book.

I asked both positive and negative questions. Examples of positive questions were: "What made you happy?" and "When have you been happy?" The reason I included positive questions was to know what they perceive as positive in their own childhood.

The questionnaire was divided into five sections:

Section 1: "Life Story", where the person is asked to write their own life story until they commit their first murder.

Section 2: "Childhood 1" consisted of two questions about positive experiences in their childhood.

Section 3: "Childhood 2" included five questions about negative childhood experiences.

Section 4: "Killing" contained two questions about the person's own perception and thoughts about being a serial killer. This includes when they first killed and what they felt and thought about committing their first murder.

Section 5: "Prevention", which contains four questions about how to prevent someone from becoming a serial killer (McLean, 2004).

# EXPERIMENTAL DESIGN: MULTIFACTOR MODEL

As I noted, there are no direct references to criminal profiling theories. However, I found possible psychological and socio-cultural theories behind or underpinning criminal profiling. In addition to this, there are several factors common to serial killers. There are always exceptions, but otherwise they are strong indicators.

Ansevics & Doweiko (1991), Hickey (2016), Norris (1992b), and Ressler et al. (1988) found that serial killers have a shared history of psychological, sexual, and/or physical abuse, neglect, and attachment problems with both family and friends.

As mentioned, some of the most significant indicators are a history of enuresis after 12, torture and/or killing of animals, arson, sadistic fantasies, and violent behavior. They see their victims as objects and perceive violence against others as legitimate (Leyton, 2000, p. 339).

Pincus (2002) estimates that a combination of brain damage, childhood abuse, which can be physical, psychological, or sexual, along with a paranoid personality type, can be seen in most serial killers. These factors are seen in adults, but some of the same factors can be found in children and adolescents. Children are mostly not diagnosed with personality disorders. But we can monitor children under the age of 18, who are on the way to developing a personality disorder, which is important, since the sooner the symptom is noted, the easier it is to intervene. Throughout my career as a psychologist, I have treated many young people under 18 years of age who are in risk for developing a personality disorder, or "lopsided character development," as some psychiatrists describe it.

The following factors are not, by themselves, determinants of serial killers. However, the factors apply to people with extremely violent criminal behavior, such as serial killers.

In my thesis from 2004, I concluded that there were 29 significant indicators of serial killers when they were children and adolescents which is in the Multifactor Model.

# 8. THE MULTIFACTOR MODEL:

Table 1.

*Frequency of problems regarding 34 serial killers (McLean, 2003)*

Problems in childhood

| **Childhood:** | n | % | **Behavioral:** | n | % | **Psychological:** | n | % |
|---|---|---|---|---|---|---|---|---|
| Psychological abuse | 4 | 12 | Animal abuse | 9 | 26% | Sadistic fantasies | 33 | 97% |
| Physical abuse | 4 | 12% | Arson | 6 | 20% | Grandiosity as an interrelation | 15 | 44% |
| Sexual abuse | 5 | 15% | Involuntary urination (enuresis) (after the 12th year) | 4 | 12% | Paranoid – narcissistic personality type | 4 | 12% |
| Attachment issues | 8 | 24% | Depersonalization of other people | 8 | 24% | Antisocial personality type | 7 | 21% |
| Rebelliousness | 7 | 21% | Cruelty towards children and adults (bullying) | 5 | 15% | Phobias | 4 | 12% |
| Running away from home | 3 | 9% | Self-destructive | 2 | 6% | Psychiatric disorders (e.g., schizophrenia and depression with psychotic aspects) | 4 | 12% |
| Brain injuries | 3 | 9% | No inhibition of violence | 6 | 20% | | | |
| Neglect | 3 | 9% | Legitimization of violence | 7 | 21% | | | |
| Isolation | 25 | 74% | Compulsive masturbation | 4 | 12% | | | |
| Nightmares | 15 | 44% | Problems with control of temperament | 16 | 47% | | | |
| | | | Chronic lying | 23 | 68% | | | |
| | | | Vandalism & theft | 23 | 68% | | | |
| | | | Grandiosity as an act | 15 | 44% | | | |

Note: This table N: Participant
%: Precent of the Participant – Rounded up or down to a whole number.

*Note. Reprint from McLean, 2004, copyright by Florence McLean, 2004.*

Looking at Ressler, Burgess, and Douglas' list (1988), the strongest indicators for serial killers were: daydreaming, compulsive masturbation, isolation, lying, enuresis, rebelliousness, nightmares, vandalism, arson, theft, and cruelty to other children. Some indicators are more compelling than others. Children often daydream or lie. However, if you see children being cruel to people or animals, commit fire setting or enuresis, something is wrong with the child in one way or another.

If you find any of the above indicators in the child or young person, you can research further in the Multifactor Model and research whether there are other factors present in the child. The way to use the Model is that the more factors the child or young person has, the more likely they are to become extremely violent.

The next section will examine how the Multifactor Model can be used to identify potential serial killers.

## USE OF THE MULTIFACTOR MODEL

It will always be controversial to use the method I have just outlined. Of course, more research is needed in this area, but I believe that the Multifactor Model can be an effective method.

There are special staff in, for example, the USA who find children with severe problems, but they do not intervene until the child is threatened. Therefore, it is critical to have methods to identify children with severe problems, and this is where the Multifactor Model comes in. The method can be applied to more than just serial killers. As mentioned, serial rapes and other serial crimes where extremely violent behavior is seen would fall into a category that could benefit from the Multifactor Model. However, before the Model can be used, more research needs to be done in this area. Once the usefulness of the method has been researched, the Model could be utilized in the same way as Hare's psychopathy list (Hare, 1972, 1999). That is, you could put the 29 factors in a hierarchy, with the most significant factors at the top. Nevertheless, as mentioned, more studies are needed. The Model can be used when working with threatened children. However, you should know the stigma associated with this method for children and young people.

## CRITICISM OF THE MULTIFACTOR MODEL

There will always be a risk of stigmatizing children when working with them. In this context, there is no need to point out that there is a risk that the child may become a serial killer or an extremely violent criminal. The category of children that you would deal with in relation to the factors seen in the Multifactor Model will already have so many problems that they are stigmatized, and you need to intervene. It is critical to find and intervene with children with such severe problems as those seen here. Once you have identified them, you can start with the right intervention.

Another criticism is that it will be difficult to identify some of the factors mentioned: sadistic fantasies, nightmares, legitimization of violence, impersonal relationships, and compulsive masturbation. These factors can be a challenge to examine. Therefore, you must rely on what people tell you. This can cause problems, as these types of children and adolescents often lie or have difficulty talking about their fantasies. Sometimes they even fear their own violent fantasies. Throughout my over 20 years as a child psychologist, children have told me about their extreme violent fantasies (about rape, mass murdering and serial killing) in confidence. It is critical to note that these fantasies can help the child to release tension, and most do not act on their fantasies.

You have the option to check through other agencies whether the information you have received is truthful (e.g., social reports, school reports and medical records) and you have the option to have a psychologist to test the child with, among other tests, a projective test like Rorschach or Thematic Apperception Test/ Child Apperception Test which are projective and personality tests, that is designed to let a person respond to ambiguous stimuli, presumably revealing hidden emotions and internal conflicts projected by the person into the test. However, there will always be uncertainty about the legitimacy of children and young people's assessments. It is not so significant if it is a lie, because there is always a reason for lying. If children lie, you must figure out why. You can then help the child through it by finding out what their problems are.

The most crucial thing about this method is examining its validity. The Multifactor Model is a proposed method (pilot project) that makes predictions based on a child's behavior, actions, and personality. The idea is that if you know what to look for, you can identify children and young people with the above problems. With the right intervention, you can prevent them from becoming extremely violent criminals.

It will always be important to how to intervene with children and young people with these problems. It's not enough to take them away from their parents. The right intervention is needed to address their problems.

Based on this, and with the criticism pointed out here, I will argue that there is potential in the Multifactor Model.

## PROBLEMS WITH THE STUDY

I encountered several problems when researching serial killers. Some serial killers claim innocence. This is also a problem for most people who interview serial killers face-to-face.

There are some serial killers who claim to have been innocently convicted. They lie about their deeds and change their stories depending on who asks them.

Several people wrote to me that they were wrongly convicted. Douglas Clark wrote that it was his girlfriend, Carol M. Bundy, who copied Theodore Robert Bundy's murder and that he himself was innocent (Case 2a, 2003).

I was advised to make a deal with the serial killers I wanted to include in my thesis. Serial killers are given something in exchange for being interviewed. You can also ask questions serial killers will want to answer. These could be questions about their murders or other things they want to discuss. You can also choose to send pictures of yourself or be their pen pal, or whatever the serial killer wishes.

Before I started the study, I decided not to make deals with them. Furthermore, I did not intend to ask them questions that would catch their attention. I was therefore aware that I could risk no one would participate in the survey. I did receive quite a few letters where serial killers try to negotiate with me. Several wanted pictures, some more special than others. Most of them sent me pictures of themselves or something else in the hope of getting pictures back from me. I declined all offers. Despite this, I did receive positive and useful responses from many of the serial killers.

The strength of the narrative method in this context is that you get to hear the person's own story. You get to hear what they think, believe, and relate to their own life and their perception of being a serial killer. This is especially true when it comes to serial killers, as few have dared to cross that line by humanizing them. This is understandable, and I had my doubts, but I concluded that if I wanted to examine prevention, I had to comprehend. The most effective way I have learned is to understand someone by going to the source and asking them directly.

## SUGGESTIONS FOR FURTHER RESEARCH IN THIS AREA

For studies of serial killers, qualitative methods have been considered, using biographical and case methods (Burgess et al., 1997; Hickey, 2016; Ressler, 1992). McKenzie (1995) believes that qualitative studies have contributed to understanding serial killers. Statistics can provide results not obtained through quantitative studies. Comparative studies of serial murderers and serial rapists could be conducted to determine whether there are similarities in terms of, for example, behavior, personality, or upbringing.

This kind of triangulation, using different research methods on the same issue, could contribute to a better understanding of serial killers. Qualitative studies could generate hypotheses for quantitative studies. In other words, you could generate hypotheses from a qualitative study and test them by conducting a quantitative study. If you don't know what hypotheses to propose, the quantitative method is an excellent way to start an investigation. When triangulating, there is a greater chance of avoiding the weaknesses that different types of research can have, as you use a variety of methods in relation to one problem.

Arthur John Shawcross was one of the 5 main cases from my thesis, which

I will discuss in the next chapter. In the quotes taken from the study, I have retained spelling errors, as Shawcross wrote them.

# 9. CASE STUDY:
# ARTHUR JOHN SHAWCROSS

**Arthur John Shawcross:**

*"There are people who use what someone else has said about me, but never what I have told them" (Case, 2003).*

This case is based on Shawcross's own words and descriptions of how he perceives himself, his life, and being a serial killer. However, I have obtained some information from other sources.

Shawcross personally contacted all his victims. He is described as normal in appearance, with nothing disfiguring or abnormal about him. Shawcross could therefore contact women easily.

*"I WAS BORN IN A TINY TOWN OR KITTERY, MAINE, IN THE YEAR OF 1945." (Case, Section 1, 2003).*

Shawcross was born on June 6. 1945, in Maine, USA, two months prematurely. He weighed five pounds and was hospitalized for 20 days at a local hospital. He was the oldest of four siblings. When he was born, his mother was 18 years old, and his father was 21.

Shawcross was called strange at five years old. He often had nightmares, enuresis, and felt he didn't get the same attention from his parents as his siblings did.

I am already seeing alarming signs of unhappiness. The fact that he is described as strange and often has nightmares and enuresis. Shawcross says that he did not feel he got enough attention. These were all reasons to examine what could be wrong with Shawcross. The fact that there is no one to intervene here is alarming.

Shawcross wrote to me that his childhood was troubled. When he was four years old, he was beaten with belts and broomsticks and sexually abused by his mother and neighbors. Shawcross writes:

*"My Mother used me as her plaything in sex. I was taught at the age of four!!! At age 7, I was very scared of my mom! At age 9, I was doing things willingly. I went from my mother to my sister and cousins in giving oral sex. Then the neighbors. What had I become of that Ms. McLean?" (Case 7a, Section 1, 2003).*

What Shawcross describes here is alarming, but no one connects the dots and puts his symptoms together and examines if there was something wrong in the family. In the case of Shawcross, he learns that there are no boundaries. He describes hating it at first but eventually accepts it. In this way, he associates sex with discomfort and pain, loose control, and a basic desire for it to stop, without having any option to say no, which, at that point, starts fantasies of killing, which he carries on into his adult life when he sexually abuses and murders two children, but also later women.

Shawcross started running away from home when he was 6 years old. He got good grades in school, but his teacher says Shawcross was lazy.

At 7 years old, Shawcross talks with imaginary friends. He talked to 2 friends. One was a blonde girl slightly younger than him, and the other was a boy of his own age. They wore silvery clothes and spoke in tiny voices. He had long conversations with them, making others believe he was talking to himself.

*"I wanted so badly someone to play with" (Case, 2003).*

He was the daily joke and was subdued to cruelty of the other children, who called him "Oddie."

When children have imaginary friends beyond the normal range that many children experience at some point in their lives, it's a strong indicator that something is very wrong. It can also be a sign of sexual abuse. What happens is that the child needs to separate themselves from the abuse. They can do this by creating other characters to interact with. Sometimes the child projects the abuse onto one of their imaginary friends (or another person) so that they are not the person being abused. This is a coping mechanism to deal with abuse. Exactly what Shawcross's imaginary friends did for him is unknown, but these are symptoms that need to be addressed and researched.

When Shawcross was eight years old, a doctor described him:

*"...attractive, well-dressed, neat in spite of his being mean to younger children, was a bully, had trouble making friends, and kept running away" (Aamodt, 2002, p.1).*

But nothing is done for Shawcross. They simply state that he is a problem for others rather than helping him. We must ask ourselves, why does he have such a hard time socializing?

His grades in school dropped when he was nine years old. His mother found out that his father had another wife and a son in Australia. The family situation gradually worsens for the whole family.

**Shawcross wrote:**

*"I hate the fact that my father did not talk much to us kids. It took me until age nine to find out why! Dad had married another woman during the World War II, and she is in Australia with a son of her own" (Case 7a, section 3., sp.2., 2003).*

*"...I have been searching for my half-brother ever since .... My mother always trying to help me, but in the wrong way of things. I was my mothers favorite for some reason. That was until I past nine years of age! Then, for any reason, she whipped me with anything that was handy, strap, broom, or stick! Then dad got home and whipped me again! Until I was old enough to put a stop to it by hitting him back!!!!" (Case, section 3, sp.4, 2003).*

*"... A messed up upbringing with an over sexual mother! Right, molested as a child of 4,7, and 9!!!!" (Case, 2004). "I hated the fact that my mother made me place my mouth upon her groin area. Sucking on her breast did not bother me, but the other did!" (Case, 2004).*

Serial killers are generally reluctant to discuss abuse. The same is true for the abused in general, where it can be many years before they tell anyone. Shawcross is no exception. He first talked about the abuse after being examined by several doctors and psychiatrists (Case, 2004).

Shawcross has a clear sexual theme. He feels abused, especially by his mother. It is difficult to know and determined whether Shawcross has been exposed to the things he reports, but he had clear symptoms that indicate that he may have been exposed to sexual abuse (including enuresis, dissociation, decreasing of intelligent and behavioral changes) and there are hospital records where he has been hospitalized with paralysis from the waist down without any apparent cause.

This can also be a sign of sexual, emotional, and/or physical abuse. But whatever has happened to Shawcross, he felt very let down; he had been left alone and not helped when struggling, he was left to defend himself, and deal with whatever his struggle was, that is, neglect. There is a reason why children repeatedly run away from home, abuse animals, and set things on fire. Early childhood is characterized by bizarre and troubling behavior. The developmental perspective is clearly seen in this case, and it is also clear how significant it is for his pathological development.

In addition to this, Shawcross was also not seen or heard by his father, who was distant, because he had another family in Australia whom he had abandoned him for. This also means that he grew up with an insecure identity and an unclear picture of who he was. He doesn't have a strong, warm identification model and must resort to others to identify with, perhaps his imaginary friends or other fictional characters. This is often seen in absent fathers and dominant mothers' constellations in homes. That often leads to low self-esteem and identity issues.

In addition to this, Shawcross states that:

*"I have brain damage" (Case, 2004).*

Shawcross got a rock in the head when he was 9 years old and was hospitalized and had stitches in his head.

Shawcross repeated fourth grade at 10. He cried easily and spoke "baby talk" when bullied by older children. He bullied the smaller children and often ran away from home. Shawcross began stealing, had nightmares, and had enuresis.

Shawcross masturbated compulsively at 11. He said he would be severely punished if his mother found out. He was threatened with a knife, and his mother stuck a broomstick up his rectum (Case 7c, 10).

Already here, I see the beginnings of antisocial behavior (bullying others and stealing), which is deeply concerning, along with regressing to an early developmental stage (crying and baby talk), all signs that Shawcross is not doing well.

Shawcross says that at 14, he had sexual relations with his cousin, his sister, and his neighbor. He further states that he was raped by an unknown person (Case 10, 2004). At this point, he began to rape various animals. Shawcross wrote about his childhood:

*"THE MOST UNHAPPY TIME IN MY CHILDHOOD WAS WHEN I was made to do something that made me sick. I have already explained the meaning of that. After I had become a teenager and as a young adult, I was taught, I got past, and sort of liked it. A tough question to speak to a woman about! All I can say is Oral sex got me where I am at, I would believe" (Case, section 3, 2003).*

I communicate via letter, but Shawcross has trouble discussing sexual abuse. This is typical of abused people.

When the rape allegedly happened, Shawcross's bizarre behavior increased, and he engaged in sexually molesting animals.

Shawcross failed 8th grade at 15. He was two years behind in school at the time. He still had nightmares, had enuresis, spoke baby talk, and set bushes on fire. Shawcross wrote:

*"...I didn't set fires as a child. I did later in life for reasons I cannot get into!" (Case 7b, 2003).*

Shawcross became more violent and tortured animals. At 15, he was described as lonely and moody.

Shawcross's worrying behavior increases, and more symptoms of anti-social behavior (arson and animal torture) appear, but no one intervenes. He is falling behind in school, and his well-being is severely threatened. Shawcross's behavior becomes increasingly worrying, so now he fulfills many components of the Multifactor Model: bullying, arson, torturing animals, enuresis, but no one does anything to help Shawcross.

By the time Shawcross was 4 years old, there were already clear signs of distress. My hypothesis is that if they had found out what was wrong in the family and connected them to a treatment center, they could have helped him. About torturing animals, Shawcross wrote:

*"...Did I kill animals? I killed Muskrats for their pelts (Furs). I killed Rabbits for food. I did kill woodchucks because they would mess up a lawn... Other than that, I didn't kill for the sake of killing. I had a .22 rifle in my late teens, and I shot some crows and a pheasants or two...in the woods near home, I did shoot Rabid (rabies) Cats that people just dropped off...it was scary to see house cats in the woods with foam around their mouths. One had to kill them..." (Case 7b, 2003). "...Loneliness is another unhappy moment in my young life. When my grama passed away, it hit me hard!..." (Case 7b, 2003).*

It is very interesting that Shawcross uses the same explanation for why he killed animals as for why he killed women.

At 16, Shawcross was still in the 8th grade. He started wrestling but was cut from the team because he became too violent when he was in fight with others. Shawcross got a discus in the head and was hospitalized for four days.

Shawcross had difficulty controlling his emotions. That is a very important skill when interacting with others. If you do not have the skill, you are at risk of getting more isolated, as Shawcross has done in the past. Here, you need to do 2 things. You need to help him regulate his emotions and find out why he can't control them.

After 16, Shawcross got big and strong, and his antisocial behavior became more pronounced and violent.

At 17, Shawcross failed 8th grade again and dropped out of school. He began burglarizing and urinated at the break-in scene.

Urinating on someone's property is very immature and demonstrates resentment and hatred towards that person. It is also a sign that Shawcross had trouble regulating his emotions properly.

Shawcross was 18 when convicted of burglary. He was on probation for 18 months. Shawcross married 20-year-old Sarah Chatterton and worked at various jobs but kept getting fired.

When Shawcross was 19, he had a son with Sarah Chatterton.

At 20, he was arrested for beating a 13-year-old boy who threw a snowball at his car. He was given a six-month suspended sentence. The psychologist who examined Shawcross wrote that he had an unstable emotional personality.

Sarah Chatterton filed for divorce. In April 1966, at the age of 20, Shawcross enlisted in the military. Here, he had some discipline problems. The military psychologist wrote:

*"...Emotionally unstable personality who reacted with excitability and ineffectiveness when confronted by minor stress..." (Aamodt, 2002).*

When Shawcross was 21 years old, he met Linda Neary. She quickly became pregnant, and they married the following year. In October 1967, Shawcross was sent to Vietnam as a supply specialist.

Shawcross wrote about military killings:

*"I was taught how to kill, not how to stop..." (Case 7a, section 1, 2003). He goes on "... Or, they can become the one who killed for no reason then "I THOUGHT I WAS IN DANGER..." (Case 7a, section 5. sp.4., 2003). "The urge to kill came on me on January the 8th of 1968 in Pleiku, Vietnam: From that moment on, I went looking for anyone whom I thought was the enemy" (Case 7c, 2004).*

Shawcross says his first murder was not cold-blooded, but he developed cold-bloodedness over time in Vietnam:

*"I cried when I shot the first person in Vietnam! It's the worst thing a Human can feel to take a person's life that easy! The second one had me feeling numb inside, but after five, you get over that feeling fast. When I killed my first female enemy, I felt good inside" (Case 7a, section 1, 2003).*

Shawcross's Vietnam reporting has been debated over the years. He was never out in combat. Some claim they didn't know who he was. It is stated that he served one tour of duty in Vietnam, where he boasted of grotesque combat exploits, such as "beheading mama-sans and nailing their heads to trees as a warning to the Vietcong" (Case, 2005). But there is no record of him being in combat. After Vietnam, he was stationed at Fort Sill in Lawton, Oklahoma, as an armorer, or a weapon specialist, as he described himself (Case, 2005).

We do not know what the appendages are. It was wartime, and many things happened that were first reported later, and some things were unreported. I am sure many things happened that we don't want to reconcile. But again, for me, it is not so important what the truth was and what was not; the most important was what impact it had had on Shawcross, and that was huge. Other hypotheses I have are that it was a way for Shawcross to talk about horrendous things, leaving out empathy for the victims.

In September 1968, Shawcross (age 23) returned from Vietnam. In October, he became mentally unstable and attempted suicide with an overdose of pills. He arranged to see a military psychiatrist. The military psychiatrist wrote:

*"...Keep him away from fire, Mrs. Shawcross. I don't want to discourage you, but this is the way he gets his sexual excitement..." (Aamodt, 2002).*

The psychiatrist recommends getting Shawcross admitted to a psychiatric hospital. Mrs. Shawcross, Arthur Shawcross's wife, Linda, did not think it was her place to get him into a psychiatric hospital. Instead, she asked Shawcross's mother, Elizabeth Shawcross, to do it. The mother's answer was: "Shawcross is fine, he doesn't have mental problems." Here, again, the mother's failure to help his son, even though she was told that there were severe problems.

When a child or adolescent has extensive troubled symptoms like bullying, arson, animal torture, and enuresis, anyone who works with children and adolescents and delinquents know that there is a high risk of potentially violent and highly aggressive behavior.

In 1969, he was discharged from the military and started to drink heavily. Shawcross killed a dog that nipped him while they played.

Shawcross got a job at a paper mill. He set fire to the mill 21 days after he was hired.

In 1967, Shawcross married Linda Ruth Neary. When Shawcross was 24 years old, in 1969, he became angry with his wife, Linda Ruth Shawcross, and beat her. She was 4 months pregnant and miscarried. Linda Ruth Shawcross left Shawcross, and he returned to breaking and entering, urinating in houses, and setting fire to buildings. Shawcross was arrested and sentenced to prison on multiple arson counts. Shawcross says he was raped in prison by a fellow inmate.

Shawcross was 26 when he was released early. He met a high school friend, Penny Sherbino, in April 1972. She became pregnant after their 5th date. Three months later, they married.

Shawcross murdered 10-year-old Jack Blake on May 8, 1972, when he was 27. Shawcross wrote to me about the first murder:

*"...you want to know when I committed my first murder? Lady, that I am unable to tell you... the first one I am on record then that would be around June the 4th of 1972... Jack Blake was the one I was accused of murdering first. But the fact is that it is not so! I was not born this way as some people think, I was made this way" (Case 7a, section 1, 2003).*

Shawcross points out here that he was not born to murder but was made this way. Whether this is the whole truth is uncertain, but there is no doubt that there are several reasons why Shawcross has become a serial killer, one of them being his upbringing, domineering mother, absent father, and sexual, mentally, and physical abuse.

About four months after the first murder, on September 2, 1972, Shawcross raped and murdered eight-year-old Karen Ann Hill. He received 25 years in prison for the two murders.

When Shawcross was 28 years old (1973), he became extremely violent in prison. He filed for divorce from his wife because she did not visit him in prison (Olsen, 1993). He divorced Penny in 1975.

At 32 (1977), he antagonized the prison psychologist. He did not comply with the rules they set for him. At this point, in prison, a psychologist described Shawcross:

*"...Functioning at a borderline level of intelligence....exhibiting defective moral and social development. When he becomes upset, he acts impulsively...... The parolee did not seem interested in any of our services" (Aamodt, 2002).*

**Dr. Haveliawala wrote about Shawcross:**

*"..shows evidence of schizoid personality feature as reflecting low self-esteem and in all probability being a personality disorder, antisocial as well as schizoid" (Aamodt, 2002).*

At 34 in 1979, he was denied parole due to his uncooperativeness and failure to comply with therapy recommendations. After that he met weekly with the counselor and followed all their instructions.

**Dr. Boyar wrote:**

*"...being of abnormal character with psychosexual difficulties..." (Aamodt, 2002).*

**When Shawcross was 38 years old, Dr. Ismael Ozyaman wrote:**

*"...in good contact with reality and in good control of his mental facilities..." (Olson, 1993).*

**When he was 40, Dr. Charles Chung wrote:**

*"...a lack of any emotional disturbance..." (Aamodt, 2002).*

Here, several psychologists point out major difficulties with Shawcross, which should lead to treatment being initiated. Whether treatment would have made a difference at this point is, of course, very uncertain. At that time, Shawcross was believed to be a pedophile. I do not agree, because a pedophile has a different profile. My hypothesis is that the reason he raped and killed the two children was as simple as that they were easy targets. I think his sexual problems were more related to childhood trauma and possible post-traumatic stress disorder (PTSD).

On April 28, 1987, Shawcross was paroled for saving a prison officer from a fire. He married his pen pal, Rose Marie Walley, and they moved to Birmingham, NY. They were run out of town because of Shawcross's past. They moved to Delhi, NY, and then Fleischmanns, NY, where they were also chased out by the locals.

When Shawcross was 41 years old, prison warden Robert Kent wrote:

*"...At the risk of being dramatic, I consider this man to be possibly the most dangerous individual to have been released to this community in many years" (Olsen, 1993).*

**A psychiatrist wrote:**

*"...he has orgasmic and ejaculatory problems... no unusual sexual fantasies...having problems with anger and experiences in Vietnam. No mental disorder requiring any specific counseling or treatment at this time" (Aamodt, 2002).*

It is incomprehensible how different the reports are. Some describe Shawcross as normal with no psychiatric problems, and others describe highly alarming problems and severe psychiatric issues with Shawcross. The fact is that it is difficult to evaluate someone from your own interaction with them, because with this profile you will see a difference in the way of interacting with people, depending on whether he likes you or not, and depending on a psychological problem is present at the time.

At 42 years old, Shawcross and Rose Marie Walley move to Rochester, NY. Shawcross also starts to date Clara Neal. Shawcross began having sexual problems with Rose and had nightmares again.

On March 15, 1988, barely a year after his parole, Shawcross murdered Dorothy Blackburn. Shawcross claimed that Dorothy laughs because he couldn't get an erection. In April, he was fired from his job because of his past (Case, 2004).

**Psychotherapist Gery Mount about Shawcross:**

"Shawcross reports extensive and what sounds like very thorough counseling, both for his post-traumatic stress disorder while in Vietnam, as well as his sexual difficulties, which led to his imprisonment. He does report extensive self-awareness and what sounds like very appropriate use of psychiatric and psychological resources while at Green Haven"
(Aamodt, 2002).

**Clinical social worker, Carl Christensen:**

*". . . suffers from post-traumatic stress disorder and severe adjustment problems in dealing with women, stemming at least in part from childhood incest and sexual abuse. No particular symptoms, discomforts, or behavioral difficulties that would benefit from mental health treatment. I find that Art [Shawcross] is a well-controlled and fairly stable individual. Although he continues to exhibit some discomfort or flashes related to anger, he is able to manage these episodes extremely well. I see no need for pursuing counseling at this time" (Aamodt, 2002).*

It is strongly recommended that he does not get help, as he is doing fine.

Meanwhile, he is well on his way to murdering more women.

Shawcross wrote to me about his murders and the reasons. It is written from what he remembers, so the dates may be slightly off. From Shawcross's own memory, he stated the following: In July 1989 (43 years old), Shawcross murdered Anna Steffen. She complained that he could not get an erection. Furthermore, she wanted to notify law enforcement that she had seen Shawcross with Dorothy Blackburn. Three weeks later, Shawcross beat Dorothy Keller, his housekeeper, to death after she threatened to inform his wife about their affair. That same year, on September 29, he killed Patty Ives, a sex worker. She tried to steal his wallet and threatened Shawcross that she had seen him with Anna Steffen. On October 23, Shawcross killed June Stott, a mentally disabled woman who told others they were having a sexual relationship. That same month, Shawcross attacked Frances Brown, also a sex worker. On November 9, he murdered Maria Welch (a sex worker) because she didn't tell him she was menstruating. On November 22, Shawcross attempted to murder Jo Ann Van Nostrand, but she had a knife and fought him off. For the first time, Shawcross ejaculated with a sex worker. On November 26, he killed Elizabeth Gibson, who was also a sex worker and had some narcotics that he gave to another sex worker. The next victim was Darlene Trippi, whom Shawcross attacked on December 4. Trippi joked that he couldn't get an erection. On December 26, he murdered Felicia Stevens. June Cicero, who ridiculed Shawcross for not getting an erection, was Shawcross's last victim (Case 10, 2004).

**Shawcross wrote about the desire to murder:**

*"...I admit I have killed Men, Boys, Woman, Woman, Girls and children whom I thought were the enemy..." (Case 7b, 2003) "...once he or she has killed, the desire to do so again may become strong in them, it did in me..." (Case 7a, section 5, Sp.4., 2003).*

Shawcross first murdered 2 children for which he was in prison for 14 years. When he got out of prison, it took about 2 years before his apparent first victims disappeared. In 1988, he killed four women, and then almost a year passed without a murder. He himself wrote:

*"I forgot about it. I was not seeing so many prostitutes at that time" (Case 10, 2004).*

But then in June 1989, he killed 7 women in 1 year. The last 2 months, he has murdered 5 women.

Shawcross indicates that he has killed more than the women he is convicted of. He wrote that he cannot tell me how many people he had killed, but he can tell me about the ones he had been convicted of. But there are indications that he became increasingly careless as time passed, more chaotic. This could be the reason he was caught. Shawcross said that he wanted to get caught. He spent more time at the crime scene after dumping the bodies in the river. Shawcross wrote that if he hadn't stayed at the crime scene, the FBI would never have found him. Serial killing can be difficult for the killer. They enter a severe depression-like state (cooling-off period) after each murder. The only thing that can get them up again is the next murder.

**Shawcross wrote:**

*"What you did not know is that the FBI did not catch me with profiling!!!! I just gave up. Reality had set in, where I realized what I was doing. Plus, after being brow-beaten in the country Jail for 14 hours did not help matters anyway" (Case 10, 2004). "I gave myself up in the parking lot where my girlfriend at the time was working. I had come to realize that I had killed two women (prostitutes in one day)!" (Case 11, 2005).*

**Shawcross's own conclusion on why he developed into a serial killer:**

*"....I have had brain damage, A messed-up upbringing with an over sexual mother! Right, molested as a child of 4,7, and 9!!!! I have what is known as a chemical imbalance in the brain. My blood type is A-RH-NEGATIVE. The FBI states that I am a 47 XYYY in my makeup, but New York State has me as 47 XY. So, who is right and who was on trial? I have a lot of knowledge of many things and skills. Over normal intelligence, maybe: At the time of my arrest, I had a high kryptopyrrole (high content of kryptopyrrole is associated with schizophrenia) in my urine, which made me stronger. Why?"*

*"I have thought about it, and I would never have been caught. I could have moved on or quit altogether. Things of this nature tend to confuse the mind. Crazy I am not and never have been" (Case, 2004).*

*"I might have a wasted personality, I have no idea. But, I say, but because of the fact that I can be very angry one moment and calm the next. You tell me" (Case 7c, April 7, 2004).*

*"I guess the best thing to look for is someone who has no consciousness! I don't feel the slightest bit guilty! Now tell me why this is so? I grew up in a house that was very hard on me! But I can fully say that my desire to kill has left me in*

*prison. WHY? I have acquired 174 certificates in job skills. What good does that do me? I am an inmate professional assistant/teacher's aide..... I have taken college courses in horticulture and now teach it to others. I don't have much to give anymore, wouldn't you agree!" (Case 12, 2004).*

*"The happiest time in my childhood was, as I've said before, being alone with my own thoughts. Exploring fields, forests, and streams. I found a lot to be grateful for."*

*"I wish I had had different parents than the ones I had. "*

*"Let me say that somewhere in my life, my will to kill was born. It could have started with my mother, as I have explained to you. There is a saying: "Different strokes for different folks" (Case 12, 2004).*

*"I would suggest that everyone check children at an early age and see who is in trouble right from the start. Every child has something to hide....not every child who has trauma in their young life becomes a murderer! Once he or she has killed, the desire to do it again can become strong in them; it did in me. All serial killers have something in common. Find it, and you might find a cure!" (Case, 2004).*

You can see a combination of different factors that contribute to serial killer development. Shawcross had a brain injury, severe abuse, and his parents also had mental health issues. These three components, along with paranoia, impulsivity, and poor judgment, create a very dangerous person, in this case, Shawcross. Even in early childhood, Shawcross notices what the problem was. He realizes that no one saw, and no one helped him. Shawcross fulfills all the factors from the Multifactor Model: emotional and physical abuse, sexual abuse, attachment issues, various abnormalities and brain damage, neglect, animal torture, arson, enuresis after 12, and paranoid personality type. Shawcross was diagnosed with schizoid personality disorder and dissociation. Shawcross has no violence inhibition, legitimizes violent acts, compulsive masturbation, experiences isolation and alienation, impersonalizes his victims, and had sadistic fantasies from when he was young.

Shawcross points out that once you've killed, the desire to kill increases, so it's very critical to prevent and find potential serial killers before they commit their first murder.

Almost all violent individuals learn about violence in their childhood, by being exposed to violence themselves and/or watching others being exposed to harmful acts. Brain damage and learning behavior together can be from being abused themselves, but also from seeing violence committed against their mother, father, siblings, or others. Children can suffer from brain damage when their parents (or others) shake them violently repeatedly, or they are hit or thrown violently around. On whether Shawcross would murder again if he were out, he says:

*"You can learn from the past, but not for the future. No one knows what's going to happen" (Case, 12, 2005).*

Shawcross died on November 10, 2008, at 63, from a heart attack in prison.

Is Shawcross telling the truth? Basically, in my opinion, it doesn't really matter, as what he says speaks volumes about his State of Mind, as living in stress for years and growing up in a threatening environment can cause an overabundance of hormones in the brain that can cause physical damage to the brain. It's certain that Shawcross is lying about something, or he remembers it as he perceives it, or he forgets it as part of a defense. However, there are several hospital documents that support most of his stories. For example, Shawcross has been hospitalized twice for weeks at a time due to paralysis from the waist down.

**Shawcross wrote:**

*".....I do not want to bring it up to my memory, it is painful, a lot of shame, and I regret it badly. I did something wrong, I put it on a shield and closed the door" (Case, 10, 2004).*

Shawcross has been examined by various neurologists, doctors, and psychologists. The following has been found. Shawcross was born with an XYY chromosome. That is, he had an extra Y chromosome. This extra Y is known to cause more physical and psychological difficulties, but this cannot explain why Shawcross became a serial killer. He had different emotional stages throughout his life. Shawcross was unstable, with low stress tolerance and low self-esteem. He received several diagnoses over 22 years. He was examined by various psychologists and psychiatrists. He was diagnosed with dissociation, dissociative identity disorder (DID), PTSD, schizoid personality disorder, antisocial behavior, and psychosexual problems. His psychological development was deficient, but Shawcross had average intelligence.

In 4th grade, a Full-Scale IQ of between 86 and 92 was found. 86 is low average, and 92 is average with a mean of 100 (Wechsler, 2008). In school, it is reported that he did OK in class, getting B's and A and he sometimes knew answers on a higher level than you would expect from his age (Olson, 2014).

IQ score distribution by Wechsler: Low average: 80-90 - Average: 90-100 - High average: 110-120 (Wechsler, 2008, 2015).

Low IQ could be another sign of trauma. It has been shown that people that are traumatized, their IQ affect the intellect in IQ points, in different repeated cognitive assessments (b = 1.36, 95% CI: 0.80–1.92, $P < .001$) than the nonexposed (b = 2.31, 95% CI: 1.92–2.71, $P < .001$; P interaction = .001) (Schizophr, 2017). So, it makes sense, when they tested Shawcross again when he was 48, he had a Full-Scale IQ of 95, a verbal IQ of 95, and a performance IQ of 107. That means he was better at doing things (IQ 107, lightly above average) than explaining himself (verbal IQ 95) (Olson, 2014).

That means, at age 48, Shawcross was properly in a calmer psychological environment, where he was not constantly provoked by an ongoing trauma. I hypotheses that the IQ score properly was the closest to his real IQ, or maybe his IQ in real could even be higher.

From the ages of 38 to 40, Shawcross was considered to have a good sense of reality testing and control of his temperament (Aamodt, 2002). But this wasn't true at all, so Shawcross was good at pretending and deceiving people, which he has done his whole life.

A few years before Shawcross started murdering women, officially, a psychiatrist wrote that Shawcross had problems with orgasms and erections. The psychiatrist believed that Shawcross had no sexual fantasies, but he had anger issues and PTSD from his time in Vietnam. Shawcross's psychiatrist said he did not suffer from mental health issues.

When Shawcross was 42 years old, a psychologist wrote that Shawcross suffered from PTSD and sexual problems. Shawcross was previously incarcerated for murdering two children because of his sexual problems, according to a psychologist. That same year, a social worker stated that Shawcross suffered from PTSD along with his sexual problems. However, the social worker found Shawcross to be calm and stable. He did not recommend psychological treatment for Shawcross. Although Shawcross displayed discomfort and anger, he was able to control these outbursts shortly, when examined. The social worker saw no reason to continue counseling. Shawcross continued to commit murder the following year.

# ANALYSIS OF CASE ARTHUR JOHN SHAWCROSS

There may have been several factors that influenced Shawcross's development at the same time. His life is influenced by physiological, psychological, social, and environmental factors. There is no single reason why Shawcross became a serial killer.

Shawcross's story is complex and extensive. Throughout this book, I have discussed and examined where interventions could have been made in his life.

Shawcross's parents deny abuse, but parents often deny abusing their children. Some parents even believe that hitting their children is not abuse.

Some see it as a normal discipline method. This was the mindset of many parents when Shawcross was growing up, but this attitude is still prevalent today. Abuse is one of the key factors in pathological development. The earlier a child experiences abuse, the more severe mental disorders they are at risk of developing. In Shawcross' case, I see reported abuse as early as 4 years old.

Shawcross denies torturing animals. He says he only killed animals when he was hungry, or they were sick (Case, 2003). But others say Shawcross skinned fish alive, tortured cats, birds, squirrels, and chipmunks. Just as Shawcross kills women, he explains why he killed animals as a child. He either wants their fur or eats them, or they are in the way.

My hypothesis is that there could be something wrong with Shawcross's attachment, especially in relation to his mother. Shawcross says women are his enemies. He had an explanation for why he committed all the murders, each woman doing something bad for him. As he wrote:

*"I saw every one of the women as my enemy... female enemy" (Case, 2004).*

His own explanation for why he murdered the women was that they humiliated him or threatened to report him to law enforcement. It's difficult to determine if he really felt threatened or if that was his excuse for killing the women. But I think that he grew up distrusting women. Shawcross felt abandoned by his mother, who was supposed to be the person, in his mind, that he should have had the most love and caring from. Shawcross ended to being unpredictable and alternately committed sexual assault, and when he tried to transfer his sexuality outward, the mother/women (in his mind) would abuse him verbally, with threats and sometimes concrete punishment.

This punishment/pleasure compounded experience could be what Shawcross experienced or transfers to his victims in his murders.

Serial killers don't wake up one day and decide they want to be serial killers, and that is also what we see in the Shawcross case. Shawcross built up his behavior and deviant personality over a long time. Symptoms were present in early childhood, and he experienced problematic relationships at an early age. Shawcross has reported mental, physical, and sexual abuse. As well as having brain injuries, Shawcross has been diagnosed with disorders such as antisocial personality disorder, sociopath, and psychiatric disorders such as schizophrenia, paranoia, and debilitating personality disorder. These problematic conditions impact serial killers' upbringing and behavioral patterns. The abuse they grew up with is passed on to their victims later. The abuse becomes a part of them; it builds up inside them and gives them a sense of fear, anger, and rage, which they take out on first dead things, then animals, and finally humans, who become the target of the serial killer's actions.

However, not everyone who experiences childhood abuse grows up to become an extremely violent serial offender or serial killer. Therefore, abuse alone cannot explain why some people become serial killers. There must be more factors present. However, there are some factors that almost all serial killers have (see the Multifactor Model in Tables 1 and 2 in Chapter 8).

It is argued (MacDonald, 1963) that the three most significant factors for potential serial killers are the MacDonald triad: animal cruelty, arson, and enuresis after 12. People who commit animal cruelty show no conscience or sympathy for the animal. They feel control and power when abusing animals. This is the same sense of power and stimulation serial killers feel when killing humans.

The MacDonald triad is still used as an indicator of risk for extremely violent behavior, but reason research has review decades of literature on the Macdonald triad turned this theory on its head (Alleyne & Parfitt, 2018). The researchers found that few people convicted of violent crimes had one or any combination of the triad. Researchers suggested that the triad was more reliable as a tool to indicate that the child had a dysfunctional home environment. Researchers who have attempted to create methods to predict whether you are dealing with potential serial killers have expanded the MacDonald triad. It is what I have done in the pilot project from 2004. If you combine the triad with several of the factors significant for serial killers' development, you get ten factors that deal with childhood problems, 13 behavioral strategies, and six psychological problems (see the Multifactor Model in Tables 1 and 2). However, more research and studies are needed in this area to say something definitively about this.

As I mentioned, serial killers are difficult to predict. Firstly, you can't be sure that children who exhibit the following characteristics will become highly violent offenders. This needs further investigation. Finding that a large proportion of children who exhibit factors from the Multifactor Model are extremely violent is not the same as saying they are serial killers. It is only in extremely rare cases that someone becomes a serial killer. My method does not state that a child or young person who has several factors from the Multifactor Model is at risk for becoming a serial killer. But what can be said with certainty is that a child who meets the symptoms listed in the Multifactor Model may be at risk of a deeply problematic life. How many symptoms the child should have and to what degree will be individual. This will depend on both what the child has in themselves and what they experience in their environment.

It can be assumed that children or adolescents who exhibit several of the factors listed in the Multifactor Model have severe problems. However, the child or young person can just as easily turn their aggression inwards, and you may not see adults with extremely violent behavior. They may have substance abuse, an eating disorder, be suicidal, or self-mutilating. When reading the various cases of serial killers, many are also self-destructive in different ways. It is just as important to intervene with introverted as with extroverted aggression.

It is important to identify early abuse and intervene right away. The earlier the better, the chance of not becoming pathological. It is much easier to prevent violence than to cure violence. This never happened in the case of Shawcross. You can see that he is unwell, runs away from home, and has deeply troubling behavior. However, no one did anything; they only punished him further and pushed him further over the edge. Eventually, he kills children and women.

Source: Aamodt, 2002, Dietz et al., 1990, Olsen, 1993, Ressler et al., 1988, Bradley et al., 1992, Schizophr, 2017 and Cases 2003-2008).

*"Once you have killed someone, the next killing is like snapping your fingers"... "I am convicted of killing 11 and suspected of 19 more...I am not going further". I can be your good neighbor next door or your worst nightmare" (Case 11, 2005).*

*"FIND A CURE LADY"* (Case 7c, 2004).

# 10. DISCUSSION AND CONCLUSION

This book researched whether the theories behind criminal profiling, psychology, and sociology could be used to design a method to identify potential, extremely violent, serial rapists or self-destructive children and young people, and ultimately serial killers before they harm themselves or others.

I have done this by examining the most dangerous persons, serial killers. I have used information from my study from 2004, which was an empirical study of several serial killers from different parts of the world. From that study, I chose one case and examined it in this book.

I started this book by examining serial killers. Studies of serial killers show that some common characteristics can be identified. Serial killers often have the same troubled background. Their personality structure is paranoid, narcissistic, or grandiose. Many suffer from psychopathy, sociopathy, and a lack of guilt or empathy. At the same time, many of them had severe problems in early childhood.

There are multiple reasons why people become serial killers. There are several psychological and socio-cultural factors that may be possible reasons why some people become serial killers. It's important to know that there is no single factor that determines whether someone becomes a serial killer. Rather, there are many factors that influence development at the same time and in different stages of life. In addition to this, there must be a vulnerability in the person that allows them to develop serial killer behavior. Several researchers (Bahn et al., 1995) suggest that this vulnerability may be genetically based. However, no evidence has been found for genetic or biological factors that are crucial for someone to become a serial killer to this day. Serial killers need imagination and fantasy. Ressler wrote:

*"Most previous researchers into the murderer's mind thought that violent behavior was rooted in childhood trauma. My research convinced me that the key was not early trauma but perverse thought patterns. These men were motivated to murder by their fantasies" (Ressler, 1992, pp. 133-134).*

In my view, fantasy is relevant to understanding serial killers' thoughts and actions, but not the reason some people become serial killers. We need to find out why some people need to escape to a fantasy world. As evidence suggests, I hypothesize that fantasies arise because of the abuse that directly leads to them. These children use fantasy to escape into a world they can control and where they can act as the abuser instead of being the target of the abuse (Jackson & Bekerian, 2001).

Druktenis (1992) suggests that these sadistic and sexual fantasies help the child control their anxiety and act as an outlet for hostility and aggression directed at significant others, such as abusive parents.

Thus, it is the cause of the child becoming entangled in a fantasy world that should be focused on, not the fantasies themselves. Fantasies can be an escape or a rehearsal for future acts. When it is an escape, it is cultivated and developed. Once the child has grown up, fantasies can overtake the person's life, and eventually, if he has nothing holding him back (e.g., conscience or empathy), he can live out his fantasies.

The path to becoming a serial killer is not only triggered by fantasies, but the killer also starts with fantasies. It often takes a psychopathic/sociopathic personality structure not to develop conscience or compassion. This puts them at risk of not stopping at fantasies and committing their first murder.

It is often debated how many serial killers are mental ill. I argue that it is critical to differentiate between mental illness and mental disorder, as many serial killers have different mental disorders, like personality disorders. But I do also estimate that there may be more psychotic individuals than what is presented in the literature. I found that most serial killers are not psychotic.

They often have different personality disorders, but the diagnosis is often given after imprisonment.

It can be difficult to understand that serial killers are not psychotic in the act when reading about what these people have done. The reason for this confusion about serial killers seemingly appearing normal, yet exhibiting bizarre behavior, could be explained by the theory that serial killers have a fractured identity disorder. The theory behind the fractured identity disorder allows them to separate the part of the person that is a serial killer from the seemingly ordinary person that they are most of the time.

Another plausible explanation could be that serial killers are latently psychotic. This means that while they commit the crime, they act out their psychotic behavior. Therefore, they do not have reality testing that recognizes the victim's humanity, so the victim is simply seen as an object for the serial killer. When they are not committing crimes, they appear normal and have normal reality testing. Whether serial killers are latent psychotic or have fractured identity syndrome requires further research. But what I found was that there is no simple explanation for why some people become serial killers. Some believe that serial killers are born evil, but no evidence supports this. If you believe serial killers are evil, it is easier to "explain" their behavior, which may seem inexplicable.

I wanted to research whether the psychological and sociocultural theories behind criminal profiling theory could be used to identify potential extremely violent, serial rapists or self-destructive children and adolescents. I couldn't find any direct references to theories that underpin criminal profiling, so I had to look at the method retrospective. The criminal profiling method is based on serial offender studies. It is possible that the method was corrected afterwards so that criminal profiling methods can be adapted, and I found various statements that criminal profiling is based on psychological and sociocultural theories, including Freudian and behavioral theories. I also locate indications of various personality and sociocultural theories that aim to explain how crime scene, autopsy reports, and victimology can be used to analyze aspects such as age, gender, recidivism risk, and personality type of the offender.

I used the personality and sociocultural theories I found by analyzing criminal profiling, together with the causal factors that are important in the development of serial killers, to propose a methodology that aim to predict whether a child or adolescent is at risk of becoming extremely violent, self-destructive, a serial rapist or, in the extreme, a serial killer. From it I made a Model "the Multifactor Model" 2004. The Model consists of 29 factors divided into three areas: childhood problems (10), behavioral traits (13) and psychological problems (6), which are factors regarding children or young people.

Studies of serial killers indicate that many serial killers feel isolated and lonely, but there are many lonely and isolated people who do not become serial killers.

You can't say it's all the mother's or father's fault either. But all serial killers have problematic family relationships in one way or another. Some serial killers have brain damage. But there are many people who have a brain injury or experienced abuse and mistreatment in childhood who do not grow up to become serial killers.

Child maltreatment and abuse, especially sexual abuse, can result in intense physiological arousal. What happens is that the abused child associate's violence with sexuality. Therefore, maltreatment can be transformed into a source of sexual arousal, and throughout childhood, violence can emerge as a central source of sexual arousal. Even in play, the child is oriented towards aggression and violence, as seen in their daydreams and fantasies. This inclination towards violence becomes more extensive over time and more significant over the years. The child may become egocentric because of violent orientation. They see adults and other children as objects they can use to satisfy themselves.

Pincus (2002) and Raine (1996) found that serial killers had brain damage. Furthermore, Buchsbaum et al., (1998) studied extreme killers on death row and found that most had frontal lobe damage.

However, it is not known whether the injury was inflicted after birth or before or during birth. Raine estimates that many serial killers suffer from brain damage. Therefore, a link exists between physical abuse and serial killers. Raine argues that it is not the psychological damage but the physical damage to the brain from abuse that causes some to become serial killers. Furthermore, it cannot be determined what the triggering factor is. It is agreed that abuse harms the child. But is violence only damaging to the brain? Or does the child also learn to become violent by experiencing violence in their environment? Several studies indicate that the environment is crucial to how we manage and encounter the world. What we learn in childhood is passed on to the next generation unless we change the social legacy through intervention. But until we can clearly separate these factors (if we ever can), it remains conjecture.

Research as Perry (2003) has shown that if an infant is under stimulated or abused, certain centers in the brain, such as those related to empathy and compassion, can negatively affect their development. In this way, the changes seen on brain scans may be changes in the brain triggered by under-stimulation of certain centers in the brain. Perry (2003) suggests that physical, psychological, and sexual abuse affect brain development.

The brain is very complex, and we do not know a lot about how the environment and the brain work together.

Serial killers have several common characteristics; they often experienced neglect, abuse, and traumatic experiences in their childhood. They often come from problematic families. Furthermore, they are individuals with severe psychological problems which can be traced back to early childhood. Serial killers may appear normal. They live a relatively normal life. Some are in relationships and have children. Others live a withdrawn and lonely life, but they don't stand out from the crowd. But they can be lonely, eccentric and some stay with their mother, even though they are well over 30 years old. Others have brain damage, personality disorder, depression, obsessive compulsive disorder, paranoia, DID or anxiety. Few are psychotic and suffer from schizophrenia.

Therefore, the conclusion is that there are many factors for someone to become a serial killer. It varies from person to person, but the act of killing other people has nearly always to do with power, control, and some psychological aspect they are reliving.

I consider the studies I have done on serial killers with the Multifactor Model as a pilot project. Therefore, more research on the Multifactor Model is needed to learn the different aspects of the method.

I would suggest research of children who fulfill several of the factors from the Multifactor Model and examine if they also grow up to be extremely violent, self-destructive, or serial rapists.

Finally, I would suggest exploring how to intervene for those children who exhibit factors from the Multifactor Model.

Children who have several of the factors included in the Multifactor Model have such severe problems that it is not enough to simply remove the child from the home, which is also a traumatic event that can make the case worse. Although the child or young person may not become violent, self-destructive, a serial rapist or murderer, they are likely to have major problems for themselves and society. You need to intervene, with massive support, otherwise it will be difficult to change the child's destructive development.

# 11. FUTURE FURTHER PERSPECTIVE - SERIAL RAPE

In this chapter, I will examine whether it is possible to compare rapists with serial killers as Turvey (2001) assesses.

American researchers (Queens Bench Foundation, 1976) estimate that less than 10% of all rapes are reported (Bay, 2002). According to Balvig (1998), the dark figures are indicated through experiences from crisis centers in Denmark together with studies made from, among others, 1991, where a representative number (the number of participants is not disclosed) of women age 15 and over were asked if they had ever been subjected to rape. 3% answered in the affirmative. Of the 15 - 24-year-olds, 7% stated that they had been exposed to rape (Balvig, 1998).

Rape is a criminal act where force and violence are inflicted on the victim and where the weapon is the sexual act (Holmes & Holmes, 2002, p. 139). The definition of serial rapist is:

Turvey's definition for serial raping (Turvey, 2001, pp. 286-287).

*"Serial rape. Two or more related cases involving rape or sexual assault behavior..."* Turvey writes further *"..The act of rape is not a motive. It is a behavior that can express other offender needs beyond those if pure sexual gratification. Any series of related rapes may also include victims who were killed, either accidentally or intentionally, by the offender. Rape or sexual assault cases who involve offenders using any amount of force can easily become homicides given the right set of circumstances"* (Turvey, 2001, p. 286)

The Danish National Police's report does not use the term serial rape crimes (Boye, 1998). But the report found that out of 668 accused rapists, 69% had at least one charge for violating the penal code, of which 20% were crimes of moral turpitude (ibid., p. 24-25). If you look at the age of the perpetrators, 25% of the 27 - 30-year-olds have been convicted of other crimes of immorality (ibid., p. 27). For the 15–18-year-olds, the report shows that 15% have previously been convicted of crimes of immorality. And for the 19-20-year-olds it is 20% and for the 23-26-year-olds it is 21% who have previously been convicted of crimes of immorality (Boye, 1998, p. 27). The age distribution of previously convicted sex offenders who commit rape is distributed in such a way that from 15–18-year-olds to 27–30-year-olds the percentage rises from 15% to 25%, and then it drops again at 31-34-year-olds (17%) (ibid.). There may be several reasons for these changes, which I will not go into here. The same figures are seen in the USA, where studies show (Queens Bench Foundation, 1976) that 25% of rapists have committed rape more than once.

The Queen's Bench Foundation's (1976) studies of rape offenders showed that you can divide the offenders into four groups: "power-assertive" rapist (Power-Assertive), "anger-revenge" rapist (Anger-Retaliation), "power-affirmation" rapist (Power-Reassurance), and the sadistic rapist (Holmes & Holmes, 2002).

Power-assertive rape, in which the rapist regards his act as an expression of his virility, mastery and dominance.

Power-reassurance rape, in which the rapist is trying to resolve doubts about his sexual adequacy and masculinity.

Anger-retaliation rape, committed as an expression of hostility and rage toward women; and Anger-excitation rape, in which the rapist finds pleasure in the suffering of his victim.

It is important that the clinical work with offenders and victims indicates that the initial impact of rape is not sexual, for either the victim or the offender. That's what I've found in over 20 years of working with both the perpetrators and the victims. Although the act itself is sexual, the victim is traumatized primarily by the life-threatening nature of the attack, their helplessness, and their experience as the object of the rapist's anger. It is noted that rape should be defined as a sexual deviance, as it is sexual behavior in the service of non-sexual needs. The potential of the proposed typology for differentiating perpetrators in identifying, predisposing, planning treatment, and prognosing is highlighted.

Turvey (2001) points out that serial rapists are like serial killers in several aspects, they have the same personality type, and the motive is the same. It applies to both types of criminals that the act itself is not the motivation, but that control and power in themselves are the motive. However, I would like to point out that there is presumably a difference between the personality of the serial rapist and the rapist who commits a single rape (Beier, 1987). The motive for a single rapist can still be power and control, but you cannot compare their personality to that of serial rapist or serial killers.

Apart from the personality, the modus operandi of serial rapists and serial killers is similar. Both criminal types can spend time selecting their victims, or they can attack in a blitz attack. They collect souvenirs from their victims, and they keep records of their deeds. Looking at background history and personality type, serial killers and serial rapists are similar. Furthermore, it is often seen that serial rapists are psychopaths, as is the case with serial killers. According to Beier (1987), there is disagreement as to whether rapists are psychopaths. Some studies show that rapists are psychopaths, others that the prevalence of psychopathy is no greater than in the general population.

Rapists are socially disadvantaged and socially maladjusted. It is a criminally charged group (Boye, 1998). But despite this, Beier (1987) considers that it is not possible to put together the personality of rapists.

When talking about the entire group of rapists, it is likely that it will be difficult to clarify a personality type that applies to all of them, but American studies indicate that it is possible to create a profile of serial rapists.

Rapists, just like serial killers, have had problems with attachment to their parents. The relationship with the father has often been sporadic, he has been distant and not involving, or he has been punishing and malicious. 20% of rapists are adopted. In the case of serial killers, it is estimated that around 16% of all serial killers are adopted (Carangelo, 2003).

The mother has often been controlling, domineering, overprotective and seductive. Many rapists are seen sharing a bed with their mother until they reach puberty. Most rapists have a bad relationship with women, 51% self-report that they wanted to gain power and dominance over the women, and 92% reported that they had planned the rape in advance. As mentioned, serial rapists have also been subjected to physical abuse. Studies indicate that 74% of the "power-confident" rapists have been abused as children. Of the sadistic rapists (Anger-Retaliation), 63% have experienced physical abuse. It is estimated that it is the sadistic rapist who ends up murdering (Holmes & Holmes, 2002, p. 155).

MacCulloch et al. (1983) found in a study of rape offenders that fantasy was an important component of the rape. Of the 62 participants, 13 out of 16 had reported back that their rape could be linked to previous fantasies they had had about rape.

The increasingly progressive fantasies that serial rapists have about women can end in murder. However, the difference between serial killers and rapists as murderers is that rapists often kill their victims by accident, or they kill to eliminate their only witness. Serial killers murder because they have a desire for full control and power over the victim. The serial rapist also rapes to gain control and power. In this way, the murder of serial killers and serial rapists is different, but the motive for each of their actions is similar. There are, however, some serial killers who are sexually stimulated by the murder, which can be explained on the basis that the mistreatment they have experienced may be at risk of being transformed into a source of sexual arousal.

As is also the case with serial killers, there can be several reasons why the criminal does not report back that they have been subjected to mistreatment. It may be that the mistreatment is repressed, but it may also be that serial killers or serial rapists do not want to acknowledge the humiliations they have been subjected to, therefore it is easier to say that they had a good childhood to avoid talking about the terrible experiences they have been exposed to. They are used to be "tough guys", and they maintain this façade.

Groth & Birnbaum (1979) found that rapists feel a lack of internal control, therefore they have a need to control others. The studies indicate that rapists suffer from psychopathy. In a study, there were 16 people who had committed rape, they also had the diagnosis of antisocial PD. Other studies (Scully, 1990) are not so convincing. In relation to serial rapists, there is uncertainty as to whether they have experienced abuse in their childhood. Groth & Birnbaum (1979) examined 500 rapists and 1/3 had experienced sexual abuse in their childhood. Scully (1990) found that 10% of 114 male rapists had experienced sexual abuse in childhood.

There is not enough research on rape and rapists worldwide. We defiantly need more research in the area will give us more insight into rapists. Newer studies show that stranger rapes, especially those involving serial rapists, are among the most difficult cases for police to solve. Recent research in the field of offender profiling has focused on making inferences between crime scene variables and offender characteristics to aid police in their investigation. This study analyses a Spanish population sample of 231 one-off and 38 serial sexual offenders, with the aim of developing an empirical model to help predict new cases of serial stranger rapists. A multivariate logistic regression model, which included eight significant crime-related variables, was able to predict whether an unknown offender was a single or serial rapist based on the victim's description alone. The predictive validity of the model was tested using a receiver operating characteristic (ROC) analysis, and the result of the AUC value indicated a moderate-level predictive ability. The final model correctly identified almost 80% of serial stranger rape cases. The implications for criminal investigation are discussed (Ramirez et al. 2022).

## CASE: Randall Brent Woodfield

### Epithets: The I-5 Bandit, The I-5 Killer

Randall Brent Woodfield was born on 26 December 1950, and is an American spree killer/serial killer, serial rapist, kidnapper, robber, burglar, and former football player who was dubbed by the media as the I-5 Killer or I-5 Bandit because of the crimes he committed along the Interstate 5 corridor that runs through Washington, Oregon, and California. Prior to his capture, Woodfield was suspected of multiple sexual assaults and murders. Although he has only been convicted of one murder, he has been linked to a total of 18 murders and is suspected of killing up to 44 people.

A native of Oregon, Woodfield was the third child of a prominent Newport family. He began exhibiting abnormal behavior in his teens and was arrested for indecent exposure while still in high school. An athlete for most of his life, Woodfield played wide receiver for the Portland State Vikings and was drafted by the National Football League in 1974 to play for the Green Bay Packers but was cut from the team during practice after a series of indecent where he exposure himself and was arrested.

Randall Woodfield was born on December 26, 1950, in Salem, Oregon, and was the third child of an upper-middle class family. His mother was a homemaker, and his father was an executive at Pacific Northwest Bell. He has two older sisters, one of whom became a doctor and the other a lawyer. The Woodfield family was 'well-known and respected' in their community.

Woodfield was raised in Otter Rock, Oregon, a small coastal town about 8 miles (13 km) north of Newport. Popular among his peers, he was a football star at Newport High School. Although his childhood was by all accounts stable, Woodfield began exhibiting sexually dysfunctional behavior during middle school, particularly with exposing himself in public. While in high school, Woodfield exposed himself to a group of teenage girls on the Yaquina Bay Bridge and was arrested. His football coaches helped cover up the incident to prevent him from being ousted from the team, although his parents forced him to go to therapy after the incident.

Woodfield left Wisconsin in late 1974 and returned to Portland as he felt dishonored by his inability to sustain his football career. In early 1975, several Portland women were attacked by a knife-wielding man, forced to perform oral sex and then robbed of their handbags. Law enforcement responded to the string of crimes by using female police officers as decoys, and on 3 March 1975, Woodfield was arrested after being caught with marked money from one of the undercover officers. When questioned, he confessed to the crimes and blamed poor sexual impulse control, which he claimed was a result of his use of steroids. In April 1975, Woodfield pleaded guilty to reduced charges of second-degree robbery. He was sentenced to ten years in prison but was released on parole in July 1979 after serving four years.

On October 9, 1980, Cherie Lynn Ayers, an X-ray technician and former classmate of Woodfield, was sexually assaulted and murdered in her apartment at SW Ninth Place in downtown Portland. Her body was discovered on October 11, by her fiancé. She had sustained severe bludgeoning and multiple stab wounds to the neck.

Ayers, a graduate of the University of Oregon, had known Woodfield since second grade, having attended the same schools in Newport.

During Woodfield's prior four-year imprisonment, he and Ayers had corresponded via letters. Ayers' family suspected Woodfield's involvement in Cherie Lynn's murder and provided his name to law enforcement. He was interrogated but declined to take a polygraph examination. The homicide detectives who investigated the case found his answers to be generally "evasive and deceptive." However, because his blood type did not match the semen found on the victim, no charges were filed.

One month later early in the morning, on Thanksgiving Day, November 27, Woodfield arrived at the north Portland home of Darcey Renee Fix, 22, with the intent of assaulting her. Woodfield had known Fix during college and was the ex-girlfriend of one of his close friends. Douglas Keith Altig, 24, was present at Fix's home when Woodfield arrived. After this event, both Fix and Altig were bound and shot to death. Also, there .32 caliber revolver was missing from the home. Due to his acquaintance with Fix, Woodfield was questioned about the murders, but law enforcement found no concrete evidence pointing to his involvement.

After committing the murders of Fix and Altig, Woodfield began a series of robberies throughout the Pacific Northwest: On December 9, 1980, Woodfield, with a false beard, held up a person at Vancouver, Washington, gas station at gunpoint. In Eugene, Oregon, four nights later, on December 13, he robbed an ice cream parlor. On December 14, he committed another robbery at a drive-in restaurant in Albany, Oregon. During one of the robberies, Woodfield wore what appeared to be a bandage or athletic tape across the bridge of his nose, like nasal strips worn by football players. On December 21, Woodfield aggressively assaulted a waitress in Seattle while wearing a false beard, trapping her in a restaurant bathroom and forcing her to masturbate him at gunpoint.

On January 8, Woodfield committed a robbery at a Vancouver gas station that he also had been targeted in December. In this instance, he forced a female attendant to expose her breasts after emptying the cash register. Three days later, on January 11, he robbed a market in Eugene. The following day, on January 12, he shot and wounded a female grocery clerk at a store in

Sutherlin, Oregon. On January 14, a man matching the description of the I-5 Bandit witch also means wearing a false beard entered by forced a home where two sisters lived, aged eight and ten. He ordered the girls to undress and sexually assaulted them, forcing the ten years old girl to perform fellatio.

Four days after, in Salem, a man matching the same description entered an office building and sexually abused two women, Shari Hull and Beth Wilmot, after that he killed Hull and wounded Wilmot, who later died of her wounds.

January 26 and 29, he traveled to southern Oregon and committed robberies in Eugene, Medford, and Grants Pass. In the latter location, two females, a clerk and a customer, were assaulted by a person resembled the previous description whit the nasal strip over the nose and false beard.

The bodies of Donna Eckard, 37, and her 14-year-old daughter, Janell Charlotte Jarvis, were found on February 3, 1981, together in a bed in their home in Mountain Gate, California, north of Redding. Both had been shot several times in the head.

Forensic tests revealed that the girl had also been sexually assaulted. On the same day in Redding, a female store clerk was kidnapped and raped during a robbery, and an identical crime was reported in Yreka, California on February 4, with the same man robbing an Ashland, Oregon motel that night.

Five days later, in Corvallis, a man matching the I-5 Bandit's description held up a fabric store, molesting the clerk and her customer before he left. On February 12, 1981, robberies committed by a man matching the I-5 Bandit's description occurred in Vancouver, Olympia, and Bellevue, Washington. The Olympia and Bellevue incidents included three sexual assaults.

After an impending visit to Portland, Woodfield planned a Valentine's Day gathering at the city's downtown Marriott Hotel, extending invitations to acquaintances from college. After no guests arrived, Woodfield proceeded to the Beaverton residence of 18-year-old Julie Reitz, with whom he had become acquainted during his tenure as a bouncer at The Faucet, a bar in Portland. Woodfield arrived at her residence at approximately 2:00 a.m. on February 15. At approximately 4:00 a.m., Woodfield perpetrated a sexual assault against Reitz, after which he fatally shot her in the head. Police investigators on the scene determined that Reitz had consumed a glass of wine with her attacker and had also begun to prepare coffee. A package of instant coffee was discovered on the kitchen counter, and water in a kettle had been left to completely boil away. By February 28, the investigation was now focused on Woodfield. However, by then the I-5 Bandit had struck three more times: in Eugene on February 18 and 21, and with another sexual assault in Corvallis on February 25. Detectives in Marion County compiled a call log indicating that Woodfield had placed calls via calling cards at payphones near the murder sites around the times they were committed.

Finely on March 5, 1981, Woodfield was brought into the Salem Police Department for an interrogation after Lisa Garcia positively identified him in a photo lineup. Two days later, on March 7, 1981, a search warrant was executed on Woodfield's apartment in Springfield, Oregon. The search yielded a spent .32 shell casing, which was found inside a racquetball bag, as well as a roll of tape that matched the tape found on the victims. On March 7, Woodfield was taken into custody after being positively identified by several Oregon robbery victims. On March 16, indictments for murder, rape, sodomy, attempted kidnapping, armed robbery, and illegal possession of firearms were initiated from various jurisdictions in Washington and Oregon.

In the summer of 1981, Woodfield was tried in Salem for the murder of Hull, as well as charges of sodomy and attempted murder (of Wilmot). Wilmot testified against him in the trial and was key in the prosecution's conviction. Chris Van Dyke, son of actor Dick Van Dyke, was the Marion County District Attorney at the time and prosecuted the case. In a subsequent interview, Van Dyke characterized Woodfield as "the coldest, most detached defendant I've ever seen. "Following a three-and-a-half-hour deliberation on

June 26, 1981, Woodfield was convicted on all counts and sentenced to life imprisonment, with an additional 90 years.

In October 1981, a second trial was held in Benton County, Oregon, during which Woodfield was convicted on charges of sodomy and weapons possession related to one of the attacks that occurred in a restaurant bathroom. The jury found Woodfield guilty and imposed an additional 35 years to his already-instated sentence. Woodfield is currently serving his sentence at the Oregon State Penitentiary in Salem. In October 1983, Woodfield sustained injuries at the hands of another inmate during an episode of prison disturbance.

Investigation in 1990 revealed the possibility of Woodfield's involvement in as many as 44 homicides, based on the discovery of additional victims. In 2001 and 2006, DNA evidence linked Woodfield to two more murders in Oregon that occurred from 1980 to 1981. Consequently, Woodfield was sentenced to life imprisonment, with an additional 99 years.

Source: The Oregonian, 2012, Rule, 1984, McPadden, 2017 and Eggers, 2017.

# EPILOGUE

It has been a real challenge to find good and newer reference that not just describe the research I have in this book, and when that was the case, I have chosen the older studies, where there are newer good sold studies, I have referenced to them.

When you look at many of the references in this book, we see a clear patten of older theory, where there was some valid newer examination, I have used them.

This tells me that we really need some more research in this field, that been about criminal profiling, serial murder or serial perpetrator.

I think, we will see more serial killers in the next 10 to 20 years, so we need to be ahead of it.

I hope I am wrong, but I do not think that cell date and DNA will not stop serial killers in the future.

It will just make them be aware of all the new technology.

# From Arthur John Shawcross:

To Florence McLean

May you do well
in your studies

Arthur John Shawcross
2003

# From other serial killers:

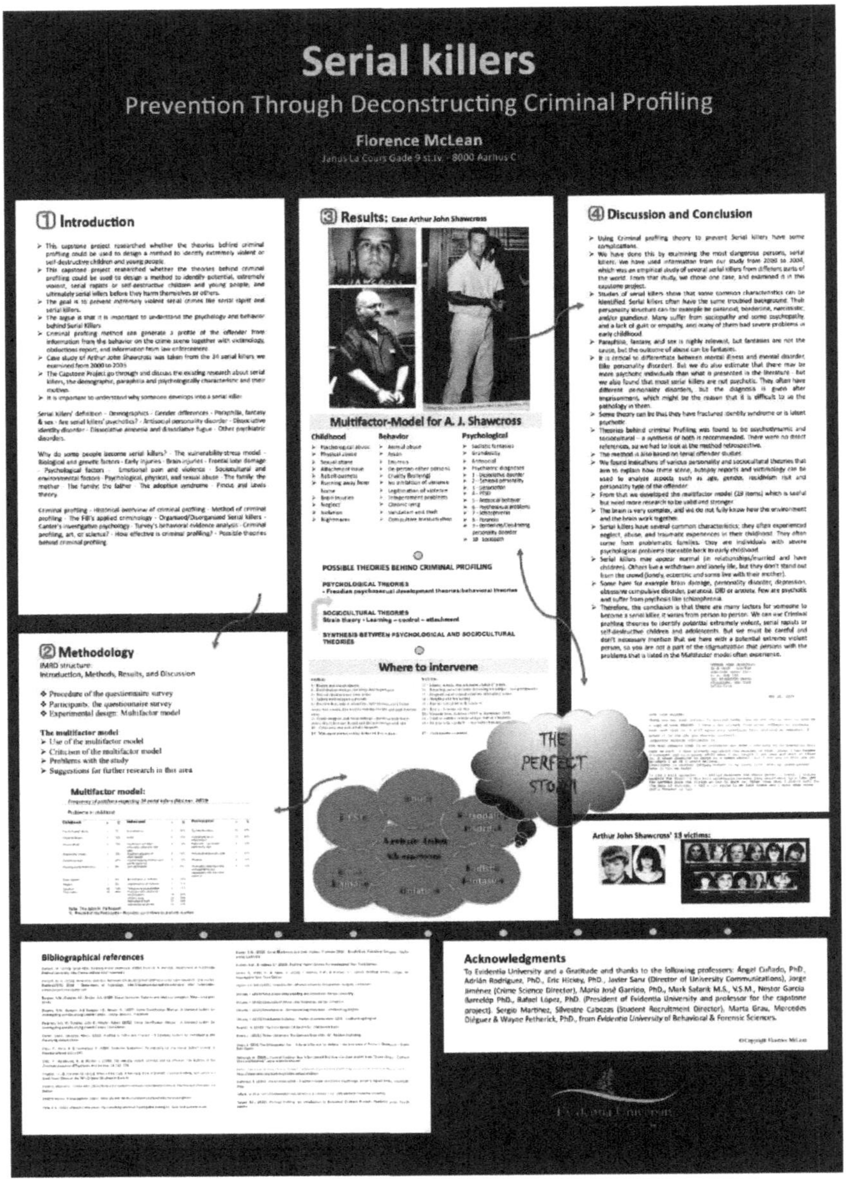

Serial killers
Prevention Through Deconstructing Criminal Profiling
Florence McLean
Janus La Cours Gade 9 st.tv. · 8000 Aarhus C
1 Introduction
2 Methodology
IMRD structure:
Introduction, Methods, Results, and Discussion
Procedure of the questionnaire survey
Participants: the questionnaire survey
Experimental design: Multifactor model
The multifactor model
Use of the multifactor model
Criticism of the multifactor model
Problems with the study
Suggestions for further research in this area
Multifactor model:
3 Results: Case Arthur John Shawcross
Multifactor-Model for A. J. Shawcross
Childhood
Behavior
Psychological
POSSIBLE THEORIES BEHIND CRIMINAL PROFILING
PSYCHOLOGICAL THEORIES
SOCIOCULTURAL THEORIES
Where to intervene
THE PERFECT STORM
4 Discussion and Conclusion
Arthur John Shawcross' 13 victims:
Bibliographical references
Acknowledgments
To Evidentia University and a Gratitude and thanks to the following professors: Ángel Cuñado, PhD., Adrián Rodríguez, PhD., Eric Hickey, PhD., Javier Sanz (Director of University Communications), Jorge Jiménez (Crime Science Director), María José Garrido, PhD., Mark Safarik M.S., V.S.M., Nestor García Barcelóp PhD., Rafael López, PhD. (President of Evidentia University and professor for the capstone project). Sergio Martínez, Silvestre Cabezas (Student Recruitment Director), Marta Grau, Mercedes Diéguez & Wayne Petherick, PhD., from Evidentia University of Behavioral & Forensic Sciences.

# BIBLIOGRAPHICAL REFERENCES

Aamodt, M. (2002). Serial Killer Timeline Arthur Shawcross. Article from Dr.

A. Aamodt, Department of Psychology Radford University: http://www.radford.edu/~maamodt/

Aamodt, M. G. (2016). Serial killer statistics. Retrieved (06.06.2023) Radford/FGCU Serial Killer Research - Site Leader, Radford/FGCU SKDB - Department of Psychology. http://maamodt.asp.radford.edu/serial_killer information center/project description.htm

Aharonovitch, Esti (2005). "To be burned". Haaretz (in Hebrew) (published August 2, 2005) https://www.haaretz.co.il/misc/2005-08-02/ty-article/0000017f-f10c-d8a1-a5ff-f18eba5d0000.

Ainsworth, P.B. (2002). Offender Profiling and Crime Analysis. Willan Publishing.

Alarid, L.; Marquart, V.; Burton, J.; Cullen, F., & Cuvelier, S. (1996). Women's Roles in Serious Offenses. Justice Quarterly 13(3): 432-54.

Allely, C. S., Minnis, H., Thompson, L., Wilson, P., Gillberg, C., (2014). Neurodevelopmental and psychosocial risk factors in serial killers and mass murderers. Gillberg Neuropsychiatry Centre Sahlgrenska Academy. Aggression and Violent Behavior, 19(3), 288-301. doi:10.1016/j.avb.2014.04.004

Alleyne, E, Parfitt, C.H. (2018). Not the Sum of Its Parts: A Critical Review of the MacDonald Triad https://orcid.org/0000-0003-4335-7176 - View all authors and affiliations - Volume 21, Issue 2 - First published online April 9, 2018 https://doi.org/10.1177/1524838018764164

Allison, R. (2015). Analysis of serial killings in the US - on SAS Learning Post July 20, 2015 - Topics | Analytics Data Visualization.

APA, (2022) American Psychiatric Association Diagnostic and Statistical Manual of Mental Disorders, Fifth Edition, Text Revision (DSM-5-TR). Washington, DC, American Psychiatric Association, 2022.

ArcGIS (2025) ArcGIS Desktop: Release 11. Redlands, CA: ESRI Environmental Systems Research Institute. https://www.arcgis.com/index.html

Ansevics, N. & Doweiko, H.E. (1991) Serial murderers: Early proposed development Model and typology. Psychotherapy in Private Practice 1991, 107-122.

Bahn, B. Hazelwood, R. Morrison, H. Ressler, R. (1995). Mind of a killer. CD-ROM.- Chatsworth, Calif: Cambrix Publishing.

Bandura, A., & Walters, R. H. (1963). Social learning and personality development. New York: Holt, Rinehart & Winston.

Bandura, A. (1973). Aggression. A social learning analysis. Prentice-Hall.

Baker, Donald P. (1998) 17-year-old sentenced to die in Fla. Penalty for young 'vampire' murderer part of national trend – published at the Washington Post on February 28, 1998

Barker, C. (2021) Warrior Genes - Mod Fiction Stud. Author manuscript, available in PMC 2021 Jan 20. *Published in final edited form as:* Mod Fiction Stud. 2020 Winter: 66(4): 755–779. doi: 10.1353/mfs.2020.0050

- PMCID: PMC7116611 - EMSID: EMS109294 - PMID: 33479549.

Barr, Alwyn (1976) "Handbook of Texas Online." Biography: Whitman, Charles Joseph (1941-1966) TSHA - Texas State Historical Association

- tshanonline.com. Published 1976. Updated September 1, 1995.

Barnes, et al., (1984) The Mind of a Murderer: Part 1+2: Directed by Michael Barnes, George Rivera. With Kenneth Bianchi, Will Lyman, Judy Woodruff. PBS Frontline: The Mind of a Murderer Part I (1984) TV episode - Ratterfat McWhiskers | Archive.org.

Bates, B. R. & Gerald, Cliff (2021) Missing from Michigan Ave: The Case of

John Eric Armstrong Paperback – Kendall hunt publishing company

Beadle-Brown, J., Richardson, L., Guest, C., Malovic, A., Bradshaw, J and Himmerich, J. (2014). Living in Fear: Better Outcomes for people with learning disabilities and autism. Main research report – January 2014 - Canterbury: Tizard Centre, University of Kent.

Beier, H. (1987). Voldtægtsforbryderen Voldtægtsforbrydelsen. Jurist- og Økonomforbundets Forlag.

Berger, T. L. (1996). Den samfundsskabte virkeligheden videnssiciologisk afhandling. Lindhardt og Ringhof.

Berk, L.E. (1997): Child Development. Allyn And Bacon.

Bernstein, E.M., & Putnam, F.W. (1986). I Ross, (1997): Dissociative identity disorder: Diagnosis, Clinical Features, and Treatment of Multiple Personality; John Wiley & Son.

Berry-Dee, Christopher, Wuornos, Aileen (2006) Monster - Inside the Mind of Aileen Wuornos - 30 Jun. 2006 - John Blake Publishing Ltd

Berthon, S. (2001) Cannibal TV - Miniseries 2001.

Bihrle, S, Buchsbaum, MS, Raine, A, Stoddard, J, (1998) Prefrontal glucose deficits in murderers lacking psychosocial deprivation. Neuropsychiatry, Neuropschology, and Behavioral Neurology. 1998: 11 1-7.

Bingham, John (2009). "Belgium 'joker' creche killer snorted with laughter in police interrogation". *The Telegraph* on 13. September 2012.

Bradley, M.M., Greenwald, M.K., Petry, M.C., & Lang, P.J. (1992) I: Christianson, S.Å., (1997). Traumatiske erindringer. Hans Ritzels Forlag. Company, Inc.

Breo, Daniel L.; Martin, William J.; Kunkle, Bill (2016). The Crime of the Century: Richard Speck and the Murders That Shocked a Nation-Skyhorse; Reissue edition (May 10, 2016) ISBN-10: 9781510708860

Brewer-Smyth, Kathleen; Burgess, Ann, W. (2019) - Neurobiology of Female Homicide Perpetrators - Research article First published online July

22, 2019 - Volume 36, Issue 19-20 https://doi.org/10.1177/0886260519860078

Brittain, 1967). I: Mitchell, E.W. (1996): The Aetiology of Serial Murder: Towards an Integrated Model. Article from "Ed Mitchell Homepage – University of Oxford": http://users.ox.ac.uk/~zool0380/home.htm. p. 38.

Borowski, John (2017) Dahmer's Confession: The Milwaukee Cannibal's Arrest Statements Paperback – October 1, 2017

Botelho, Greg (2013). "Serial killer, rapist Richard Ramirez – known as 'Night Stalker' – dead at 53". CNN. p. 3. Updated June 9, 2013. https://edition.cnn.com/2013/06/07/justice/california-night-stalker-ramirez-dead/

Brophy, John (1966) The Meaning of Murder (1966). ID:59008 - Published: Ronald Whiting & Wheaton.

Brown, S.E. (1984). Social class, child maltreatment and delinquent behavior.

Criminology, 22 (2), pp. 259-278.

BT (2023) Sagen om den 37-årig – hvad ved vi og hvad mangler vi at vide. BT online den 7. juli 2023.

Burgess, A.W.; Hartman, C.R.; Ressler, R.K.; Douglas, J.E., & McCormack, A. (1986), Sexual homicide: A motivational model. Journal of Interpersonal Violence, 1, 251-272.

Burgess, A.W.; Douglas, J.E.; Ressler, R.K. (1988). Sexual Homicide: Patterns and Moti- ves. Lexington, Mass.: Lexington Books.

Burgess, A.W.; Burgess; A.G Douglas, J.E.; Ressler, R. (1997). Crime Classification Manual. A Staqndard System for Investigating and Classifying Violent Crimes – Jossey-Bass Inc., Publishers.

Burgess, Ann W, Douglas, John E., Ressler, Robert (2012). Crime Classification Manual - A Standard System for Investigating and Classifying Violent Crimes, Third Edition.

Burgess A N, Groth; A. W., Holmstrom L. L. (1977) Rape - power, anger, and sexuality. NCJ Number: 43688. Journal. American Journal of Psychiatry Volume: 134 Issue: 11, Dated: (NOVEMBER 1977) Pages: 1239-1243 - Date Published 1977

Burgess, R.R., & Hazelwood, A.W. I: O'Connor, T. (2003b). History Of Profiling.

Artikel from "Criminal Justice" http://faculty.ncwc.edu/toconnor/ Butterfield, Michael, since (1990) – The Zodiac Killer facts https://zodiackillerfacts.com/

Butterfield, Michael (2025) The Zodiac Killer: The Story of America's Most Elusive Murderer Paperback – Publiser Sirius - ISBN-10 1398851779 ISBN-13 978-1398851771

Canter, David, Laurence, Alison. (2012). Profiling in Policy and Practice - A Standard System for Investigating and Classifying Violent Crime.

Carangelo, L. (2003). Chosen Children - Adopted Killers. Access Press.

Carlo, Philip (2009) The Ice Man: Confessions of a Mafia Contract Killer Mass Market Paperback – April 28, 2009, Publisher: St. Martin's Paperbacks ISBN-10 0312938845

CASE NO. SC00-1199 (2001) In the Supreme Court of Florida Case NO. SC00-1199 Aileen C. Wuornos, Appellant, v. State of Florida, Appellee.

Chesler, Phyllis. (1972). Women and madness. Doubleday. Chesler, Phyllis. (1991, January 16). Personal communication with Aileen Carol Wuornos. Transcript/videotape Chesler, Phyllis. (1993). A woman's right to self-defense: The case of Aileen Carol Wuornos. St. John's Law Review, 66(4), 933–977. https://scholarship.law.stjohns.edu/lawreview/vol66/iss4/1/

Chesler, Phyllis. (2020). Requiem for a female serial killer. New English Review Press. 6 Issue 3 Article 2 5-2021 Profiling a Unique Female Serial Killer: Aileen Wuornos' Life of Violence - Phyllis Chesler Organization

Chesler, Phyllis (2021) Dignity: A Journal of Analysis of Exploitation and

Violence Volume

Christianson, S.Å., (1997). Traumatiske erindringer. Hans Ritzels Forlag.

Company, Inc.

Chun, R. (2019). Modern Life Has Made It Easier for Serial Killers to Thrive https://www.theatlantic.com/magazine/archive/2019/10/are-serial-killers-more-common-than-I-think/596647

Clark County Prosecuting Attorney (CCPA, 2008) "Aileen Carol Wuornos". Archived from the original on September 14, 2008. Retrieved September 26, 2008.

Clary, Mike (1991). "A Mother's Love". Los Angeles Times. Archived from the original on May 27, 2020. Retrieved December 17, 2019

Clay - PMID: 31984012 - PMCID: PMC6876420 - Flippin, Perry (2007). "UT

tower shooting heroes to be honored". gosanangelo.com. Archived from the original on September 5, 2007.

Colorado Judicial Branch (gov)_document, 2013 - 2014-12-09 People's Submission of List of Charges (P-100) .pdf - Case No. 12 CR 1522

Cook, Chris, (2024) Peter Sutcliffe: The Full Crimes of The Yorkshire Ripper Pen and Sword True Crime

Cooper, Alexia & Smith, L. Erica (2011) (Bureau of Justice Statisticians) PAT TERNS & TRENDS Homicide Trends in the United States, 1980-2008 Annual Rates for 2009 and 2010 - U.S. Department of Justice Office of Justice Programs Bureau of Justice Statistics

Court record, (2001) R v Harris 20. December 2000 - NSWCCA 469 (20 December 2000), Court of Criminal Appeal (NSW, Australia) Supreme Court of New South Wales - Court of Criminal Appeal

Court TV and Scripps News Fort Myers, FOX4, (2024). FL v. Wade Wilson: Strangled Women Murder Trial https://www.courttv.com/news/fl-v-wade-wilson-strangled-women-murder-trial/

Cullberg, J. (1996). Dynamisk psykiatri - København: Hans Reitzels Forlag. Crystal, Ponti (2020). "'The Iceman': An Undercover Agent Reflects on Taking

Down Notorious Hitman Richard Kuklinski". A&E. June 20, 2020.

Dahmer, Lionel (1994) - A Father's Story – publisher January 1, 1994 - William Morrow and Company, Inc.

Dahmer, Lionel (2021) - A Father's Story – Echo Point Books & Media, LLC. Dahmer, Dahmer & Phillips, (1994), Jeffry Dahmer, Lionel Dahmer & Phillips,

Stone (1994) "Jeffrey Dahmer - Confessions of a Serial Killer" Stone

Philips interview from Dateline NBC with serial killer Jeffrey Dahmer recorded in 1994.

Davis, C. A. (2001). (IPM, dist.) ISBN 0-7490-0535-1 from Women Who Kill: Profiles of Female Serial Killers Rotella, Allison & Busby.

Dahl, A.A., & Dalsegg, A. (2002). Charmør og tyran – et indblik i psykopaternes og ofrenes verden. Munksgaard Danmark.

Denzin, N.K. (1978). The Research Act. 2nd edn., New York: McGraw-Hill.

De Young, R. (1999). Environmental Psychology Environmental Psychology. In D. E. Alexander and R. W. Fairbridge [Eds.] Encyclopedia of Environmental Science. Hingham, MA: Kluwer Academic Publishers.

Dhinoj Dings (2017) Rodney Alcala The Dating Game Killer: A Psychological Profile

Published https://www.ibtimes.com/rodney-alcala-dating-game-killer-psychological-profile-2623321 12/04/17 AT 6:05 AM EST

Dietz, P., Harry, B. & Hazelwood, R. (1986). Detective Magazines: Pornography for the Sexual Sadist? Journal of Forensic Science 31(1): 197.
Dietz, P.; Hazelwood, R., & Warren, J. (1990). The sexually sadistic criminal

and his offenses. The Bulletin of the American Academy of Psychiatry and the Law, 18, 163-178.

Discovery Channel, (2002a). Discover My World. Watch the, 29.07.2023.

Discovery Channel, (2002b). FBIs arkiver. Discovery Nordic (Fakta). Watch the 31.01.2023.

Discovery Channel, (2003a). På sporet af en morder: The Hillside Stranglers.

Discovery Nordic (Fakta). Watch the 29.07.2023.

Discovery Channel, 2003b). Gerningsstedet. Discovery Nordic (Fakta). Watch the 03.04.2023.

Discovery Channel (2004). Beltway Sniper, Discovery Nordic (Fakta). Watch the 02.01.2022.

Douglas, J.E., & Olshaker, M. (1995). Mindhunter: Inside the FBI's elite serial crime unit. London: Mandarin.

Douglas, J.E., & Olshaker, M. (1998). Obsession: A Lisa Drew Book – Scribner. Douglas, J.E., & Olshaker, M. (2001). The Cases That Haunt Us - Pocket Books

Douglas, J.E., & Olshaker, M. (2022). When a Killer Calls: A Haunting Story of Murder, Criminal Profiling, and Justice in a Small Town (Cases of the FBI's Original Mindhunter Book 2).

Dover, Kristina Robb (2023) A Killer's Mind: Kristen H Gilbert – article posted on October 24, 2023 "Restore Mental Health" https://restore-mentalhealth.com/a-killers-mind-kristen-h-gilbert/ Druktenis (1992). I O'Connor, T. (2002a): The role of childhood trauma as a cause of serial killing. Article from "Criminal Justice" http://faculty.ncwc.edu/toconnor/

Egger, S. (1998). The killer among us: An examination of serial murder and its investigation. New Jersey: Prentice Hall

Eggers, Kerry (2017). "'I-5 Killer' played for PSU before taking dark turn". Article in Portland Tribune. Retrieved January 24, 2017.

Emamzadeh, A. (2019) psychopathy - You May Be Able to Identify

Psychopaths by Their Speech 6. Changing the subject when they're not in control.

Psychology today – online https://www.psychologytoday.com/intl/blog/finding-a-new-home/201904/you-may-be-able-to-identify-psychopaths-by-their-speech

Esparza, Manuel A., Turvey Bent (2016) Behavioral Evidence Analysis International Forensic Practice and Protocols, 1st Edition.

Eysenck, H. J. (Hans Jurgen) (1982) Personality, genetics, and behavior: selected papers 1916-1997. New York Praeger 1982

Falcon, Gabriel (2010) Convicted serial killer won on 'Dating Game' CNN's AC360.

FBI (1933) Records: The Vault – The Zodiac Killer - Part 1 - Part 7/final – 1933-1934 .

https://vault.fbi.gov/Bonnie%20and%20Clyde/Bonnie%20and%20Clyde%20Part%2001/view

FBI (1969) Records: The Vault – Bonnie and Clyde - Part 1 - Part 6/final – 1969-1991 https://vault.fbi.gov

FBI (1988) Records: The Vault – Jack the Ripper - Part 1/final – 1988 -

https://vault.fbi.gov/Jack%20the%20Ripper/Jack%20the%20Ripper%20Part%2001%20%28Final%29/view

FBI (2005). Federal Bureau of Investigation (2005). Serial Murder: Multi-Disciplinary Perspectives for Investigators.

Fears, D. & Thomas-Lester, T (2002): Blacks Express Shock at Suspects' Identity –Most Say They Expect a Serial Killer to Be White. Washington Post Staff Writers, Saturday, October 26, 2002; Page A17.

Feldman, P. (1993). The Psychology of crime. Cambridge University Press. Fournier, Gregory A. (2016) Terror in Ypsilanti: John Norman Collins

Unmasked Paperback – August 1, 2016. Publisher Wheatmark

Francois, Z. (2024) - Schizotypal Personality Disorder - editor: Tyler J. Torrico – for National Institutes of Health - Brochures and Fact Sheets - Department of Health and Human Services - Last Update: May 7, 2024.

Freckelton, Ian & Scott, Russ (2017) Narcissistic Rage and the Murder of Allison Baden-Calligeros, Marissa, 2014, "Gerard-Baden-Clay-consummate-salesman-narcissist-and-killer". Brisbane Times. 19 July 2014. Archived.

Freud, S. (1899) *Die* Traumdeutung - puplised: Franz Deuticke, Leipzig & Vienna. 1913 (Macmillan, translation of the German third edition) *The Interpretation of Dreams*

Freud, S. (1917). Introduction to Psychoanalysis (Vorlesungen zur Einführung in die Psychoanalyse) FISCHER Taschenbuch.

Freud, S. (1995). Psykoanalysen i grundtræk. Det lille forlag.

Fries, J. F. (1821) Letter of 6 January in Gunther Nicolin, Hegel in Berichten seiner Zeitgenossen, Felix Meiner, Hamburg, 1970, p. 221.

Füllgrabe, U. (1992). Sadistische Mörder. Kriminalistische Studien, 5, 125-

156.

Gabbard, G.O. (1994). Psychodynamic psychiatry in clinical practice: The DSM-IV edition, Washington D.C.: American Psychiatric Press.

Gallagher (1987). I: Mitchell, E.W. (1996). The Aetiology of Serial Murder: Towards an Integrated Model. Article from www.forensic.to.

Geberth, V. J. (1996). Practical Homicide Investigation: Tactics, Procedures and Forensic Techniques. Boca Raton: CRC Press.

Ginsberg, Arthur & Spain, Tom (directors) Kuklinski, R. (1992) - The Iceman Tapes: Conversations with a Killer – HBO (Home Box Office Home Video) three true-crime TV documentaries - Episodes aired in 1992

Ginsberg, Arthur, (2003) Richard Kuklinski, Park Dietz - The Iceman and the Psychiatrist (Documentary, Crime) Home Box Office Home Video (HBO)

Giorgi, A. (1975). An Application of Phenomenological Method in Psychology. I: A. Giorgi, C. Fischer, and E. Murray (Eds.), Duquesne Studies in Phenomenological Psychology. Vol. 2, pp. 82 -103. Pittsburgh, Pennsylvania: Duquesne University Press.

Goldberg, A. (1975). A fresh look at perverse behavior. International Psycho-Analysis, 56, 335-342.

Goldscheider, C., & Frances, K. (1998). The Effects of Childhood Family Structure on Leaving and Returning Home. Journal of Marriage and the Family 60:745-756. (PQ, ASE).

Graham, K.C, Roslyn, Jay & Zola, Emily (2024) The Appeal of the Night Stalker: The Railroading of Richard Ramirez Paperback – August 21, 2024 - Publisher: Independently published (August 21, 2024) ISBN-13 979-8878572934

Graysmith, Robert (2002) - Zodiac unmasked the identity of America's most elusive serial killer revealed – A Berkley Book

Gresham, A. C. (1993). The insanity plea: A futile defense for serial killers.

Law and Psychology Review, 17, 193-208.

Gresswell, D.M., & Hollin Clive, R. (1994). "Multiple Murder: A Review. "British Journal of Criminology, 34(1): 1-14.

Grinell, Richard (2023) The autopsy findings of Cecelia Shepard - https://www.zodiacciphers.com/zodiac-news/the-autopsy-findings-of-cecelia-shepard)

Groth, N.A., & Birnbaum, J.H. (1979). Men who Rape. The Psychology of the Offender. Plenum Press: New York.

Gudjonsson, G., & Copson, G. (1997). In: Wrightsman L.S. (2001). Forensic Psychology. Wadsworth-Thomson Learning.

Hammerbrink (2003) I: Larsen, J.S., & Bering, M. (2003). Sexmordere benægter skyld. "Jyllands-Posten", 19 juli, 2003.

Hare, R.D. (1972). Psykopati – teori og forskning. Hans Reitzel.

Hare, R.D. (1999). Without Conscience: The Disturbing World of Psychopaths Among Us. New York Guilford Press.

Harrison, M. A. (2023) Just as Deadly – The Psychology of Female Serial Killers. Cambridge university press.

Harrison, S. (1993). The Diary of Jack the Ripper: The Chilling Confessions of James May- brick. London: Smith Gryphon.

HBO (2002). Cannibal Killers, America Undercover documentary, monday

25. november, 2002 - TV 2.

Heide, K.M., Hubbell, J.T., Wagers, S.M., (2021) Adopted children who kill their adoptive parents: An examination through the lens of attachment theory - PMID: 34131962 - DOI: 10.1002/bsl.2529

Heiman, 0. (1978). Nordisk Kriminalraportage. Nordisk Politi-idræts-forbund. P57-78.

Hermann, D. H., Morrison, H. L., Sor, Y., & Norman, J. A. (1983). People of the State of Illinois vs. John Gacy: The Functioning of the Insanity Defense at the Limits of the Criminal Law. W. Va. L. Rev., 86, 1169.

Hellman, D.S., & Blackman, N. (1966). Enuresis, fire setting and cruelty to animals: a triad predictive of adult crime. American Journal of Psychiatry; 122: 1431-1435.

Hemmingsen, R.; Birket-Smith, M., & Forchammer, H. mf. (1998). Menneskets Bevidsthed; Munksgaard.

Hickey, E.W. (1991). Serial Murderers and their victims. Brooks/Cole Publishing Company, Pacific Grove, California.

Hickey, E.W. (2002a). Inside the Criminal Mind. Discovery Channel den 24.10.2002.

Hickey, E.W. (2002b). I: O'Connor, T. (2003a). Female serial killers. Article from "Criminal Justice" http://faculty.ncwc.edu/toconnor

Hickey, E.W. (2003). Understanding Murder. Discovery Channel, den 05.12.2003.

Hickey, E.W. (2016). Serial Murderers and their victims. 7 edition 2016 - Brooks/Cole Publishing Company, Pacific Grove, California.

Hickey, E.W. (2023a) Presentation live lecture/masterclass. Week 9, Section

1. Lecture 1. CP PRO635 Inductive Profiling in Serial Criminal: Serial Criminality - Sexual Homicide – paraphilia e.g. Necrophilia, pedophilia. LMS Platform Evidentia University.

Hickey, E.W. (2023b). Presentation live lecture/masterclass. Week 10. Section 2. Lecture 2. CP PRO635 Inductive Profiling in Serial Criminal: Differences Between Sexual and Nonsexual Homicides of Women in the United States Semester 3. LMS Platform Evidentia University.

Hickey, E.W. (2023c). Presentation live lecture/masterclass. Week 11. Section 1. Lecture 3. CP PRO635 Inductive Profiling in Serial Criminal: Serial offender. Semester 3. LMS Platform Evidentia University.

Hickey, E.W. (2023d). Presentation live lecture/masterclass. week 12. Section 1. Lecture 4. CP PRO635 Inductive Profiling in Serial Criminal: *Case study.* Semester 3. LMS Platform Evidentia University.

Hickey, E.W. (2023e) Presentation live lecture/masterclass. Week 13. Section 7. Lecture 5. CP PRO635 Inductive Profiling in Serial Criminal: *Case Study.* LMS Platform Evidentia University.

Hirschi, T. & Gottfredson, M.R. (1990). A General Theory of Crime. Stanford: Stanford University Press.

Holmes, R. M., & DeBurger, J. (1988). Serial murder. Thousand Oaks: Sage.

Holmes, R. M., Holmes, S.T., & Hickey, E. (1991). Female Serial Murderesses: Constructing Differentiating Typologies. Journal of Contemporary Criminal Justice. 7(4): 245-256.

Holmes, R. M., & Holmes, J. Tewksbury, R. (1999). Fractured Identity

Syndrome - A New Theory of Serial Murder August 1999. Journal of Contemporary Criminal Justice 15(3):262-272: 10.1177/1043986299015003004 - University of Central Florida Differentiating Typologies. Journal of Contemporary Criminal Justice. 7(4): 245-256.

Holmes, R.M., & Holmes, S.T. (2002). Profiling Violent Crimes: An Investigative Tool. Third Edition.

Holzman, Eli (executive); Russell, Tiller; Saidman, Aaron; Skolnick, Paul; Walsh, Tim (producers) (2021) The *Night Stalker: Searching for a Serial Killer*. TV Miniseries for Netflix – January 13, 2021

Honeycombe, Gordon (2009). Murders of the Black Museum 1875–1975. London, England: John Blake Publishing. ISBN 978-1-84454-715-

9. Kennedy (1961).

Hougaard, E.; Diderichsen, B., & Nielsen, T. (red.) (1998). Psykoterapiens hovedtraditioner. København: Dansk Psykologisk Forlag.

Howitt, D. (2002). Forensic & Criminal Psychology. Prentice Hall. ICD-11 (2023) WHO-ICD-11: https://icd.who.int/en

Igninla, Biodun (2019) The Story of Veronica Compton Paperback – July 13, 2019.

Jackson, J.L., & Bekerian, D.A. (2001). Offender Profiling: Theory, Research and Practice.4. oplag. John Wiley & Sons.

Jenkins, P. (1994). Using Murder – The Social Construction of Serial Homicide. Aldine De Gruyter-New York.

Jesse, F. T. (1957) Trials of Timothy John Evans and John Reginald Halliday Christie - ISBN13: 004599 - ISBN: 004599 - Published: November 1957 - Publisher: William Hodge and Company, Limited

Johnson BR, Becker JV (1997), Natural born killers?: the development of the sexually sadistic serial killer. J Am Acad Psychiatry Law 25(3):335-348

Jones, Barbara (1996) Voices from an Evil God. Published at Blake Pub

Kasindorf, Jeanie Russell (1993). "The Bad Seed". New York - New York Magazine. Vol. 26, no. 31. pp. 0, 3, 38–46. Published August 9. 1993.

Keatley, A. D., Marono, A. J., Reid, S. & Yaksic, E. (2020) A Behavior Sequence Analysis of Serial Killers' Lives: From Childhood Abuse to Methods of Murder - Psychiatr Psychol Law - PMCID: PMC7144278 - PMID: 32284784 - 2020 Feb 6; 27(1):126–137. doi:10.1080/13218719.2019.1695517

Kelleher, M., & Kelleher, C. (1998). Murder Most Rare: The Female Serial Killer. NY: Dell. Who Track Them. Academic Press.

Keller, Erin (2024-08-08). "Wade Wilson's 'Troubled' Early Years: The Making of A Convicted Killer". Newsweek. Published Aug 08, 2024, and Updated 27. August 2024.

Kennedy, Ludovic - Ten Rillington Place. London, England: Victor Gollancz Ltd. pp. 23–24. ISBN 978-0685032640.

Keppel, R. D. & Birnes, W.J. (2003). The Psychology of Serial Killers And The Investigators Who Track Them. Academic Press.

Kevles, B.H., & Nissenson, M. (2000). Picturing DNA. Article from: Genomic Art: www.- genomicart.org/

King, T. L., Scovelle, A. J. Meehl, A, Milner A. J., & Priest, N (2021) - Gender stereotypes and biases in early childhood: A systematic review - First published online March 31, 2021 - Volume 46, Issue 2 - https://doi.org/10.1177/1836939121999849

Kirschner, D., & Nagel L. S. (1988). Antisocial behavior in adoptees: Patterns and dynamics. Child and Adolescent Social Work, 5, 300-314.

Kirschner, David (2006) Adoption: Uncharted Waters Paperback – September 15, 2006 - Juneau Press

Kirschner, David (2009) "Adoption Forensics: The Connection Between Adoption and Murder," article in Crime Magazine: https://www.crimemagazine.com/adoption-forensics-connection-between-adoption-and-murder

Kocsis, R., Orwin, H., & Hayes, A. (2000). I: Holmes, R.M., & Holmes, S.T. (2002). Profiling Violent Crimes: An Investigative Tool. Third Edition.

Kruuse, E. (1999). Kvalitative forskningsmetoder – i psykologi og beslægtede fag. Dansk psykologisk Forlag.

Kvale, S. (1997). InterView- En introduction til det kvalitative forskningsinterview. Hans Reitzels Forlag.

Kuter, Rachel and Ramsland, Katherine (2015) Multiple Personalities: Crime and Defense https://www.crimelibrary.org/

Leake, John (2009). Entering Hades: The Double Life of a Serial Killer.

Publisher: Berkley - ISBN-10: 0425228010 ISBN-13: 978-0425228012

Laderer, Ashley (2023) Is It the Silent Treatment or Passive-Aggressive Personality Disorder? 27. December 2023 – at Charley Health - https://www.charliehealth.com/post/passive-aggressive-personality-disorder

Lane, B. & Gregg, W. (1996). The New Encyclopedia of Serial Killers. Headline Books.

L.A. Times Archives (1985) - Suspect's Dad Puts Blame on Drug Use - Sept. 1, 1985 12 AM PT - https://www.latimes.com/archives/la-xpm-1985-09-01-mn-25710-story.html

Lavergne, Gary M. (1997). A Sniper in the Tower. Publisher: University of North Texas Press. ISBN 10 1574410296 ISBN 13 978-1574410297

Law & Crime Network (2024) LIVE: Cape Coral Killing Spree Murder Trial (full trail)— FL v. Wade Wilson (2024)

Levin, J., & Fox, J. (1985). I: Mitchell, E.W. (1996). The Aetiology of Serial Murder: Towards an Integrated Model. Article from "Dr. Zeno's Forensic Page" www.forensic.to

Leyton, E.H. (1986). I: Hickey, E.W. (1991): Serial Murderers and their victims. Brooks/Cole Publishing Company, Pacific Grove, California.

Leyton, E.H. (ed.) (2000). Serial Murder - Modern Scientific Perspectives.

Ashgate, Dartmouth.

Liebert, J.A. (2000). Contributions of Psychiatric Consultation in the Investigation of Serial Murder. I: Leyton, E.H. (ed.) (2000). Serial Murder - Modern Scientific Perspectives. Ashgate, Dartmouth.

Lifton, Betty Jean, (1995) Journey of The Adopted Self Paperback – May 6, 1995

Lindboe, O. (2002). Mord på stribe: en bog om seriemordere. Kbh.: Big City Books.

Lo, R.; Rosewood, J. (2017) The Big Book of Serial Killers Encyclopedia of Serial Killers Volume 1 - LAK Publishing.

Lo, R.; Rosewood, J. (2019) The Big Book of Serial Killers Encyclopedia of Serial Killers Volume 2 - LAK Publishing.

Lindsey, Robert (1979) Special to The New York (October 23, 1979). "One of Two Seized as 'Hillside Strangler' Pleads Guilty and Gets Life". The New York Times

Lo, R.; Rosewood, J. (2019) The Big Book of Serial Killers Volume 2 - Another 150 Serial Killer Files of the World's Worst Murderers - Independently Published

Lowenstein (1989). I: Mitchell, E.W. (1996) The Aetiology of Serial Murder: Towards an Integrated Model. Article from "Dr. Zeno's Forensic Page" www.forensic.to

MacDonald, J. M. (1963). The threat to kill. American Journal of Psychiatry, 120, pp. 125-130.

Martell, Joseph L & Martell, Joey (2021) – "Psychological Profile of a Criminal Offender: Richard Ramirez part 1 & 2" - January 2021 - https://www.researchgate.net/publication/354172508_Psychological_Profile_of_a_Criminal_Offender_Richard_Ramirez

Martell, Joseph L & Martell, Joey (2021) Analysis of the Psychopathic Traits of Richard "The Iceman" Kuklinski - August 2021 - Saint Leo University

Martens, W.H.J. (2001). Effects of antisocial or social attitudes on neurobiological functions. Medical Hypotheses 56(6):664-671.

Marston, Edward (2007). John Christie. London, England: A&C Black Business Information and Development. p. 7. ISBN 978-1905615162.

Martens, W.H.J. (2002). The Hidden Suffering of the Psychopath. Psychiatric Times. January 2002 Vol. XIX Issue 1.

Masters, Brian (1986). Killing for Company: The Case of Dennis Nilsen.

Publisher Stein & Day Pub House. ISBN-13 978-0-812-83104-7.

Masters, Brian (1993). The Shrine of Jeffrey Dahmer. London, England: Hodder & Stoughton. ISBN 978-0-340-59194-9.

McClary, Daryl (2008) After he murders two Bellingham women, police arrest serial killer Kenneth A. Bianchi on January 12, 1979. Posted 7/26/2008 - HistoryLink.org Essay 8613.

McEvoy et al., (2023) By Biography.com Editors and Colin McEvoy "Jeffrey Dahmer". Biography.com. A&E Networks. Archived from the original on September 15, 2023.

McPadden, Mike (2017). -"Randall Woodfield: The Green Bay Packer Who Became the I-5 Killer". CrimeFeed. Investigation Discovery. Archived June 26, 2017.

McKenzie, C. (1995). Study of Serial Murder. International Journal of Offender Therapy and Comparative Criminology. 39(1): 3-10.

McLean, F. (2004) Serial Killers Understanding and Prevention. Thesis from psychology study at Aarhus University, Denmark.

McLean, F. (2012). Case study of Arthur John Shawcross. Aarhus University. McLean, F. (2021) Seriemordere – Mennesket bag Monsteret – Lindhardt og

Ringhof - ISBN13 9788727122113

McLean, F. (2023a) Ondskabens Psykologi – Profiler af seriemordere. 2023 – Lindhardt og Ringhof - ISBN139788727155692

McLean, F. (2023b) SERIAL KILLERS - Prevention Through Deconstructing Criminal Profiling - August 7th, 2023 - UNIVERSITY: Evidentia University of Behavioral & Forensic Sciences. 111 E. Monument Ave. Unit 401-09 - Kissimmee FL 43741 – Capstone Projekt Year 2021

McLean, F. (2025) Et forstyrret sind – Bag seriemorderens maske. 2025 – Lindhardt og Ringhof - ISBN13 9788727157764

McLeod, S. (2024) Eysenck H., Allport G., & Cattell (2024) Theories of Personality. Updated on January 29, 2024. https://www.simplypsychology.org/personality-theories.html

McQuigge, M (2017) Lawyer advised Wettlaufer to take murderous secrets to her grave – PUBLISHED JUNE 2, 2017.https://www.ctvnews.ca/

McQuiston, John T. (1994) "Expert Says Rifkin Is Sick But Is Not Legally Insane" - Published May 5, 1994 - https://www.nytimes.com/

MCU, ME, & KLD (2009) De Standaard Online - Standaard.be - 'Ouders De Gelder vroegen al opname psychiatrie'" published 27. January 2009

Mello-Klein, Cody (2023) Why are there fewer serial killers now than there used to be? Published: april 26, 2023 - https://news.northeastern.edu/

Meyer, G. J.; Eblin, J. J. (2012). "An Overview of the Rorschach Performance Assessment System (R-PAS)". Psychological Injury and Law. 5 (2): 107–121. doi:10.1007/s12207-012-9130-y. ISSN 1938-971X. S2CID 143393022.

Meyer, L. F., & Valenca, A. M. (2021). Factors related to bias in forensic psychiatric assessments in criminal matters: A systematic review. International journal of law and psychiatry, 101681. https://doi.org/10.1016/j.ijlp.2021.101681

MMP (2022) Mike Mathis Production (2022) Conversations with a Killer:

The John Wayne Gacy Tapes - TV Mini Series - TV-MA

Miklowitz, David J. (2019) The Bipolar Disorder Survival Guide: What You and Your Family Need to Know Third Edition – Publisher: The Guilford Press - ISBN 10 - 1462534988

Miller, A. (1998). Childhood Trauma. presented article as a lecture at the Lexington 92nd Stre- et YWHA in New York City on October 22, 1998.

Mitchell, E.W. (1996): The Aetiology of Serial Murder: Towards an Integrated Model. Article from" Ed Mitchell Homepage – Unuversity of Oxford": http://users.ox.ac.uk/~zool0380/home.htm.

Mladinich, Robert (2002) From the Mouth of the Monster: The Joel Rifkin Story – publisher Pocket Books February 10,2002.

Moesgaard, K. (1999). Mishandling og overgreb mod børn. Article Det Kriminel præventive råd.

Money, J. (1990). Forensic Sexology: Paraphilic Serial Rape (Biastophilia) and Lust Murder (Erotophonophilia). American Journal of Psychotherapy. Vol. XLIV (1) pp. 26-36.

Morrison, J. (1995). DSM-IV Made Easy - The Clinician's Guide to Diagnosis.

Guilford Pres.

National (The) Archives, Kew (1953) Trial of John Reginald Halliday Christie: transcript - Reference: CAB 143/13 - Description Trial of John Reginald Halliday Christie: transcript – date: 1953 – held by: The National Archives, Kew original department: C9-10 record open: 15 October 2002

Newsroom, the (2008) "The hitman and her: Barbara Kuklinski". The Scotsman - Published 12th Mar 2008, 11:56 BST - Updated 12th Mar 2008, 15:22 BST

Newton, M. (2000). The Encyclopedia of Serial Killer. Checkmark Books.

Nielsen, H. B. & Rudberg, M. (1991). Historien om piger og drenge - kønssocialisering i et udviklingspsykologisk perspektiv. Gyldendal.

NIH (2025) National Institutes of Health - Brochures and Fact Sheets

- Bipolar Disorder U.S. Department of Health and Human Services -- NIH Publication No. 25-MH-8088 - Revised 2025.

Nilsen, Dennis & Pettigrew Mark (2021) History of a Drowning Boy: The Autobiography Paperback – May 1, 2021 – publisher RedDoor Press - ISBN-10 1913062538

Noe, Denise (April 27, 2007). "Augusta Gein, the woman who drove a man Psycho". Men's News Daily.

Norris, J. (1989). Serial Killers. Anchor. Reprint edition. Norris, J. (1992a). Jeffrey Dahmer. New York: Kensington Pub.

Norris, J. (1992b). Arthur Shawcross: The Genesee River Killer. NY: Windsor Publishing.

O'Brien, Darcy (2017) The Hillside Stranglers - The Inside Story of the Killing Spree That Terrorized Los Angeles. ISBN139781504047883, publicer: Open Road Media

O'Connor, T. (2002a). The role of childhood trauma as a cause of serial killing.

Article from "Criminal Justice" http://faculty.ncwc.edu/toconnor/

O'Connor, T. (2002b). Advanced applied criminology. Article from "Criminal Justice" http:// faculty.ncwc.edu/toconnor/

O'Connor, T. (2003a). Female serial killers. Article from "Criminal Justice" http://faculty.n- cwc.edu/toconnor/

O'Connor, T. (2003b). History Of Profiling. Article from "Criminal Justice" http://faculty.n- cwc.edu/ toconnor/

Oates, Jonathan (2013) - John Christie of Rillington Place - Biography of a Serial Killer- Barnsley, England: 19-01-2013 · ISBN139781845631413 · Publisher: Wharncliffe Books

Olson, J. (1993) The Misbegotten Son – A Serial killer and his Victims – the true story of Arthur J. Shawcross – Headline books.

Olson, J. (2014) The Misbegotten Son – A Serial killer and his Victims – the true story of Arthur J. Shawcross – Crime Rant Classic.

O'Neill, Ann; Cabrera, Ana, & Weisfeldt, Sara (2015) CNNus "A look inside the 'broken' mind of James Holmes". CNN. June 10, 2015.

Orne, Martin T.; Dinges, David T.; Orne, Emily Carota (1984). "On The Differential Diagnosis of Multiple Personality In The Forensic Context 1,2". *The International Journal of Clinical and Experimental Hypnosis*. Philadelphia, Pennsylvania: Taylor & Francis: 118–

169. DOI:10.1080/00207148408416007. PMID 6469414.

Paton, Jean M. (1954) The Adopted Break Silence, 1954 (Philadelphia: Life History Study Center, 1954), 3, 6-8, 49-51, 143, 148, 151-152, 155.

Paulus, C. (1998). Serial killers: Causes and development of extreme aggression. University of Saarbruecken, Germany. Article from "Universität des Saarlandes": www.uni-saarland.de

Payne K. & Fischer D. (2025) "Florida State gunman used deputy mom's former service weapon to kill 2 and wound 6, authorities say". Associated Press. April 17, 2025. Retrieved April 17, 2025. Updated 4:26 AM CEST,

April 18, 2025

People v. Alcala (1992) [No. S004724. Crim. No. 25693. Dec 31, 1992.] (Superior Court of Orange County, No. C-42861, Donald A. McCartin, Judge.)

Perri, Frank S; Lichtenwald, Terrance G (2010). THE LAST FRONTIER: Myths & the Female Psychopathic Killer Forensic Examiner; Springfield Vol. 19, Iss. 2, (Summer 2010): 50-67.

Perry, B.D. (2003). Maltreated children: experience, brain development and the next generation - W.W. Norton.

Petherick, W. (1999a). Criminal Profiling: Fact, Fiction, Fantasy, and Fallacy. Article from "Crime Library – Criminal Mind and Methods": www.crimelibrary.com

Petherick, W. (1999b): Criminal Profiling: How It Got Started And How

It Is Used. Article from ”Crime Library – Criminal Mind and Methods”: www.crimelibrary.com

Petherick, Wayne. (2022). Presentation live lecture week 1-8. Section 2, lecture 4, CP PRO505 - Introduction to Criminal Profiling. Semester 1. LMS Platform Evidentia University.

Phelps, William M. (2003). Perfect Poison: A Female Serial Killer's Deadly Medicine. Pinnacle Books. ISBN 9780786015504.

Piccotti, Tyler (2023) Biography.com EditorsRichard Ramirez - Updated: May 17, 2023.

Pincus, J.H. (2002). Base Instincts: What Makes Killers Kill? W. W. Norton & Company.

Potter, N. (2002). The Mind of a Killer Patterns Seen in Murderers' Brains.

Article from ”ABC News”: http://abcnews.go.com/

Prentky, R.; Burgess, A.; Rokous, F. mf. (1989). The presumptive role of fantasy in serial sexual homicide. American Journal of Psychiatry, American Psychiatric Association.

QGIS (2025) QGIS Development Team, number 3.42.1. QGIS Geographic Information System. Open-Source Geospatial Foundation Project. http://qgis.osgeo.org

Quinn, K.M. (2000). Violent Behavior Animal abuse at early age linked to interpersonal violence. Article from ”The Brown University Child and Adolescent Behavior Letter”: www.childresearch.net/

Raine, A. (1999). Murderous Minds: Can I See the Mark of Cain?

Published: April 1, 1999.

Raine, A. (2003). Understanding Murder. Discovery Channel den 05.12.2003. Raine, A. (2013). The Anatomy of Violence: The Biological Roots of Crime.

Publisher: Pantheon.

Ramirez MP, Framis AG, Gonzalez-Alvarez JL, Castro JES. (2022) J Interprets Violence. 2022 Predicting Serial Stranger Rapists: Developing a Statistical Model from Crime Scene Behaviors - Oct;37(19-20):NP18888-NP18907. doi: 10.1177/08862605211044968. Epub 2021 Sep 11. -

Affiliations Expand - PMID: 34510955 - DOI: 10.1177/08862605211044968

Ramsland, K. (2000). Efren Saldivar: Hospital executioner. Article from "Crime Library – Criminal Mind and Methods": https://mail.crimelibrary.org/

Ramsland, K. (2002): The Criminal Mind – A writer's Guide to Forensic Psychology. Writer's Digiest Books, Cincinnati, Ohio.

Ramsland, K. (2003). The Genesee River Strangler. Article from "Crime Library –Criminal Mind and Methods": https://mail.crimelibrary.org/ Ramsland, K. (2006). Inside the Minds of Serial Killers: Why They Kill. ABC-CLIO, LLC. p. 17. ISBN 9780275990992.

Ramsland, Katherine (2013). "A True Necrophile". Crime Library. Archived from the original on December 2, 2013 - https://mail.crimelibrary.org/ Ramsland, Katherine. (2015) "Angels of Death: The Female Nurses". Crime Library: Criminal Minds and Methods – 2015

https://mail.crimelibrary.org/

Ramsland, K. (2015) John Norman Collins: The Co-Ed Killer. Crime library: Criminal Minds and Methods - https://mail.crimelibrary.org/

Ramsland, K & Safarik, M. (2019) Spree Killers 1st Edition - CRC Press

Rappaport (2020) Making a monster (2020) Interview was recorded July 2019. With Dr. Richard Rappaport About the case: John Wayne Gacy with Dr Richard Rappaport - 16 MAR 2020 · Making A Monster: The Tapes.

Ravindran, T. (2022) - Paraphilia and Its Psychological Implications and medically reviewed by Dr. Vishal Anilkumar Gandhi - Published on Sep

16, 2022, and last reviewed on Mar 08, 2023.

Rayman, G & GO Staff (2016) The Iceman's Daughter and interview with Merrick Kuklinski - The Cultural Roadmap for City Girls Everywhere (GO) Published June 15, 2016.

Redondo, Santiago and Garrido, Vicente et al (1997) - *"Adoption & Murder"* (from Psychology and Law" p.274-280, 1997, NCJS 176632)

Ressler, R., & Burgess, A.W. (1985). The men who murder. FBI Law Enforcement Bulletin, 54(8): 2-6.

Ressler, R. K., & Shachtman, T. (1992). Whoever fights monsters. New York: Pocket Books.

Root, Neil (2011). Frenzy!: Heath, Haigh and Christie. Preface Publishing. ISBN 978-0-099-55776-0.

Rothschild and Watts (2020) 'Butcher Baker' Prosecutor Frank Rothschild Shares the Serial Killer's Breaking Point – Marina Watts Newsweek - SEP 02, 2020.

Rule, Ann (1984) The I-5 Killer Mass Market Paperback – March 1, 1984 – publisher Berkley – ISBN-10 1848093179

Ryan, C. (1985). "Carroll Cole, who romanced at least 10 women before..." *UPI*. CARSON CITY, Nevada: United Press International, Inc. Published 5 December 1985

Safarik, M. (2010) Criminal Landscape - S1.E4 · Joel Rifkin - Criminal Mindscape (TV Series 2009–2010) Julie Almendral (associate producer)

- 2 episodes • 2009–2010 - Lloyd Fales (producer), Vicki Sufian (executive producer).

Safarik, M. (2022a) Presentation live, Section 2. Lecture 9 - – CP RO510. Modus Operandi, Ritual, and Staging II. Lecture 8D to 9 - Criminal Profiling

- Behavioral Manifestations - Modus Operandi and Ritual. Case Study. LMS Platform Evidentia University.

Safarik, M. (2022b) Presentation live, Section 2. Lecture 3-9 – CP RO510.

Crime Scene Investigation – Case Study. LMS Platform Evidentia University.

Safarik, M. (2022c) Presentation live, Section 3. Lecture 1-9 – CP RO510. Serial killers - sexual homicide – link analysis, victimology and killer instinct – Case Study. LMS Platform Evidentia University.

Saferstein, R. (1998). Criminalistics: An introduction to forensic sciences.

New Jersey: Simon and Schuster.

Sands, Stella (2011). The Dating Game Killer: The True Story of a TV Dating Show, a Violent Sociopath, and a Series of Brutal Murders. New York City: St. Martin's True Crime. p. 367.

Santi, Angela Delli (2023) Associated Press 'Dating Game' serial killer accused of 2 NYC deaths

Schechter, D. S., Moser, Wang, Marsh et al., (2011) An fMRI study of the brain responses of traumatized mothers to viewing their toddlers during separation and play PMCID: PMC3501701 PMID: 22021653

Schechter, H. (2018) - Hell's princess: The mystery of Belle Gunness, butcher of men. Little A.

Schechter, Susan. (1982) - Women and male violence. South End Press.

Schneider, E. and Jordan S. (1978) - Representation of women who defend themselves in response to physical or sexual assault, 4 Women's Rts. L. Rep. 149.

Schizophr, B. (2017) Mar; 43(2): 316–324. Evidence That the Impact of Childhood Trauma on IQ Is Substantial in Controls, Moderate in Siblings, and Absent in Patients with Psychotic Disorder Published online 2017 Feb

8. doi: 10.1093/schbul/sbw177 PMCID: PMC5605269 - PMID: 28177077.

Schorsch, E. (1978). I: Paulus, C. (1998). Serial killers: Causes and development of extreme aggression. University of Saarbruecken, Germany. Article from "Universität des Saarlandes": www.uni-saarland.de

Schmidt, G. (1983). Motivationale Grundlagen sexuellen Verhaltens. I: H. Thomae (Hrsg.): Psychologieder Motive Enzyklopädie der Psychologie, Bd. C/IV/2. Göttingen: Hogrefe, S. 70-109.

Scott, S.L. (2003). What Makes Serial Killers Tick? Article from Crime Library – Criminal Mind and Methods": www.crimelibrary.com

Sears, D. J. (1991). To Kill Again: The Motivation and Development of Serial Murder. Wilmington, DE: Scholarly Resources Books.

Sifuentes, K. (2001). Arthur Shawcross A Man Driven by the Ravages of War.

Article from "Crime Web":http://members.fortunecity.com/

Stanfield, Frank (1998) - "Doctor: Ferrell's Lies A 'Game'" www.OrlandoSentinel.com – February 14. 1998.

Stoller R. J. (1975) The Erotic Form of Hatred Pantheon Books, 1975.

Stone, Michael H. (2006). Personality-Disordered Patients: Treatable and Untreatable. American Psychiatric Publishing ISBN 978-1-58562-705-9.

Stone, Michael H. & Brucato, Gary (2019). The New Evil: Understanding the Emergence of Modern Violent Crime. Publisher: New York: Prometheus Books.

Summers, C. (2002). The Hillside Stranglers. Article from "BBC News Online": www.bbc.co.uk/crime/caseclosed/

Tapia, F. (1971). Children who are cruel to animals. Child Psychiatry and Human Development 1971; 2(2): 70-77.

Tayler, S. (2023): Serial Killer Statistics - March 4, 2023 - Data & Social Science News. The Lonely Head-Hunter: Ed Kemper - Murder Casebook: Published January 1991.

Teten, H. (1995). Offender profiling, Pp. 475-77 in W. Bailey (ed) The Encyclopedia of Police Science. NY: Garland.

Time, 1966) Nation: The Madman in the Tower – Time Magazine, August 12, 1966.

The Oregonian Staff (2012). "Serial killer Randy Woodfield's legacy: pain, preening and pointlessness". Published, May 13. 2012 - The Oregonian live.

Turvey, B.E., (1995). The Impressions of a Man: An Objective Forensic Guideline to Profiling Violent Serial Sex Offenders. Article from Knowledge Solutions": www.corpus-delicti.com/

Turvey, B.E., (2012). Criminal Profiling: an introduction to Behavioral Evidence Analysis. Academic press. Fourth edition.

Tuckman, Jo (2006) The Lady killer – The Guardian – Published 19. May 2006 – article - https://www.theguardian.com/ United States Court Of Appeals For The First Circuit - 181 F.3d 152 (1st Cir. 1999) - UNITED STATES, Appellee, - KRISTEN GILBERT, Defendant, Appellant. No. 98-1563 - Heard March 3, 1999 - Decided June 21, 1999

United States v. Gilbert, (2000) 120 F. Supp. 2d 147 (D. Mass. 2000) US District Court for the District of Massachusetts - 120 F. Supp. 2d 147 (D. Mass. 2000) November 14, 2000 - 120 F. Supp. 2d 147 (2000) UNITED

STATES of America v. Kristen GILBERT - No. 98-CR-30044-MAP - United States District Court, D. Massachusetts. - November 14, 2000.

Van Sant, Peter (2024) CBS News - 48Hours - Serial killer Rodney Alcala's trail of murder - Updated on: November 10, 2024 / 2:17 AM EST / CBS News - https://www.cbsnews.com

Vaknin, S. (2003). Serial Killers as a Cultural Construct. Article from "Philosophical Essays and Musings": http://samvak.tripod.com/

Verrier, Nancy Newton (2003) Primal Wound – Understanding the Adopted Child ISBN139780963648006 - Published: Verrier Publishing

Vestergaard, P., & Sørensen, T. (1998). Psykiatri, en lærebog om voksnes psykiske sygdomme. Foreningen af danske lægestuderendes forlag-københavn-Århus-Odense.

Vronsky, Peter (2004) Serial Killers: The Method and Madness of Monsters – Publisher Berkley books ISBN-10 0425196402.

Wark, Jake (2015) The Zodiac Killer https://www.crimelibrary.org/ TM &

© 2015 Turner Entertainment Networks, Inc. A Time Warner Company.

Walsøe, K. (2003). Dødsporno skal undersøges. Kristelig dagblad. 29. september 2003.

Webmd (2024) https://www.webmd.com/

Wechsler, D. (2008) Wechsler Adult Intelligence Scale | Fourth Edition – Pearson.

Wechsler, D. (2015) Wechsler Intelligence Scale for Children | Fifth Edition, Integrated – Pearson.

Williams, S.L. (2003). Social Construction of Serial Murder. Article from "Department of Sociology, Anthropology, and Social Work" http://www-personal.ksu.edu/~lswilli/

Wilson, P. R.; Lincoln, R. & Kocsis, R. (1997). Validitiy, Utility and Ethics of Criminal Profiling for Serial Violent and Sexual Offenders. Psychiatry, Psychology and the Law, 4 (1), 1 – 12.

Wilson, P. R., & Soothill, K. (1996). Psychological profiling: Red, green or amber? The police journal, 12 – 30.

Williams, Chitsabesan, Fazel, McMillan, Hughes & James (2018) Traumatic brain injury: a potential cause of violent crime? Published February 26, 2018, DOI: 10.1016/S2215-0366(18)30062-2

Winton, Richard (2013). "'Night Stalker' Richard Ramirez died of complications from lymphoma". *The Los Angeles Times*. Archived from 2013.

Wrightsman, L.S. (2001). Forensic Psychology. Wadsworth-Thomson Learning.

Yi, Daniel (1999) Ng Would Fit Well Into a Prison Life, Defense Says –

April 13, 1999 Los Angels Times archive: https://www.latimes.com/

Ziporyn, M and Altman, J. (1967) Born to Raise Hell: The Untold Story of Richard Speck The Man, The Crime, The Trial – January 1, 1967 – Grove press.

# From Same Author

Books and Research Papers

*"Serial Killers – Understanding and Prevention"* (2004) Thesis from Aarhus University, Denmark.

*"Prevention: A Case Study of Arthur Shawcross"* (2012) Research report through Aarhus University, Denmark.

*"Serial Killers - The Man Behind the Monster"* (2021) Danish, German, Swedish, and Italian Bestseller book published by Lindhardt & Ringhof publisher.

*"Serial Killers - Prevention Through Deconstructing Criminal Profiling"* (2023) Capstone Project with Evidentia University, USA.

*"The Psychology of Evil - Profiles of Serial Killers"* (2023) Danish - Bestseller book Published with Lindhardt & Ringhof publisher.

*"A Disturb Mind – Behind the Serial Killer Mask"* (2025) Danish - Bestseller listed book Published with Lindhardt & Ringhof publisher.

Podcasts

*The Human Behind the Monster* (Arthur John Shawcross) – Season 1 – Danish (2024) with Sage Egmont.

*The Human Behind the Monster* (Douglas Clark) – Season 2 – Danish (2025) in press with Sage Egmont.

# About the Author

Florence McLean is a psychologist and a specialist in clinical psychology, psychotherapy, and child neuropsychology and an approved supervisor.

She has an MSc in criminal profiling. She holds a professional diploma in criminal profiling and crime scene analysis, as well as a certified diploma in criminal profiling. For over two decades, she has worked with children, young people, and adults. She is an approved specialist in clinical psychology, psychotherapy, and child neuropsychology and an approved supervisor.

Since 1997, she has been dealing with serial killers, culminating in a 2004 thesis "Serial Killers: Understanding and Prevention", and a 2012 research report, "Prevention: A Case Study of Arthur Shawcross" and from 2021 she has published 3 books about serial killers.

Since her thesis, Florence McLean has communicated with many serial killers and investigated over 100 of them. She has interviewed some of them and reviewed their cases. She also read court transcripts, looked at walkthrough, watch some of their legal proceedings, watched interrogation recordings, and read interviews with them to gain a deeper understanding of serial killers.

She is still in contact with some of the serial killers and can draw on their knowledge when appropriate.

Florence McLean is an experienced speaker and author of 3 books about serial killers. She has appeared in several TV series, including as a host in the TV documentary: *"Are they too dangerous for freedom?"* She has also acted as an expert in many programs, e.g., *"When men kill women," "Women who kill," "Criminal,"* and *"When crime shakes us."*

In addition, she has appeared in several radio programs, newspapers, and magazines, and she has her own podcast: *"The Human Behind the Monster."*

She is often invited to be an expert in different TV programs, news stations, podcasts, talks, and radio programs in Denmark, Sweden, Norwegian, and Germany.

Made in the USA
Columbia, SC
02 June 2026

83742813R00174